I0799409

IMAGES
of America

AQUIDNECK ISLAND AND HER NEIGHBORS

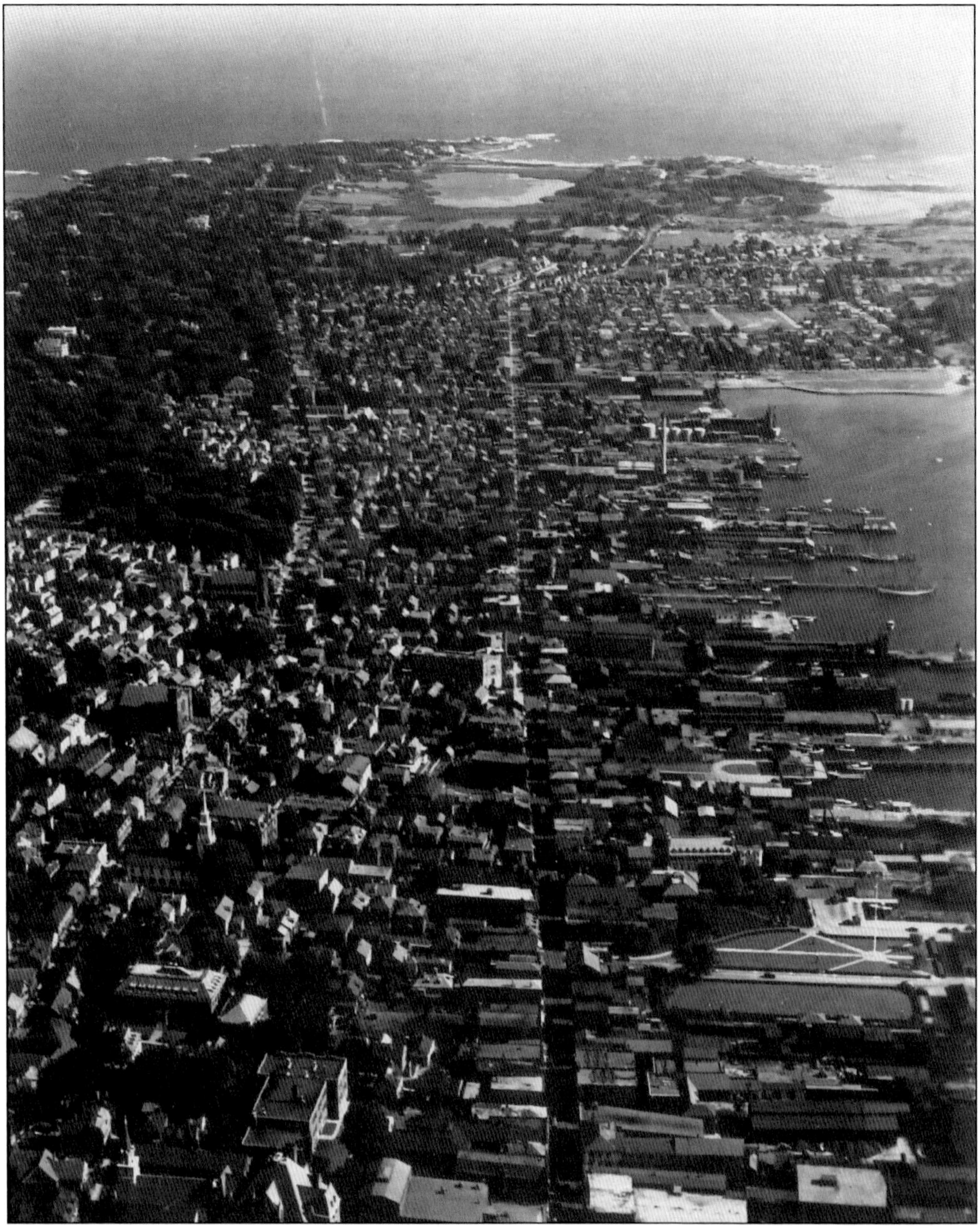

Aerial view looking down Thames Street and continuing past Ocean Drive. This photograph was taken in July 1937 by H.H. Harris. (Photograph courtesy of the William Bachus Collection)

IMAGES
of America

AQUIDNECK ISLAND AND HER NEIGHBORS

Rob Lewis

ARCADIA
PUBLISHING

ISBN 978-0-7385-9035-6

Published by Arcadia Publishing
Charleston, South Carolina

Printed in the United States of America

For all general information contact Arcadia Publishing at:
Telephone 843-853-2070
Fax 843-853-0044
E-mail sales@arcadiapublishing.com
For customer service and orders:
Toll-Free 1-888-313-2665

Visit us on the Internet at www.arcadiapublishing.com

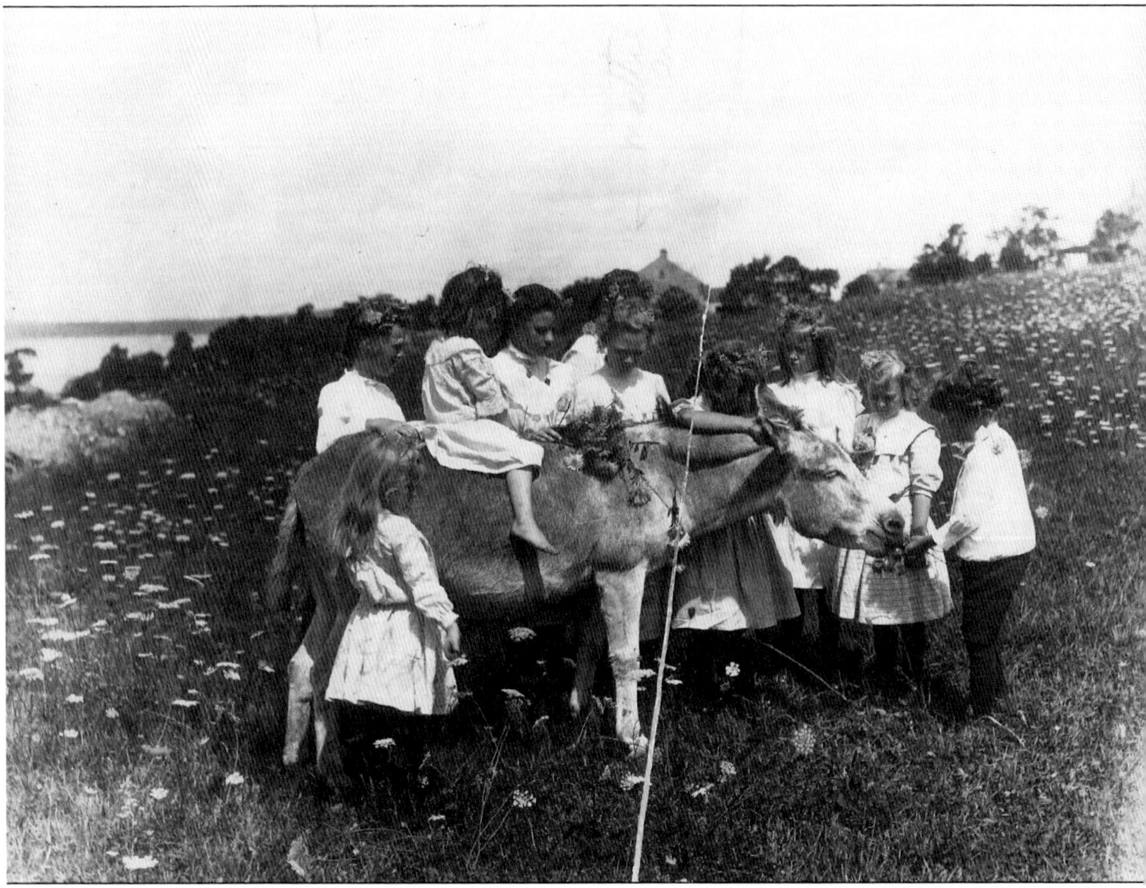

The children of Benjamin and Annie Hall and some of their friends in 1905. (Photograph courtesy of Lorraine Davol)

Contents

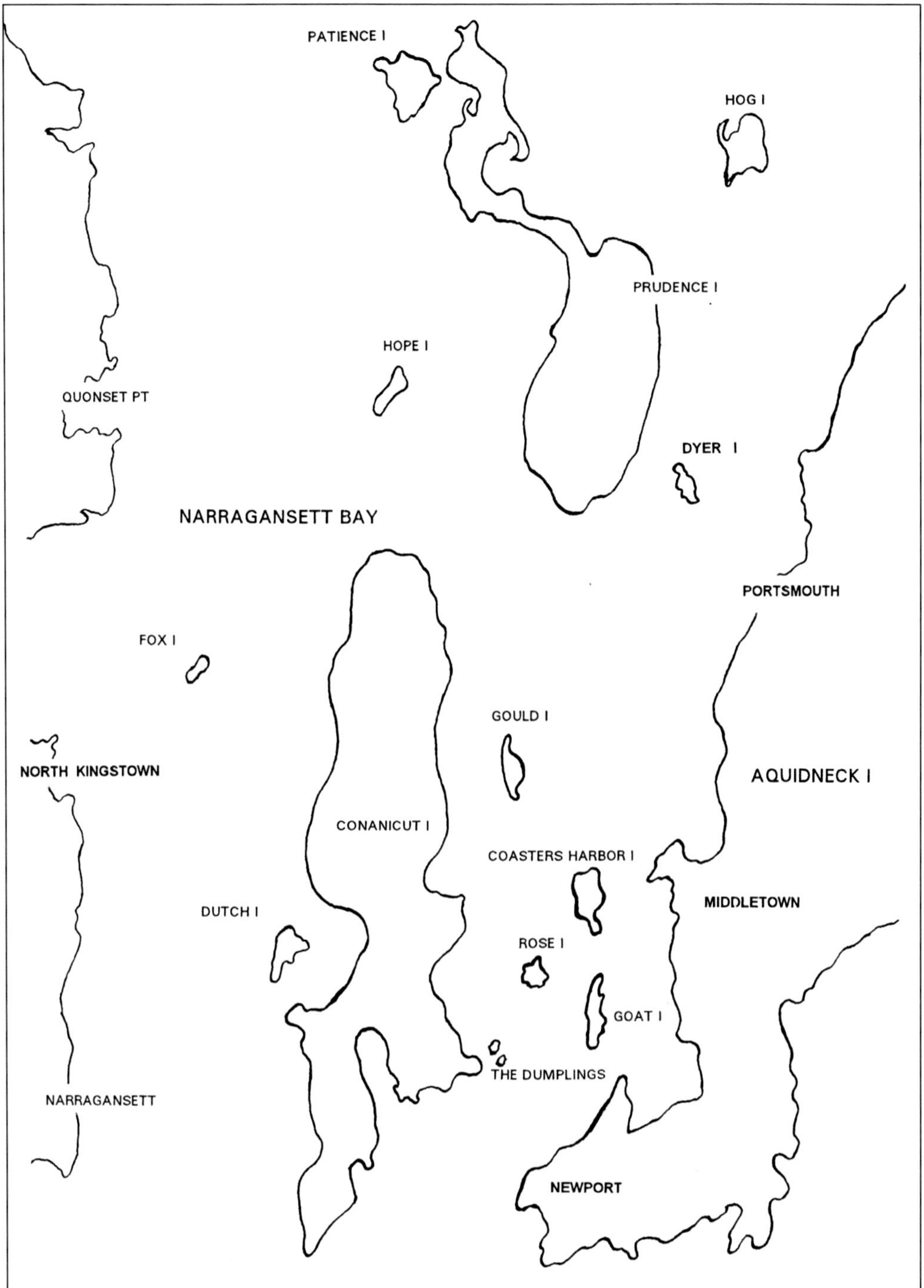

AQUIDNECK ISLAND AND HER NEIGHBORS

Introduction

In March of 1638, a group of men—William Coddington, William Hutchinson, John Clark, William Dyre, and others—left Boston for Providence. In Providence they met with Roger Williams, and then proceeded to Plymouth; it was here that, after conferring with authorities, they decided to purchase the Island of Aquidneck.

After arriving on Aquidneck they met with Wannumetonomey, a local sachem, who introduced them to the chief sachems, Conanicus and Miantonomi, and the island was purchased in late March 1638. The first Rhode Island town was the Pocasset settlement, May 1638, at the northern end of the island. In 1639 Newport was founded at the southern end of the island. Middletown was part of Newport until 1743, when it formed its own township.

Her Neighbors

*Conanicut (Jamestown) was named after the Narragansett Sachem Conanicus. In 1656 Benedict Arnold and a group of men purchased the island from the Narragansett Indians.

*Prudence Island is nicknamed "whale in the bay" because of its shape. The Native Americans called the island Chibachuwese, which translates to "separation of passage." It was purchased by Roger Williams around 1637 and became part of Portsmouth in May 1647.

*Aquopimokuk was the Native American name for Gould Island. Thomas Gould purchased the island in 1657 to use as pasture land.

*Chisewewnok (Hog Island) was purchased in 1646 from the Wampanoags to pasture swine.

*In addition, Rose Island was obtained by Benedict Arnold in February 1659 to be used as animal pasture.

*Coasters Harbor Island, known as Woonachaset by area Native Americans, was purchased in 1654.

Narragansett Bay and the surrounding area is steeped in history; some events happened here first and some originated elsewhere and rippled by us. This book is a compilation of photographs, some from the archives of the Newport Restoration Foundation, and many from private family albums, that captures moments in history. I hope that you enjoy the browse through time, remembering some things and seeing others, long lost, with wonder.

One

Newport

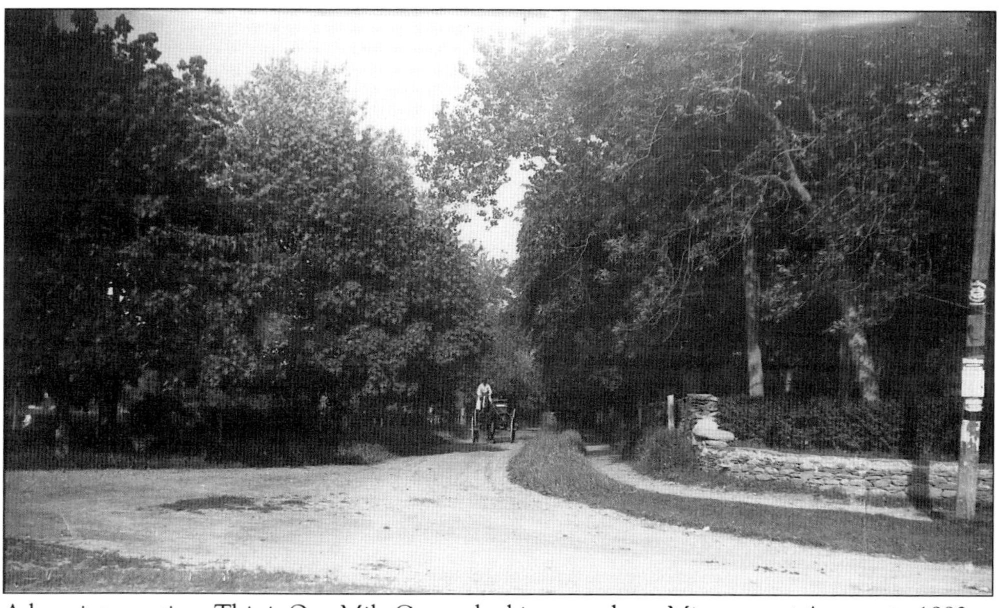

A busy intersection. This is One Mile Corner looking east down Miantonomi Avenue in 1880.

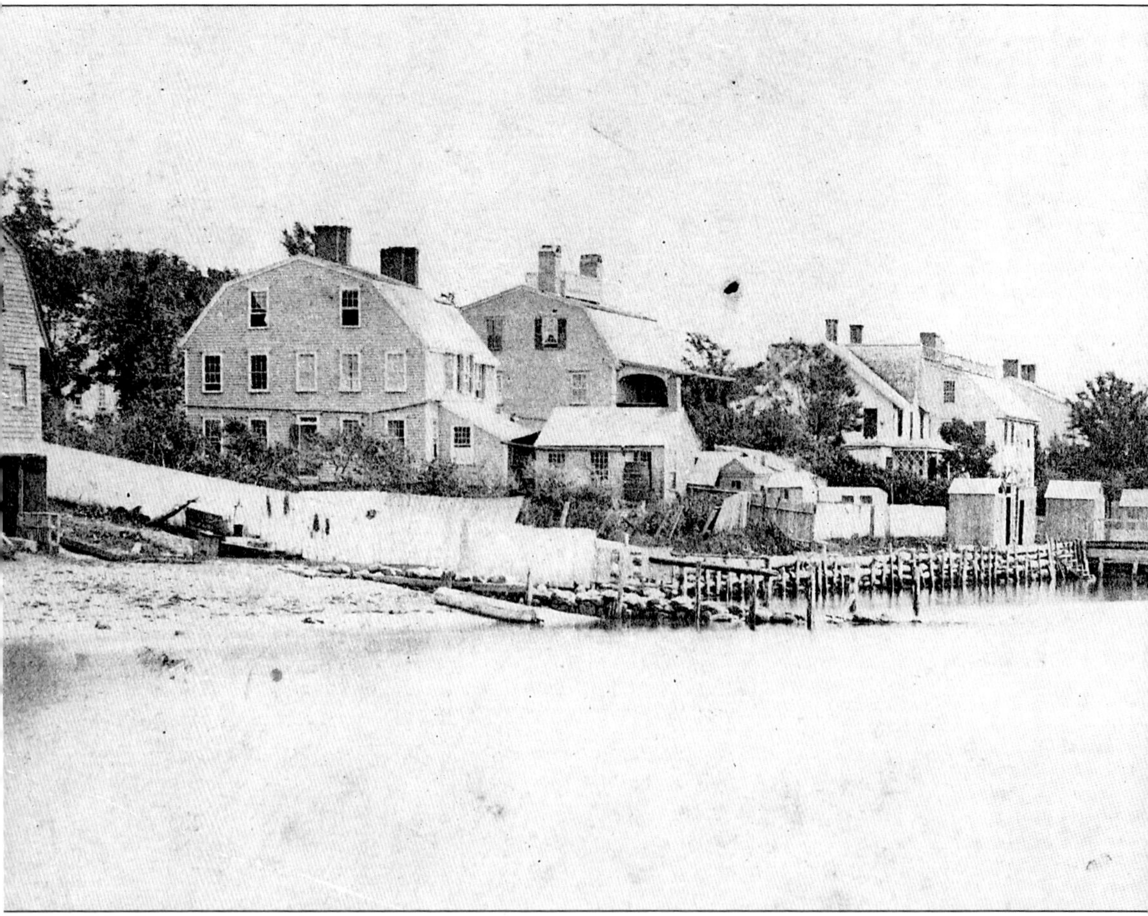

The Washington Street shore in 1865 from the area called Blue Rocks. Nicholas Easton was one of the nine incorporators of Newport and was also one of the original eleven proprietors. In the first division of land among the proprietors, Easton was given about 65 acres, which became Eastons Point. Today the area is known simply as "the Point."

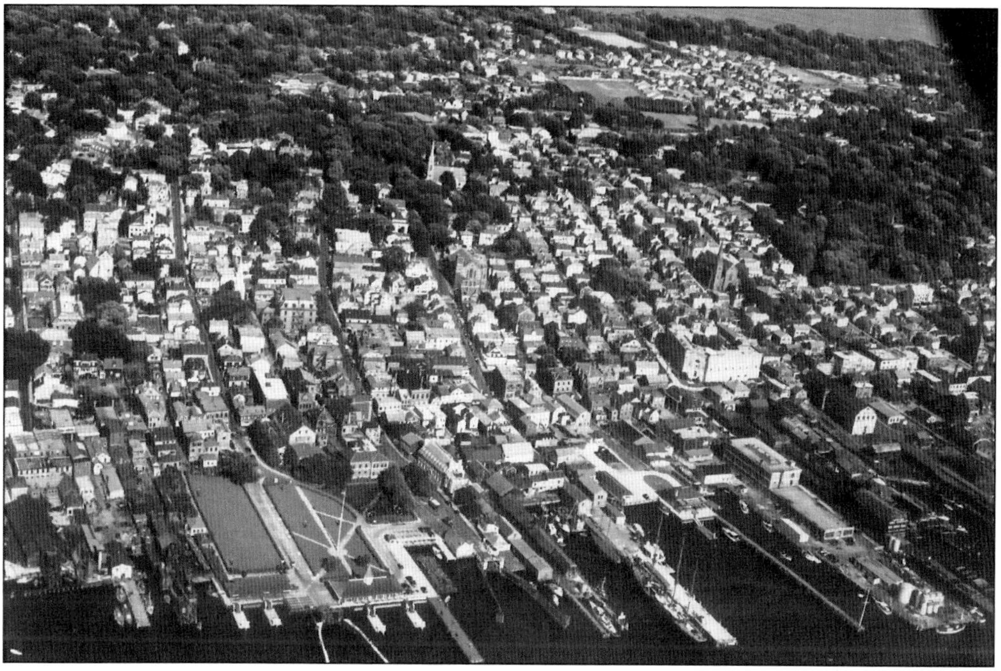

An aerial view of Government Landing and the surrounding area, taken in July 1937 by H.H. Harris. (Photograph courtesy of the William Bachus Collection)

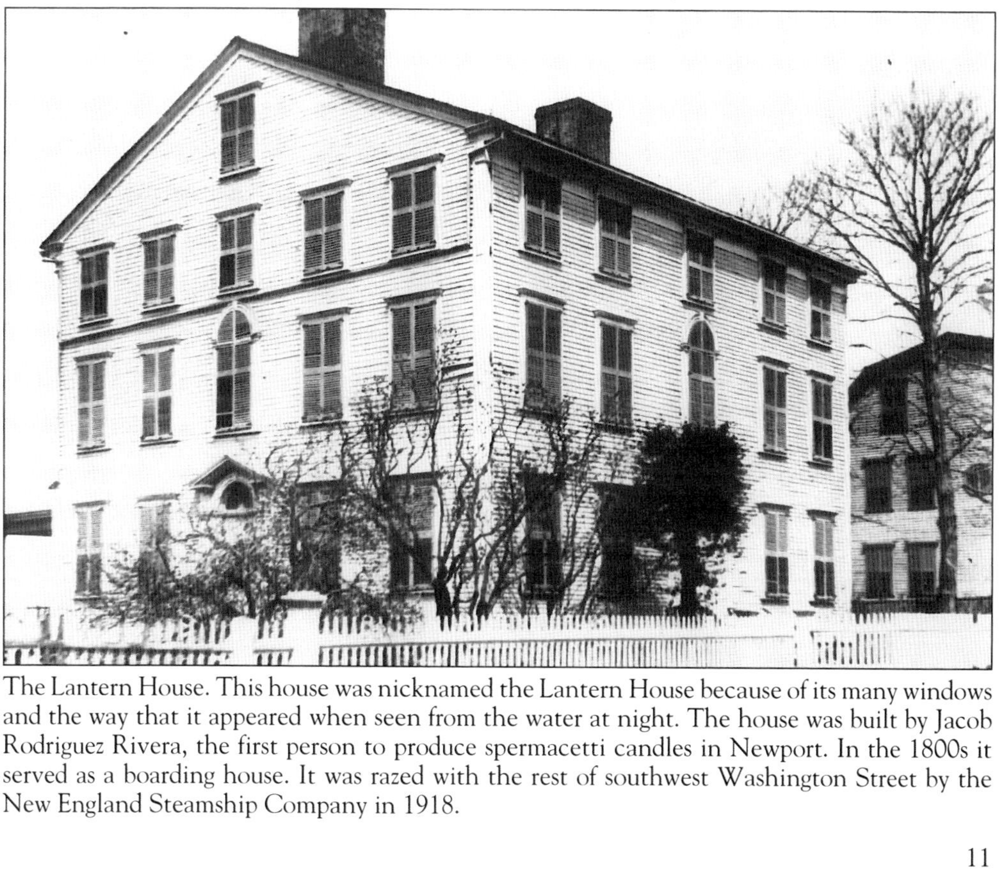

The Lantern House. This house was nicknamed the Lantern House because of its many windows and the way that it appeared when seen from the water at night. The house was built by Jacob Rodriguez Rivera, the first person to produce spermacetti candles in Newport. In the 1800s it served as a boarding house. It was razed with the rest of southwest Washington Street by the New England Steamship Company in 1918.

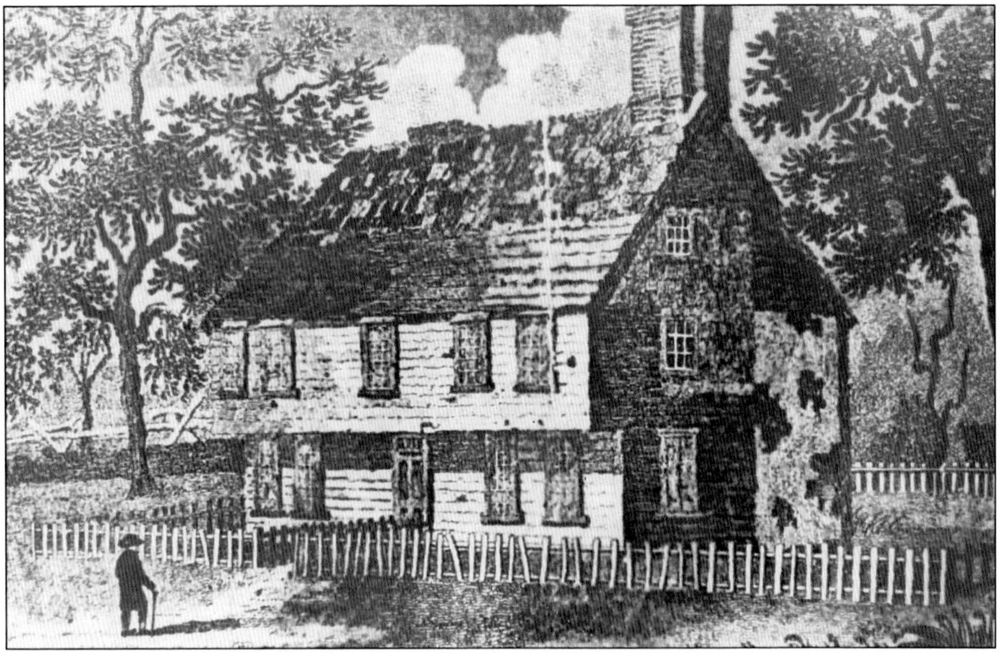

The Governor William Coddington House, built in 1641 on Marlborough Street, from an old woodcut. Coddington served as governor from 1640 until 1647 and again from 1674 to 1676. He died on November 1, 1678. The house was taken down in 1835 by Clarke Burdick, a decision he later regretted.

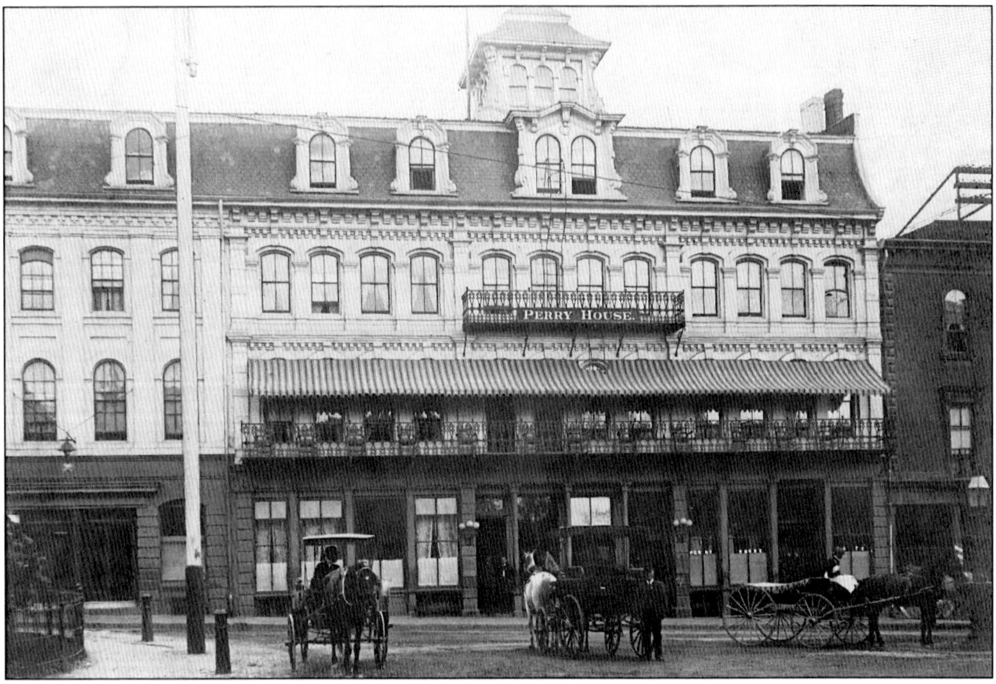

The Perry House Hotel on Washington Square. This structure, built by P.C. Shanahan in 1865 and named in honor of Commodore Perry, was demolished in the mid-1920s and replaced by the Horgan building, which remains standing to this day.

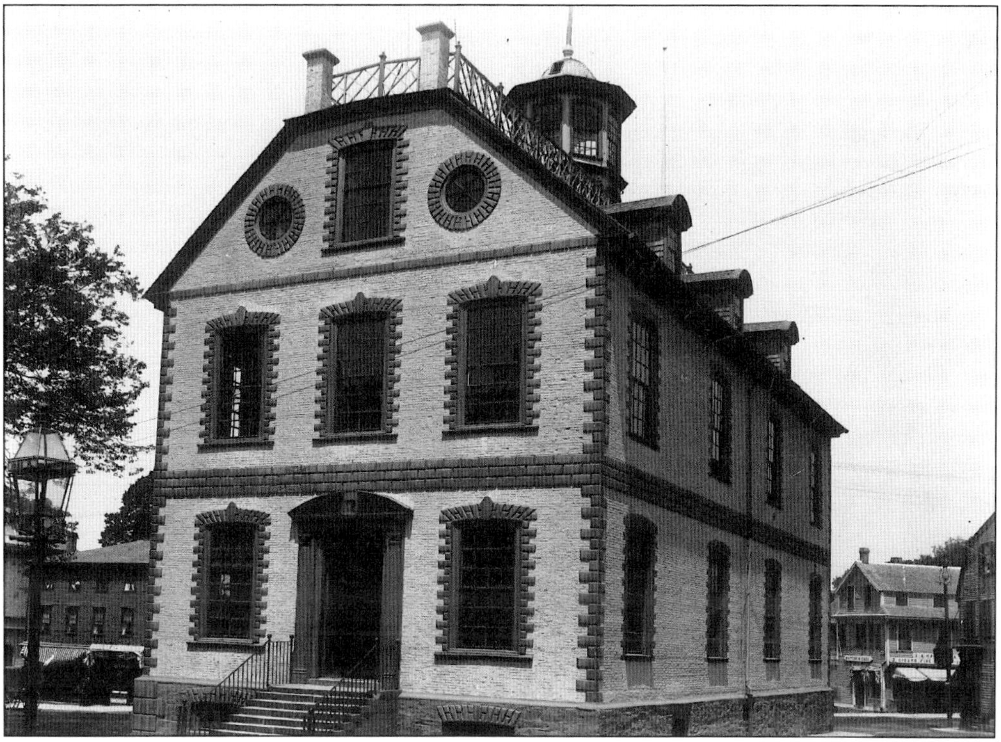

The Old Colony House viewed from the south in the 1890s. It was built in 1739 and designed by Richard Mundy. On May 4, 1776, from the balcony on the front of the building, Rhode Islands' declaration of independence was proclaimed two months before the other colonies. (Photograph by P.H. Caswell)

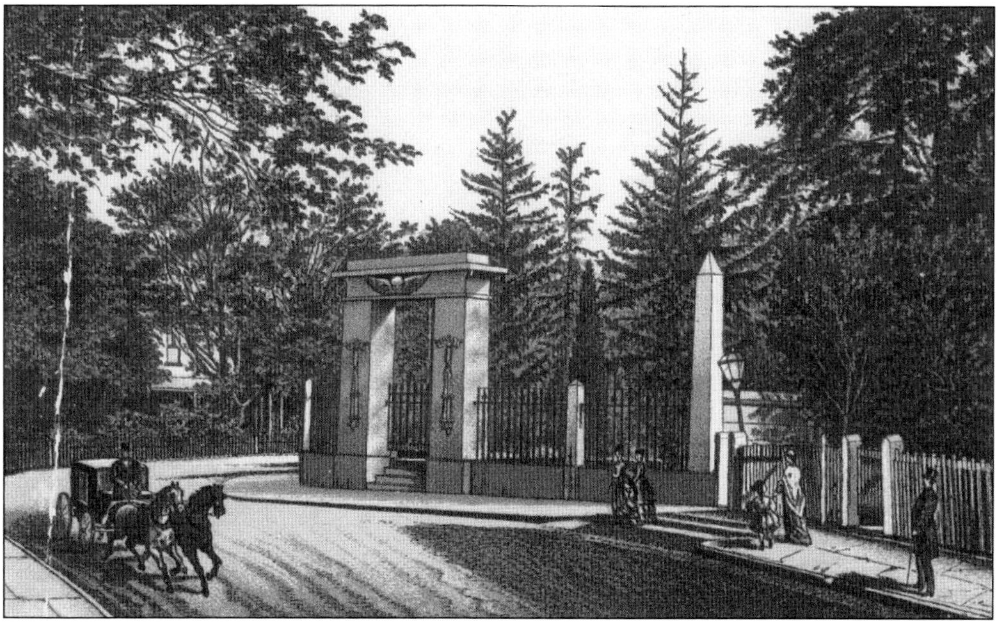

An early lithograph of Touro Cemetery at the intersections of Bellevue Avenue and Touro and Kay Streets. First used as a cemetery in 1677, it was restored in 1842.

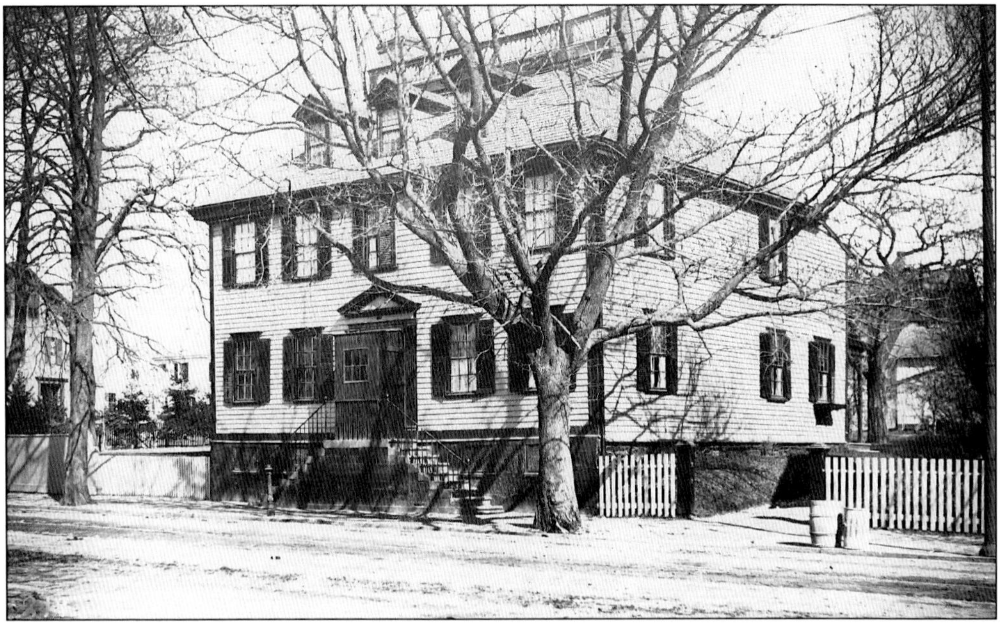

The Doctor John P. Mann House on Broadway. Born in Attleboro, Massachusetts, in 1755, Mann was a graduate of Brown University. After graduating, he resided and practiced in Newport, where he died on September 24, 1837.

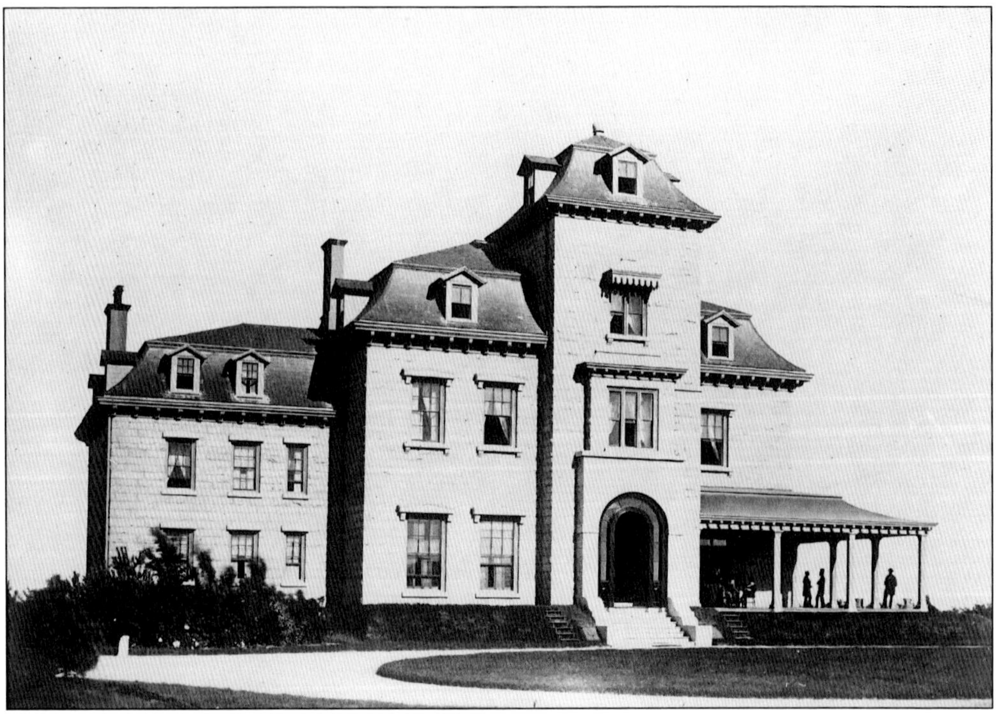

Chateau Sur Mer on Bellevue Avenue, built in 1851 by William S Wetmore, in a photograph taken before 1872. In 1872 Richard Morris Hunt was commissioned to enlarge the mansion; while doing so changed the roofline of the tower and house, and moved the front door to the left.

A view of Eastons Beach by H.H. Harris taken in July of 1937. At the top of the photograph is the roller coaster that was swept into Eastons Pond by the tidal surge from the "Hurricane of '38." (Courtesy of the William Bachus Collection)

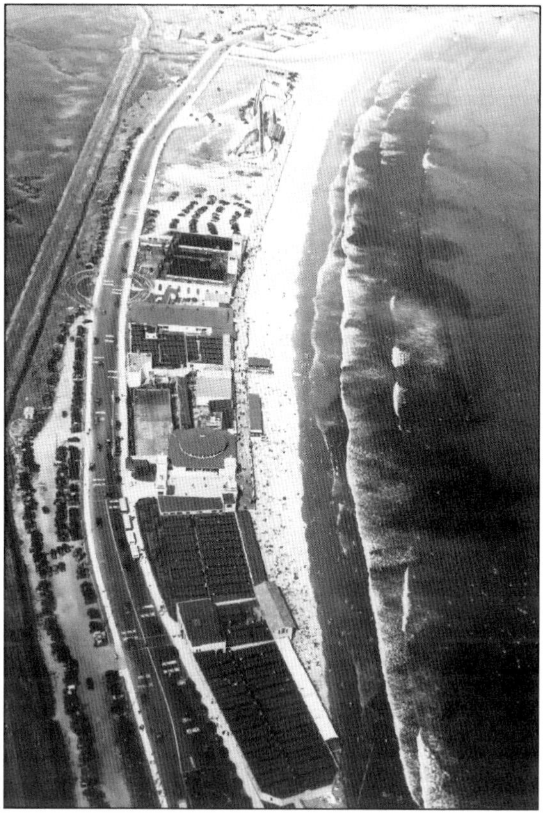

The Cliff Hotel in 1899, overlooking Eastons Beach. On June 8, 1908, it was consumed by fire.

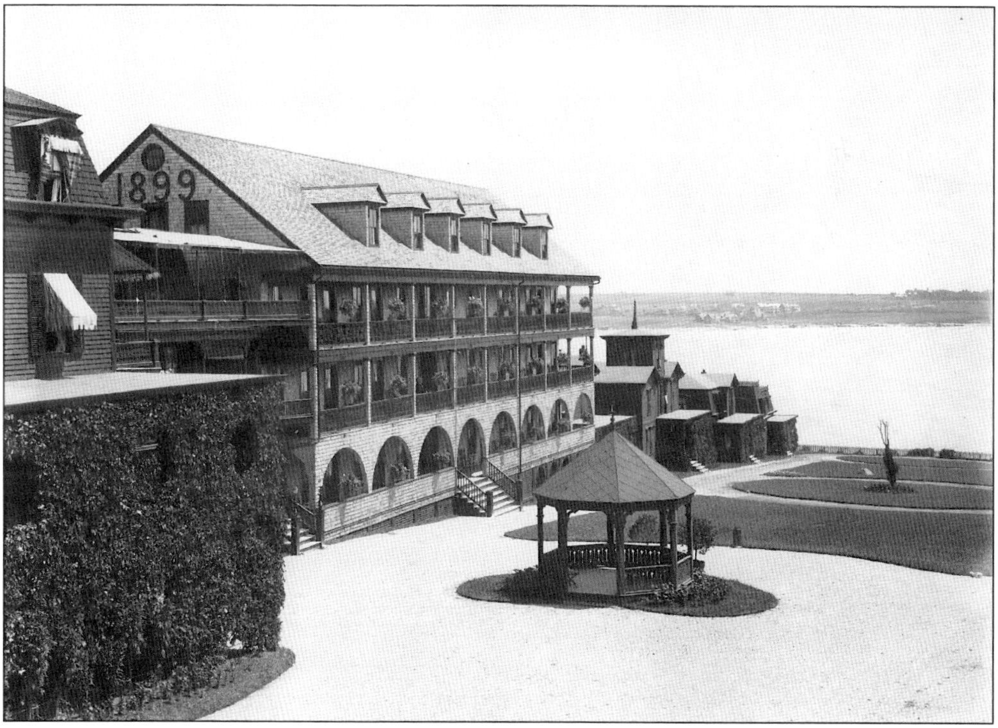

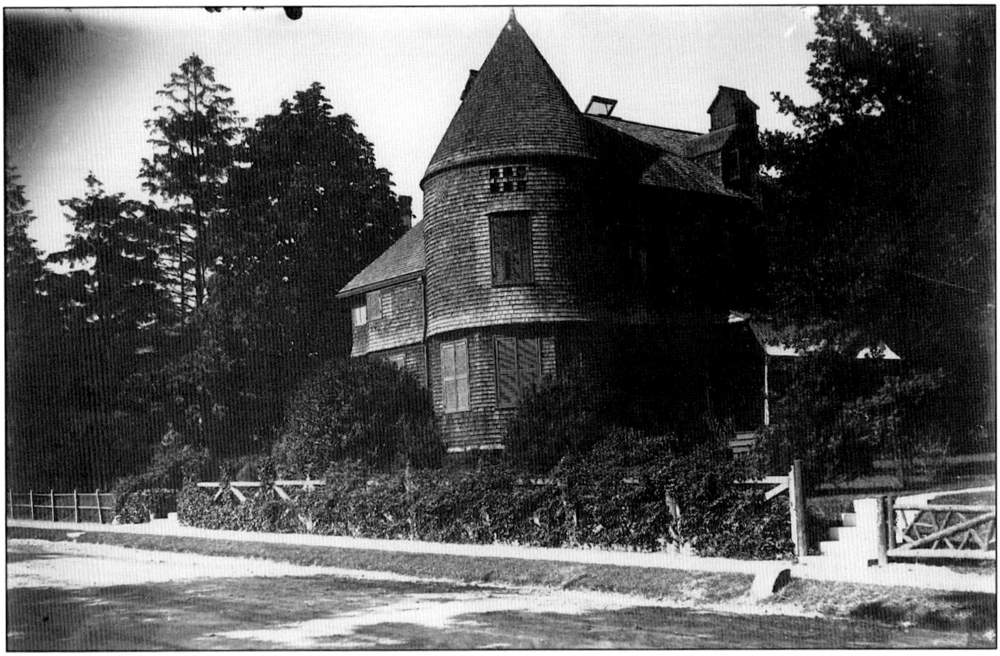

The Skinner House as it appeared in 1895. The house was built in 1882 on Red Cross Avenue.

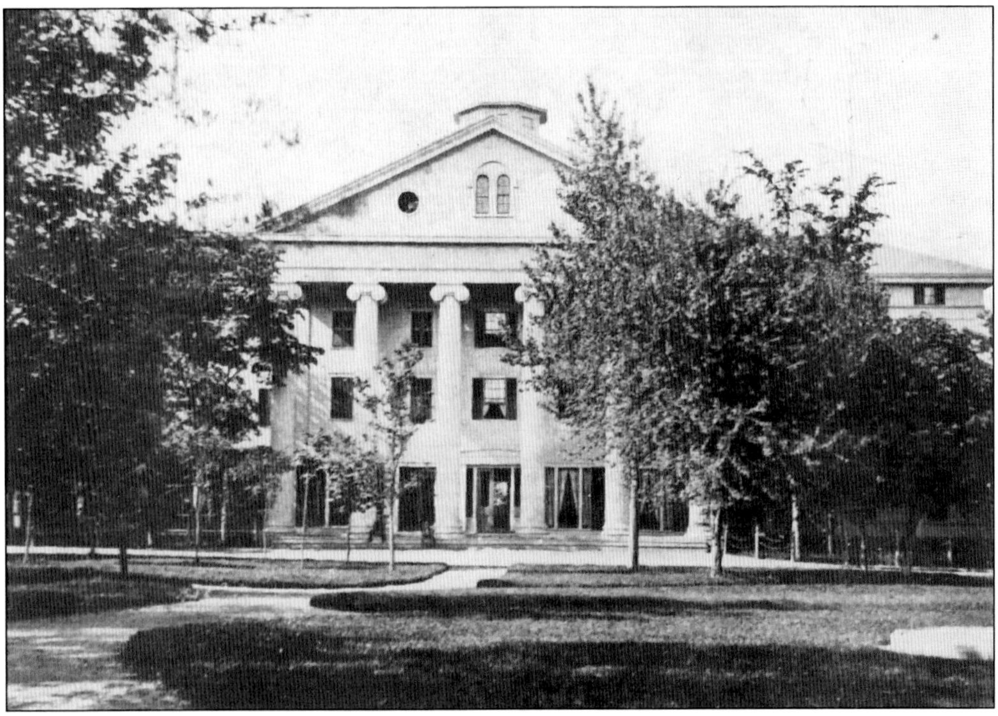

The Atlantic House at the corner of Bellevue Avenue and Pelham Street. Built in 1844, this was one of the most popular hotels in Newport. In 1861 the War between the States was declared. On May 8, 1861, the frigate *Constitution* removed 130 midshipman from Annapolis, being too close to the hostilities. The Atlantic House was taken by the federal navy to house them. The hotel closed in 1874 and in 1877 it was broken up and taken away.

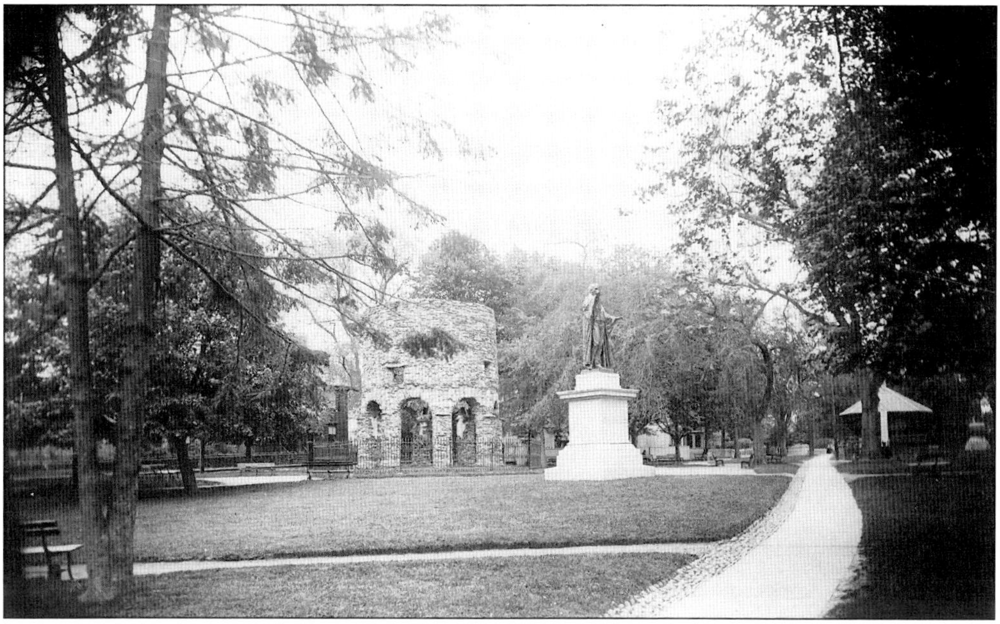

Touro Park looking southwest in 1895. The stone mill and the statue of William Ellery Channing are visible. The statue was created by W.C. Noble, and was a gift from William G. Weld in 1893.

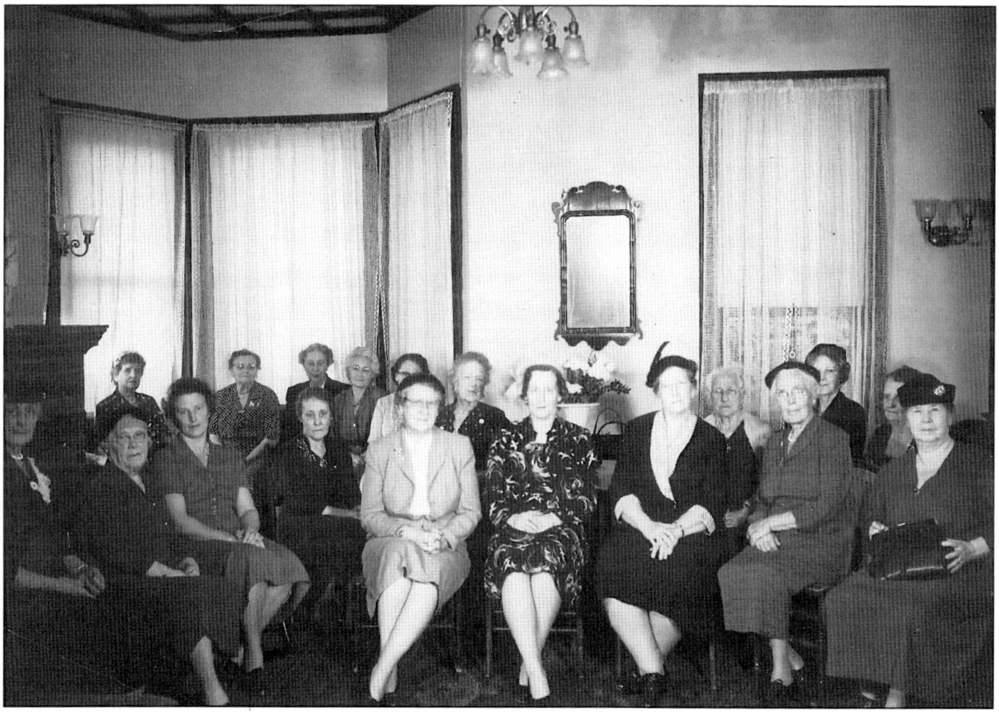

Channing Girls. The Channing Memorial Church was erected in 1881. The belfry chimes consisted of nine bells, the largest weighing 2,170 pounds, and were the first in Newport. This group photograph taken in the early '50s was a women's organization who met at the church and were known as the Channing Girls. (Photograph courtesy of the Peter H. Sherman family)

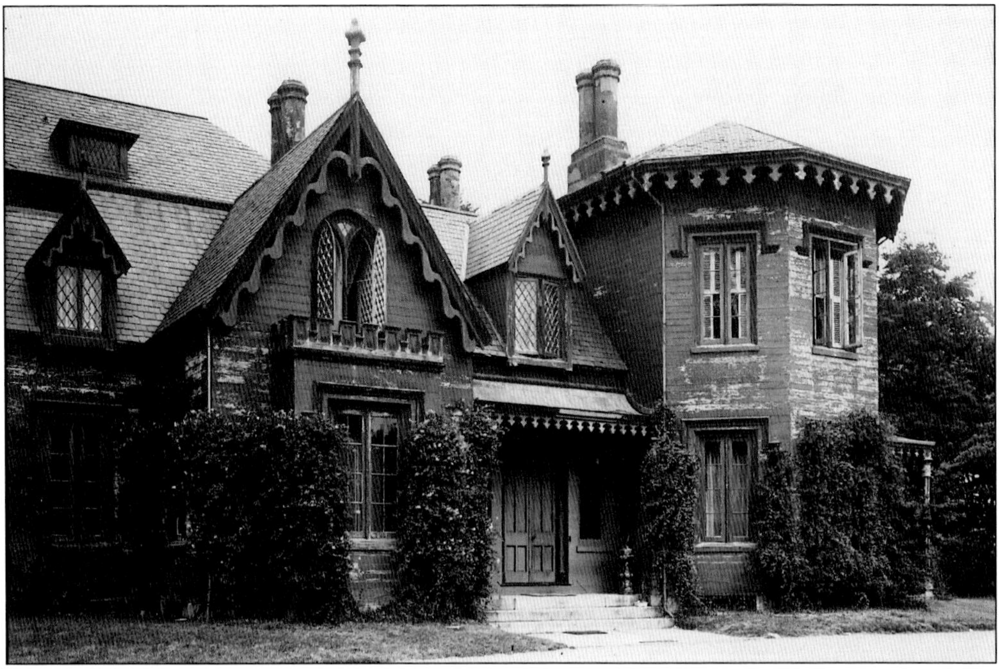

KingsCote at the corner of Bellevue Avenue and East Bowery Street. The mansion was built by Noble Jones, a Savannah native who summered in Newport, and was designed by Richard Upjohn in the early 1840s. Today, owned by the Newport Preservation Society, it has been restored and is open for tours. This photo shows the house before restoration. (Photograph by Meservny)

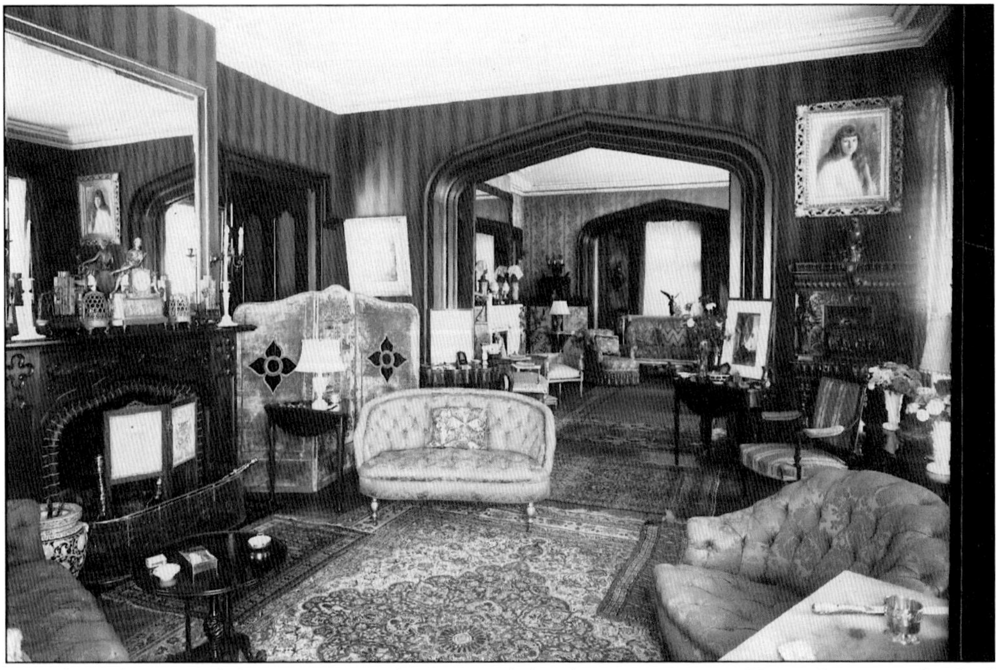

Another photograph by Meservny, this time of the drawing room at KingsCote as it looked in 1949.

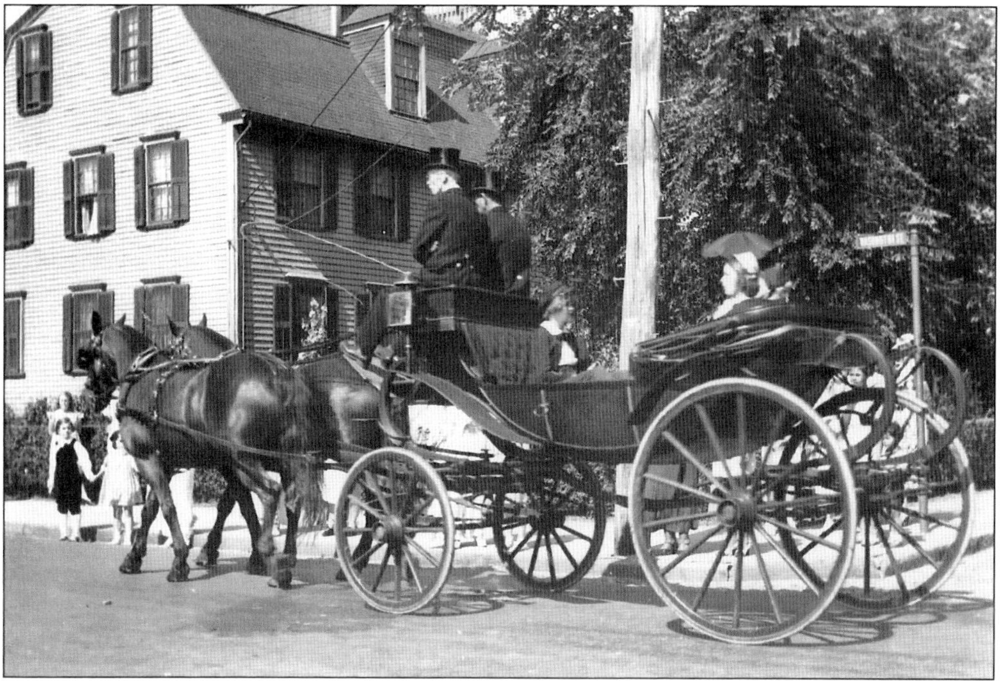

Old Port Days on the Point in 1925. The building in the background is the Dennis House, built in 1740. For the celebration, residents on the Point dressed in colonial costumes and many of the houses were open to display antiques and family heirlooms.

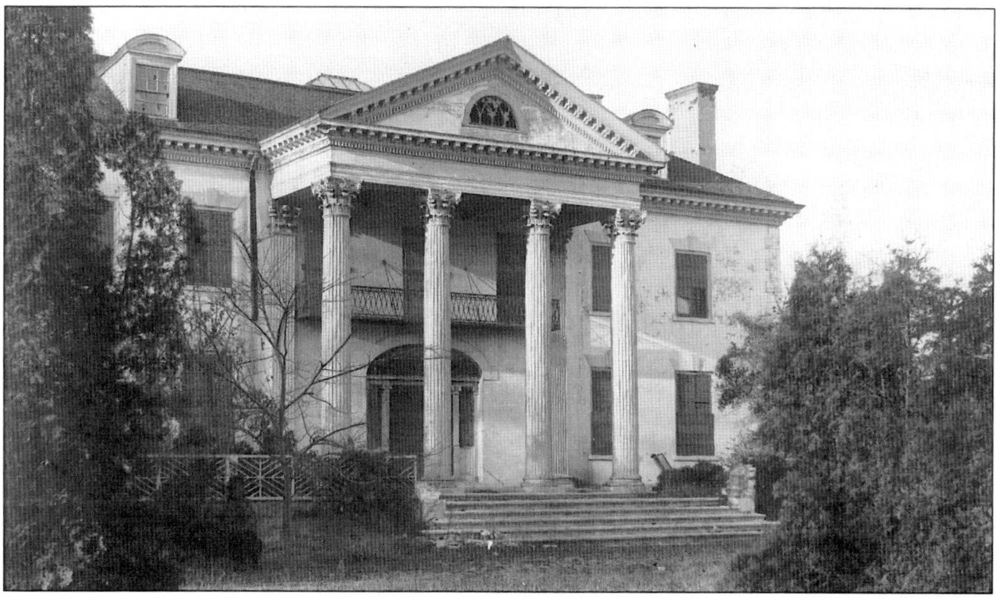

Whitehall, built in the latter part of the 1800s by Dexter Bradford at the corner of Rhode Island Avenue and Catherine Street. Martin J. Murphy tells the story of the Coogan family who acquired this house in 1903. The family had planned a huge affair for their daughters coming out party. On the night of the party not one guest showed up. It seems that the Coogans were snubbed by Newports 400. It is said that the Coogans walked out of the house that night and returned to Manhattan, never to set foot in Newport again.

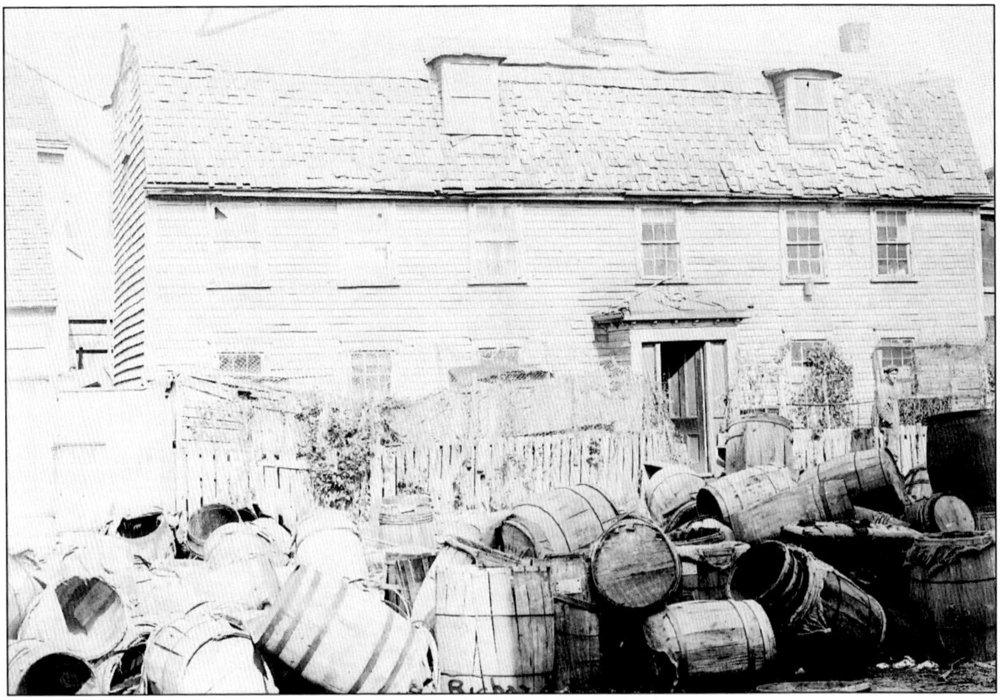

The Richardson House on Whittier Pass at Thames Street. Built in 1715, it was torn down in 1940. This photograph was taken in 1873. (Photograph by W. Shea)

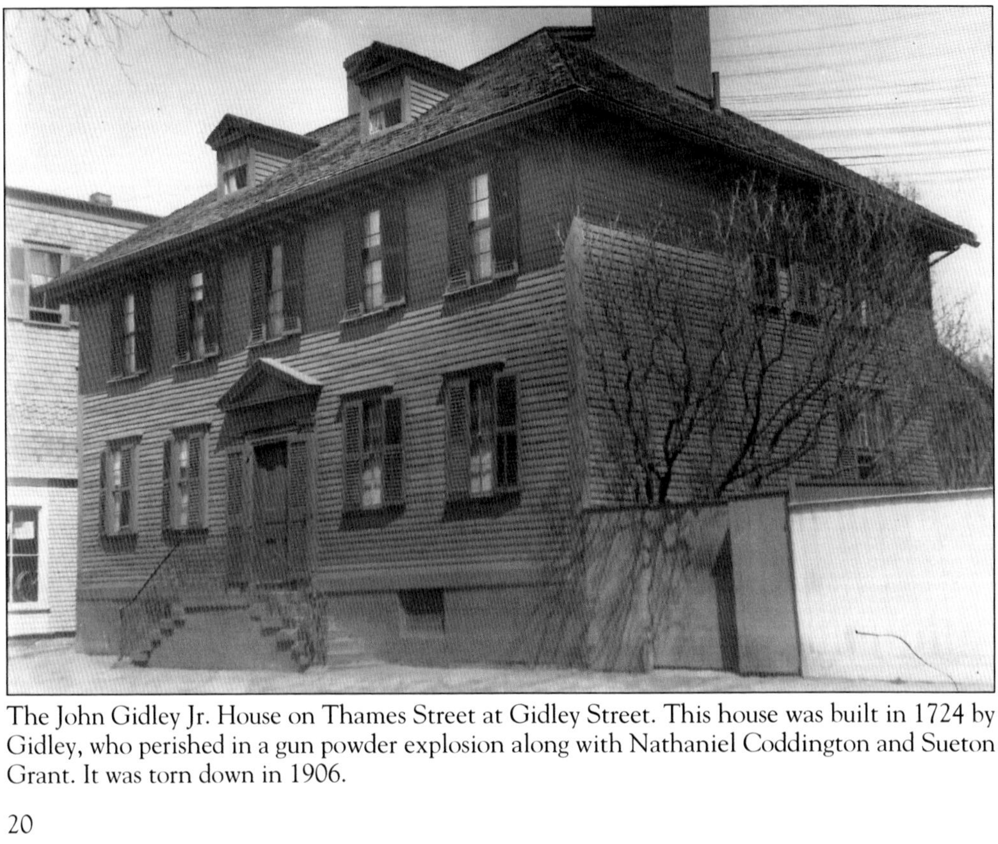

The John Gidley Jr. House on Thames Street at Gidley Street. This house was built in 1724 by Gidley, who perished in a gun powder explosion along with Nathaniel Coddington and Sueton Grant. It was torn down in 1906.

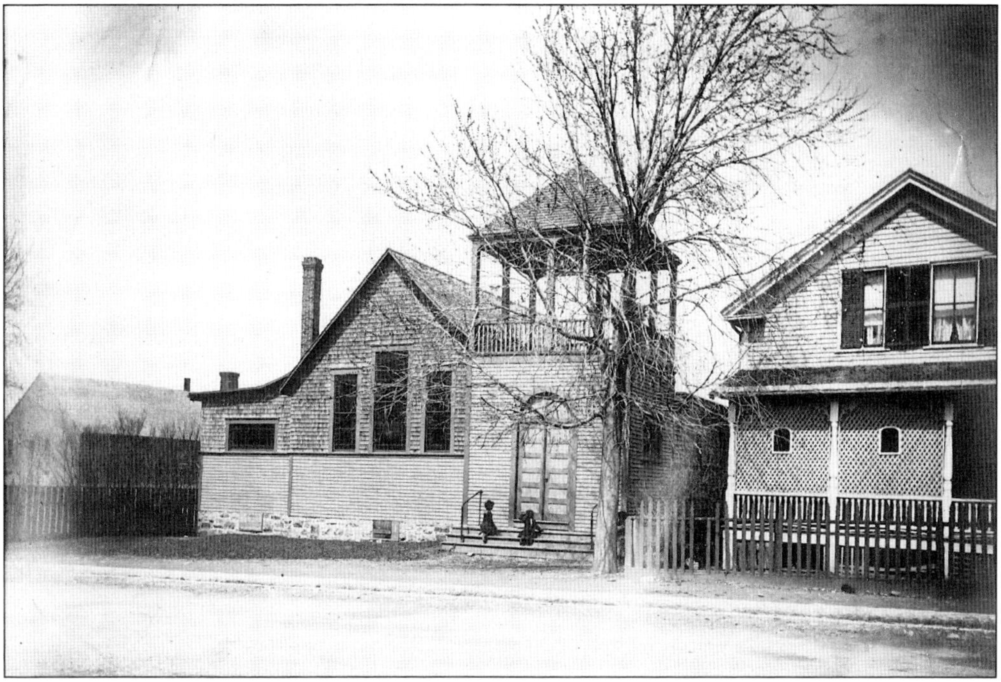

Home of the Hibernians, formerly the Grace Chapel, built in 1888 on Wellington Avenue. Since the early 1900s it has served as the home of the Ancient Order of the Hibernians.

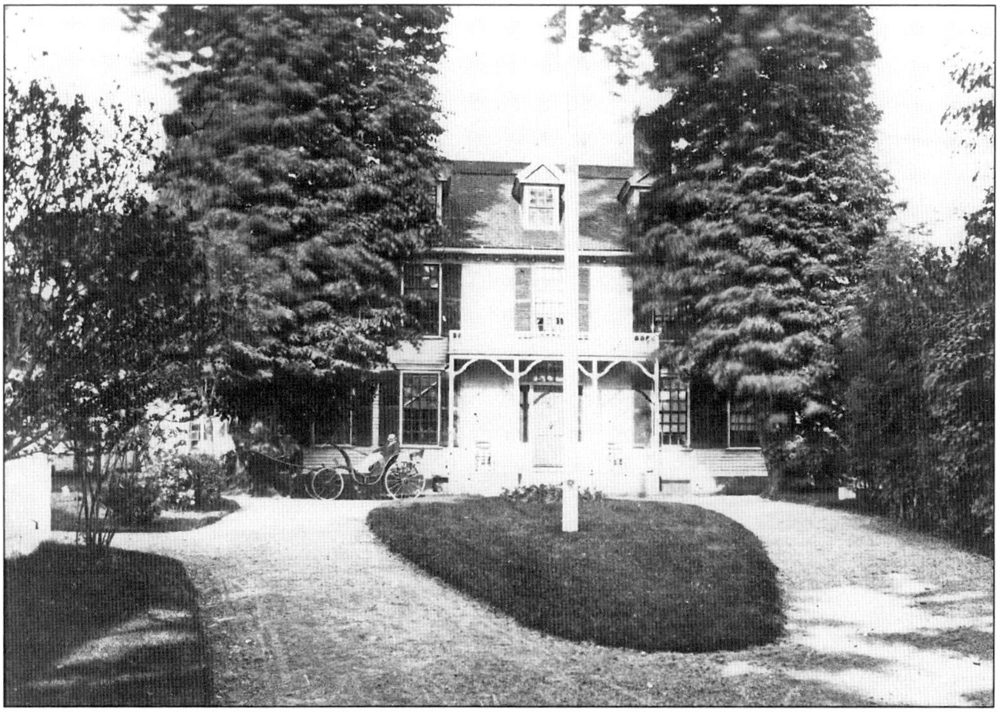

The Jahleel Brenton House on Thames Street. Built by Brenton in 1720, possibly on a design by Richard Mundy, this building was razed in the 1920s. Brenton also owned a summer estate on the site of Fort Adams.

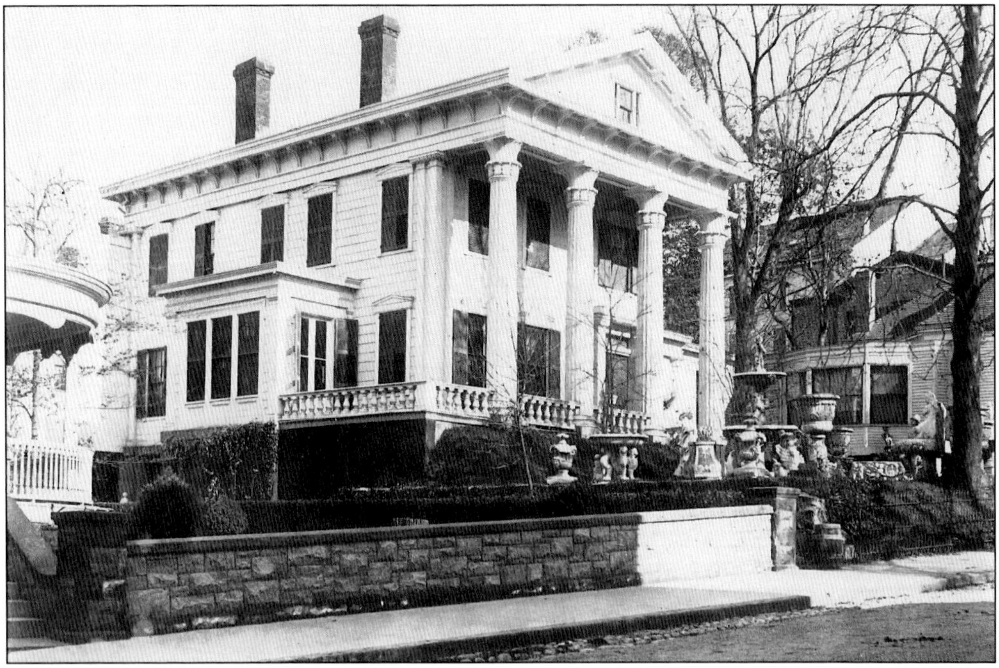

The Charles Van Zandt House. In 1838 a mariner named Captain Augustus Littlefield commissioned John Ladd to build this residence on Pelham Street. Governor Charles Van Zandt was the next owner. Behind the house is a cemetery (not open to the public) where Governor Benedict Arnold was buried in 1677.

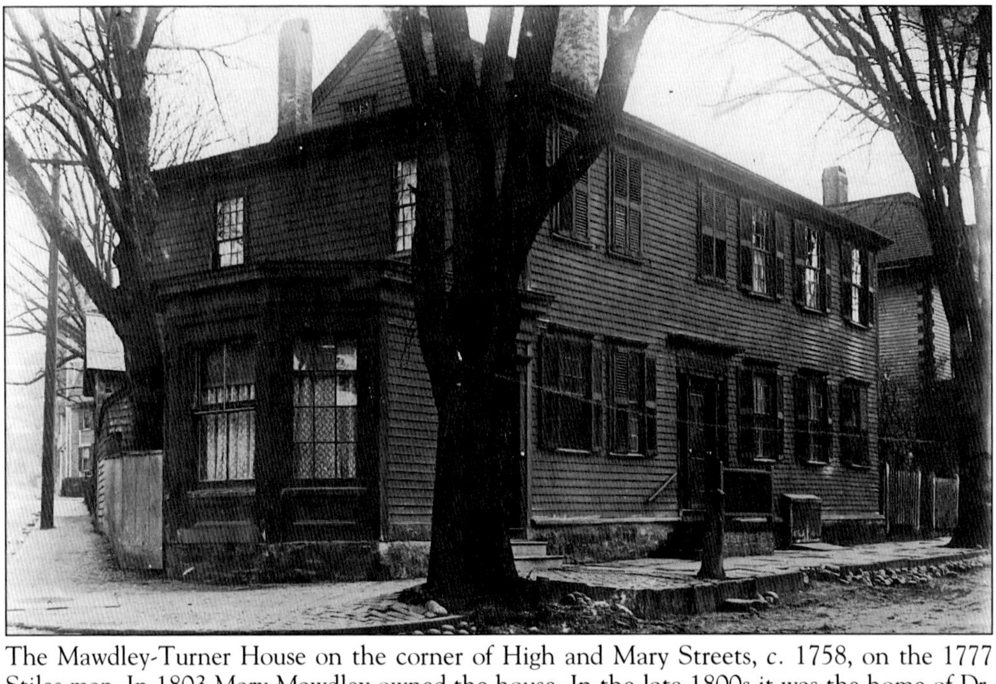

The Mawdley-Turner House on the corner of High and Mary Streets, c. 1758, on the 1777 Stiles map. In 1803 Mary Mawdley owned the house. In the late 1800s it was the home of Dr. Turner, who was with Admiral Perry at the Battle of Lake Erie in 1812. The house still stands on its original site.

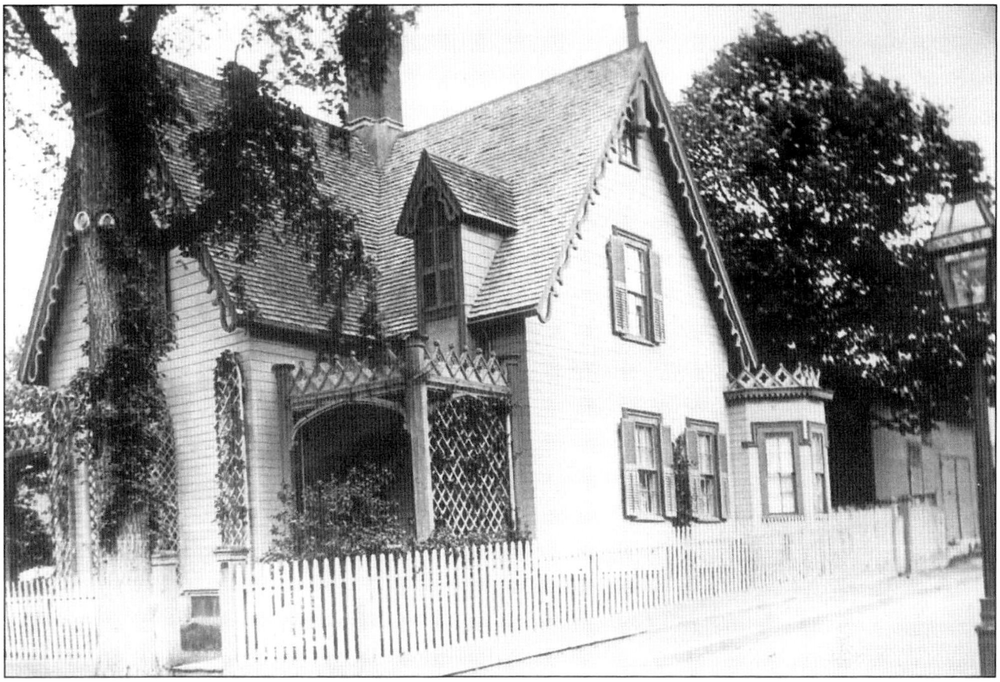

The Benjamin Marsh House, built in 1840. The house stands on the northeast corner of School and Mary Streets. In recent years it has been painstakingly restored by June and Don Occaso. (Photograph courtesy of Adam Occaso)

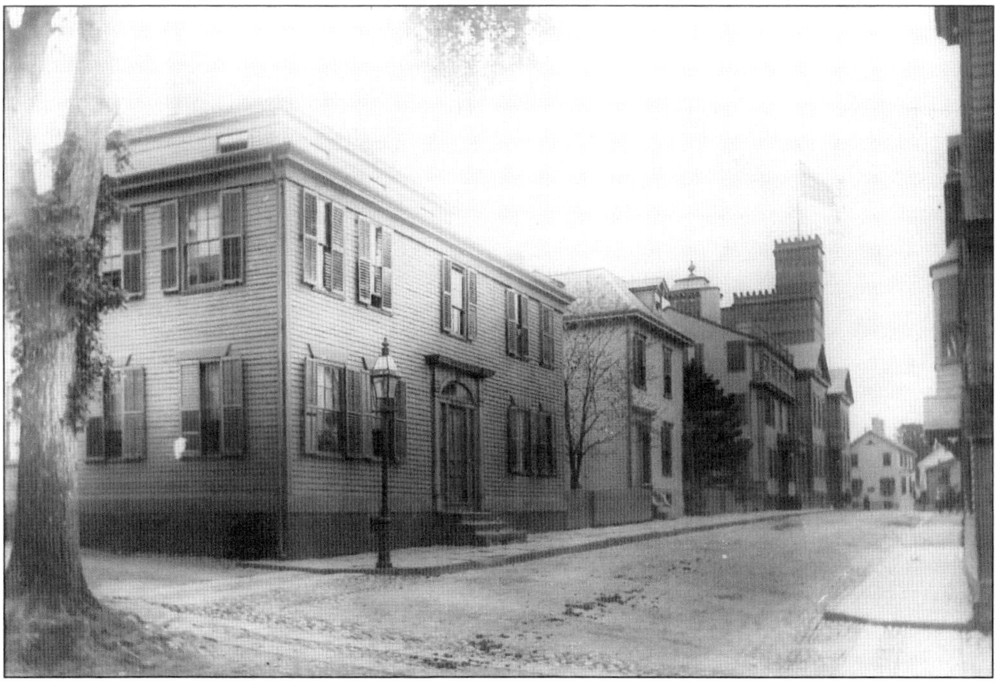

The house at the southeast corner of School and Mary Streets, built around 1750. This was the birthplace of William Ellery Channing, founder of the Channing Memorial Church. In 1866 it was opened as the Home for Friendless Children.

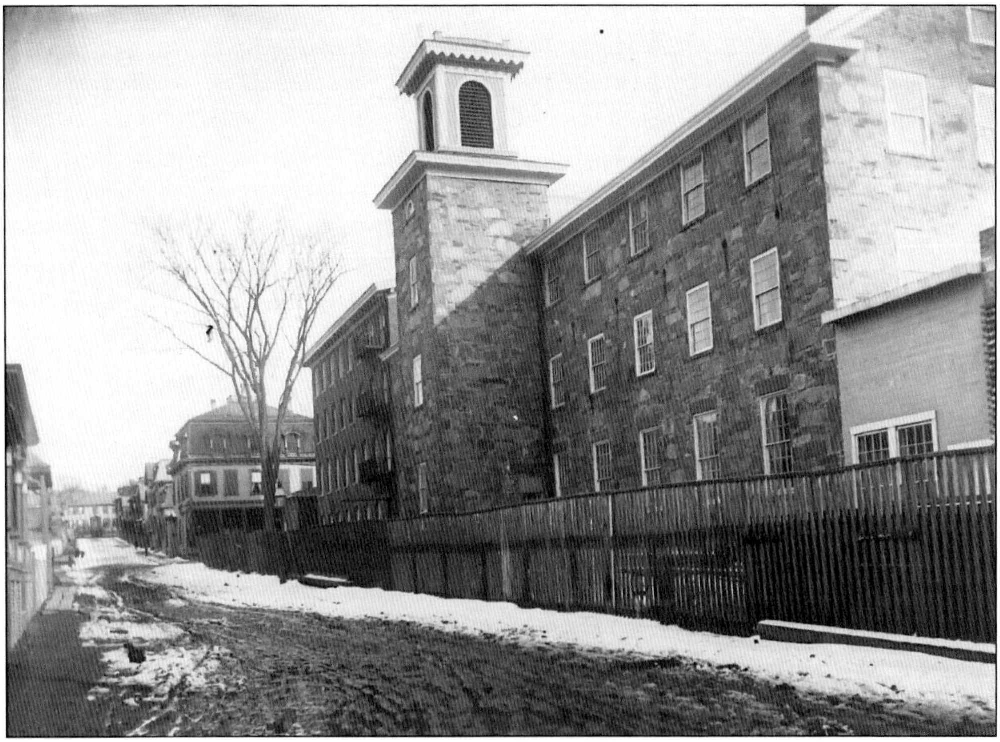

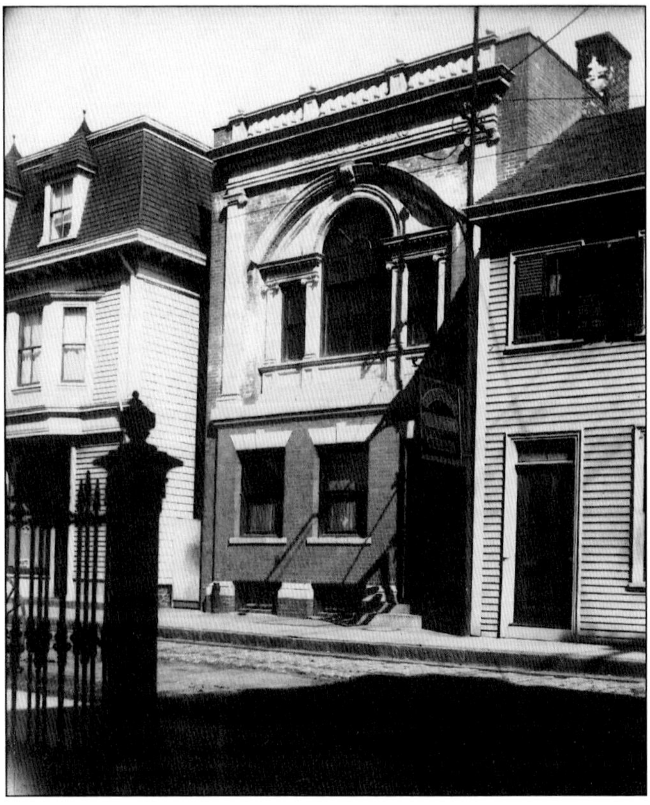

The Aquidneck Mill on Thames and Howard Streets. The mill was constructed as the Newport Steam Mill in 1831 and enlarged in 1865. Its purpose was to spin cotton purchased from southern ports. During its operation it employed over 100 people and had 6,000 spindles running. The mill ceased spinning cotton in 1883; this photograph dates to 1880.

The Telephone Exchange Building, built on Spring Street in 1890. In 1877 the first telephone agency was started by Henry Cozzens and Henry Bull Jr. The first connection was with Fall River. Mr. Lyman Freeze sang a song whose words were clearly heard on this end.

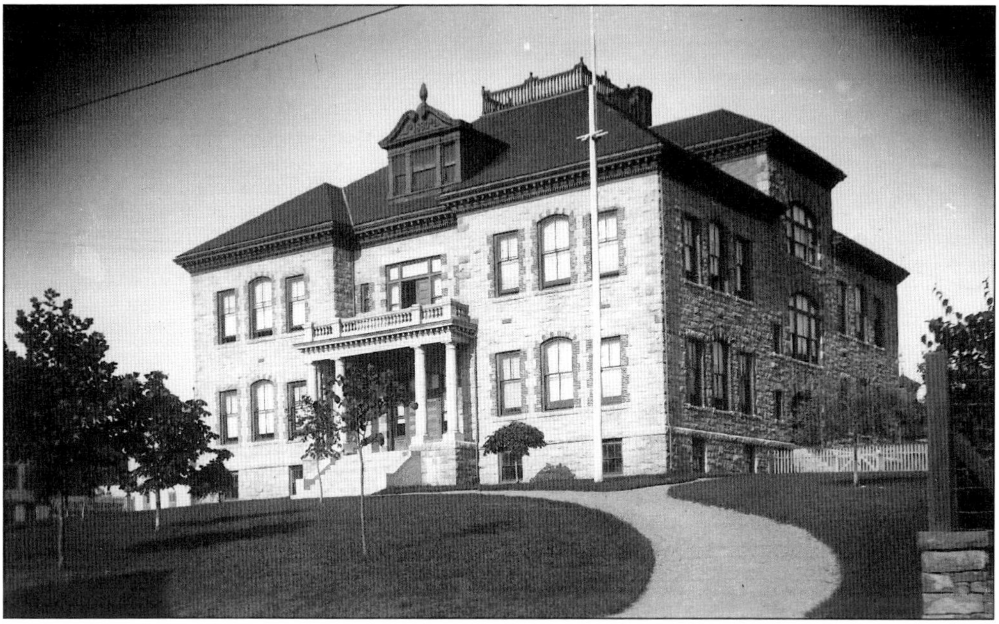

The Lenthal School on Spring Street as it looked in the 1890s. Designed by James Fludder and members of the school committee, it was built in 1886 and dedicated the following year.

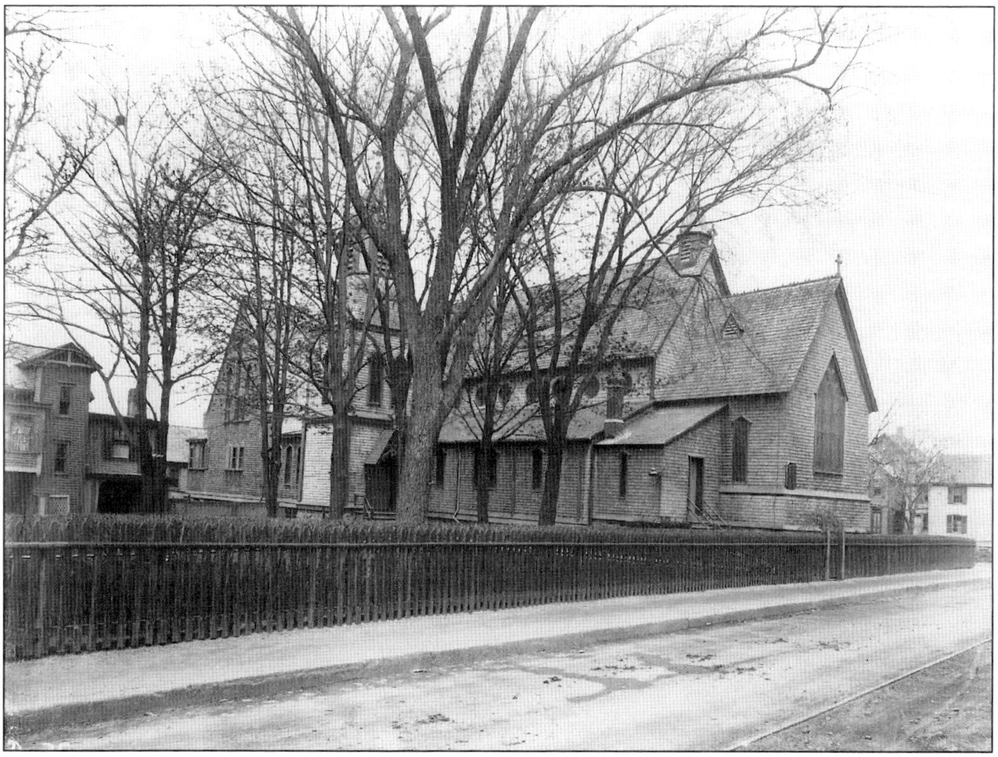

The old Emmanual Church on Spring Street at the corner of Dearborn Street in 1890. The church was consecrated in 1858. A new church was consecrated in 1902, a gift from Mrs. John Nicholas Brown.

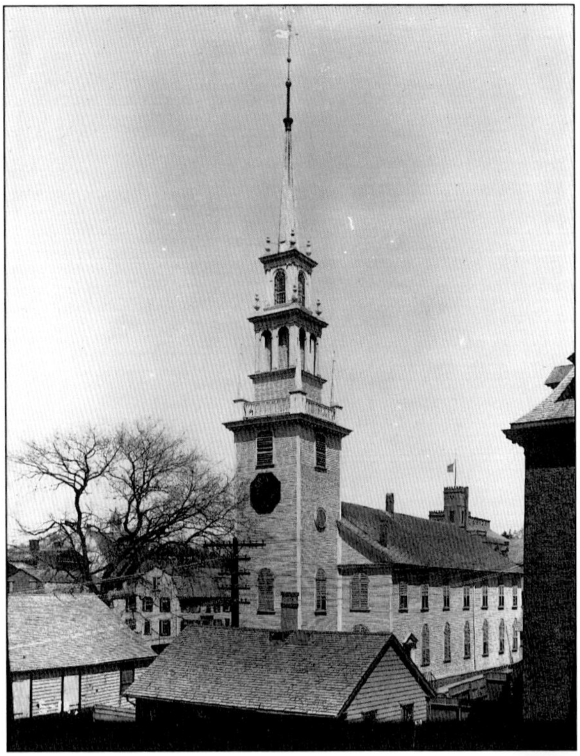

The second Trinity Church building, designed by Richard Mundy. The first Trinity Church building was erected in 1702. By 1725 the congregation had grown too large for the building and the building shown here was built soon after. The spire was designed in 1725 but not erected until 1741. After a severe gale in 1768 it was dismantled and reconstructed. This photograph was taken *c.* 1880. (Photograph by P.H. Caswell)

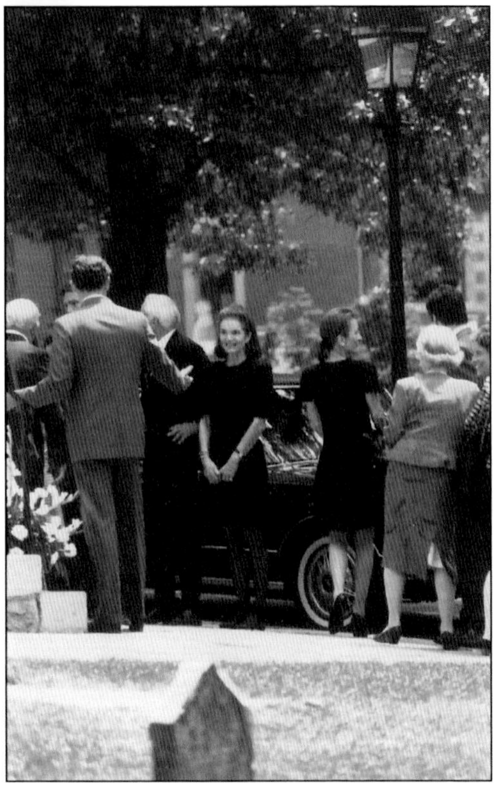

Jacqueline Kennedy Onassis at the funeral services for her mother, Janet Lee Auchincloss, at Trinity Church on July 27, 1989. Mrs. Auchincloss was a member of the church since the early 1940s. (Photograph courtesy of Doug Baker)

The original Trinity Church organ, in a photograph taken from the south gallery before 1929. This early organ was signed by Robert Bridges, London and dated 1733. It was a gift from Dean George Berkley (see p. 73). In 1929 the present organ was installed.

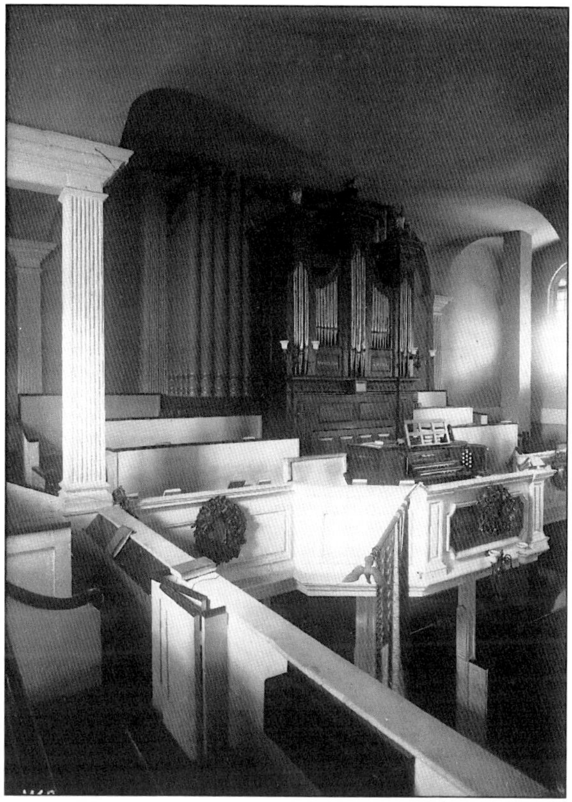

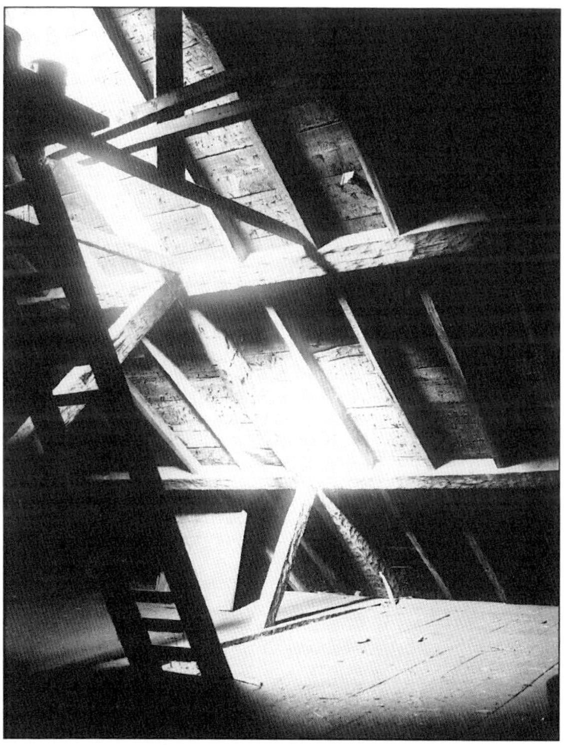

A 1920 photograph of the church showing the roof trusses on the south side. In 1762 the church was cut into two pieces and lengthened by two bays, increasing its length to seven bays.

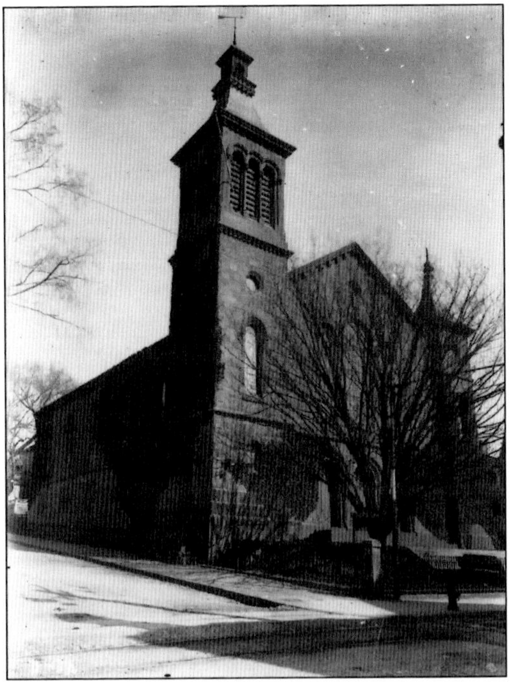

The United Congregational Church on Spring and Pelham Streets. In 1855 the cornerstone was laid, and the following year the church was completed and the pews sold at auction.

The United Baptist Church on Spring Street. Founded in 1638, this building was erected in 1846 and rebuilt in 1949. It rests on the site of the meetinghouse built in 1738. It is the fourth church built by the Baptists on Aquidneck Island. The first was on Green End Avenue, the second on Tanner Street, and the third and fourth on this site.

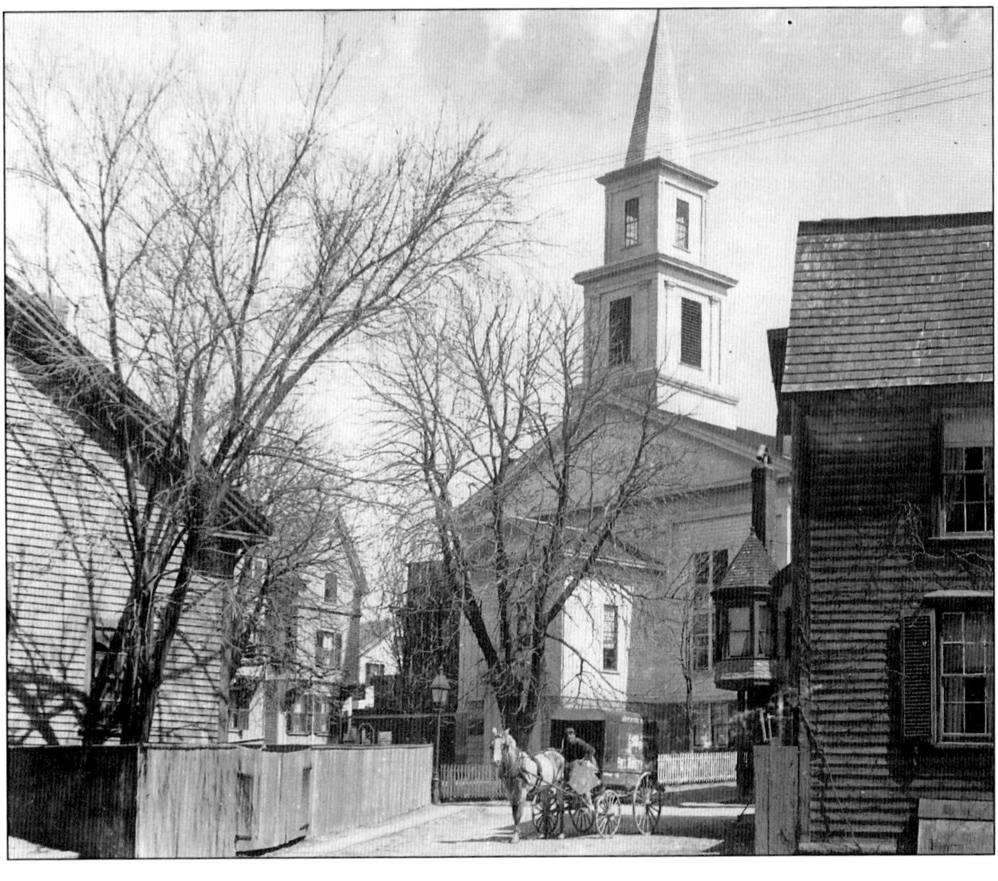

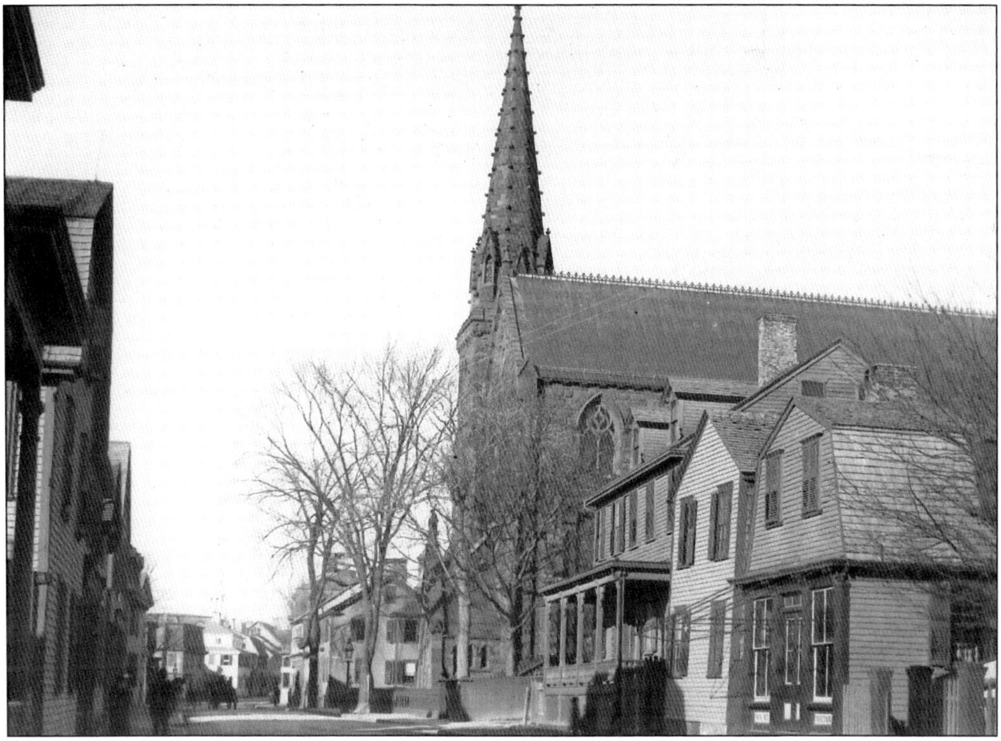

Saint Marys, Lady of the Isle, looking north from Ann Street. On April 8, 1828, Father Woodly purchased land and a building on Barney Street to use as a church; this was the origin of Saint Josephs parish. The congregation soon outgrew its house and in 1848 Patrick C. Keely designed the present structure on Spring Street. On July 25, 1852, the church was dedicated as Saint Marys, Lady of the Isle.

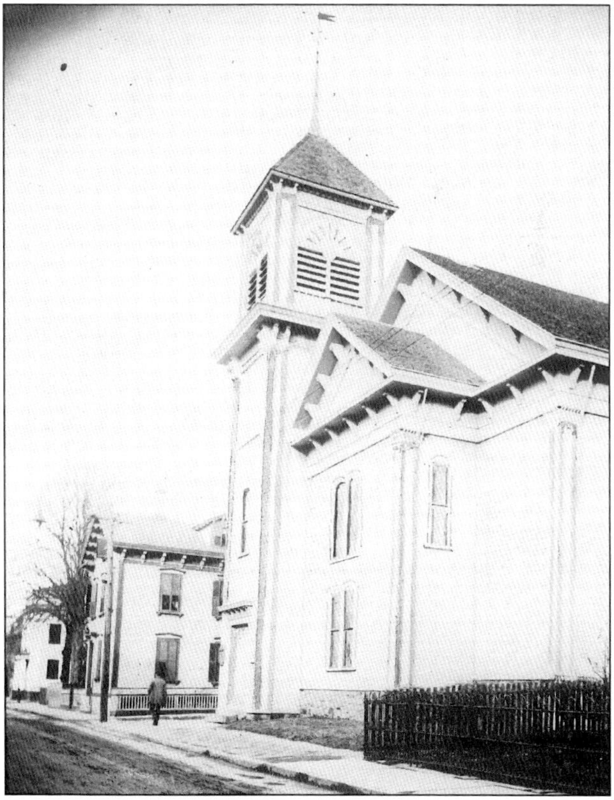

Saint Spyridon. The Greek community purchased this building in 1924 from the Methodists, who had moved to a new building on Marlborough Street. It was renovated and reconsecrated in the name of Saint Spyridon.

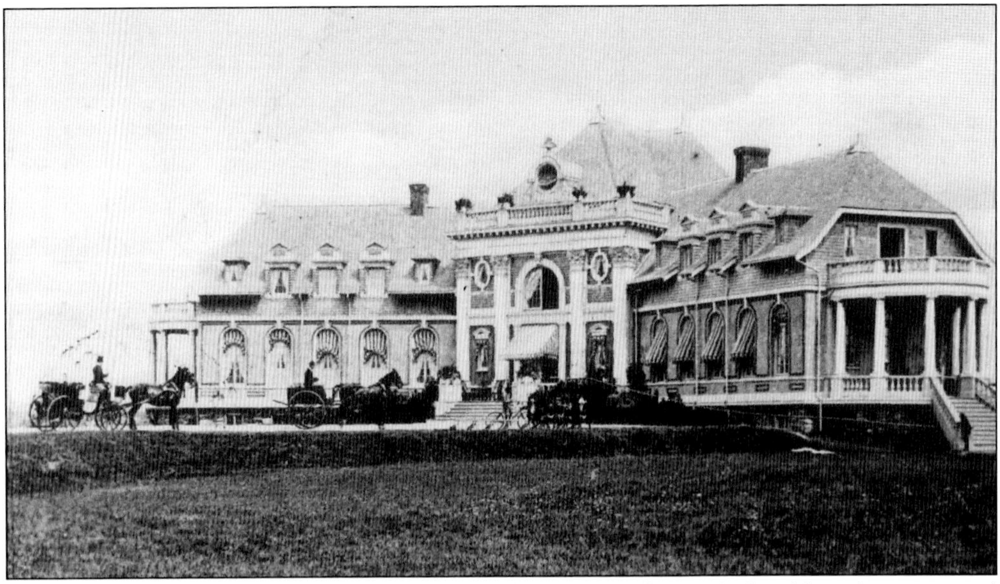

The Newport Country Club, established in 1893 by a group of New York golfers who summered here. The clubhouse was built in 1894 on a design by Whitney Warren. The golf course is among the oldest in America.

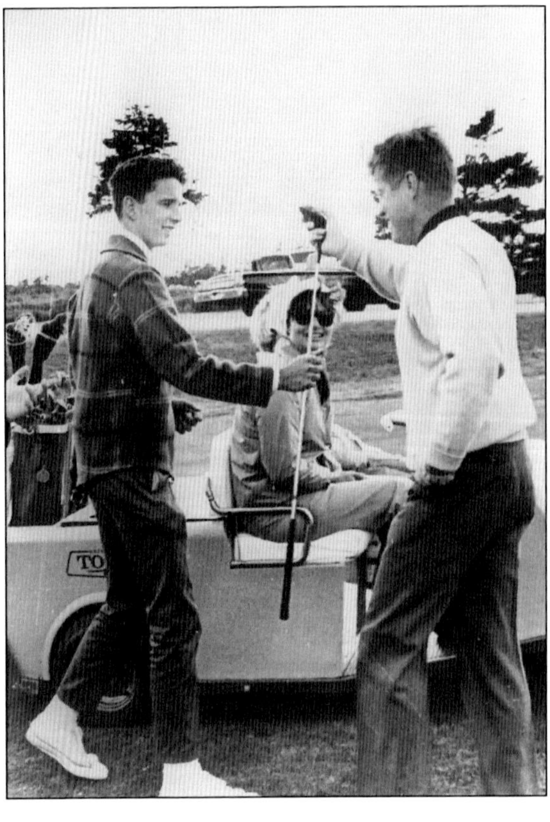

Ronald Hogan, Jacqueline Kennedy Onassis, and President Kennedy in early September 1963. During the Kennedy administration the first family frequently visited Newport, and Hammersmith Farm was dubbed the summer Whitehouse. The president enjoyed golf at the country club whenever he was here. (Photograph courtesy of Dot Hogan)

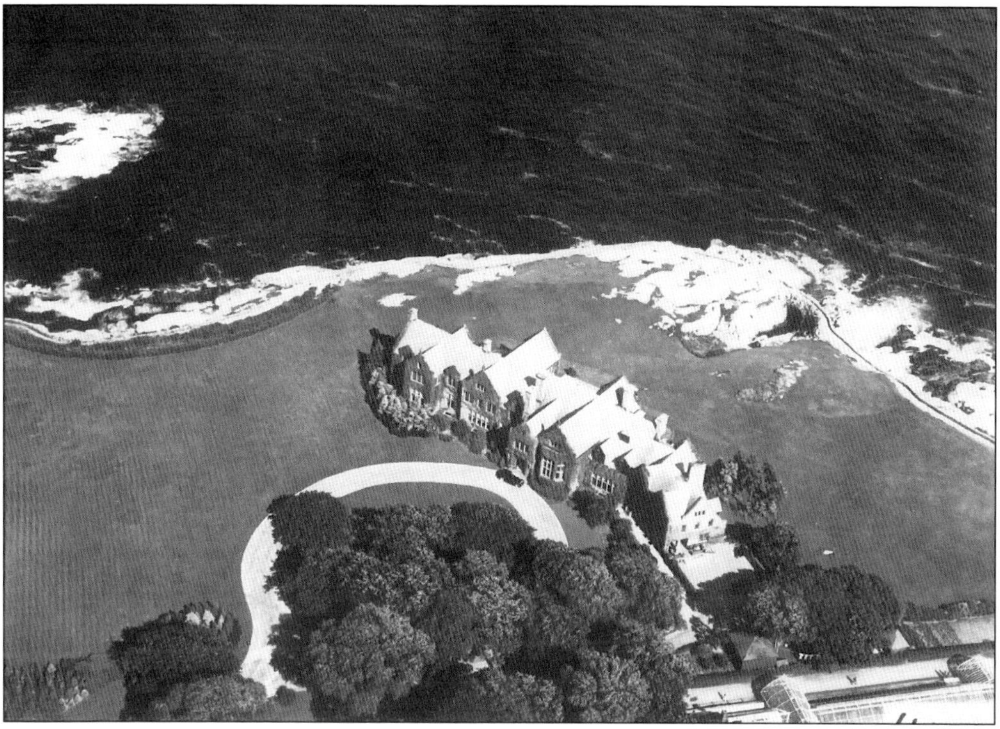

An imposing stone structure (formerly a wooden villa), built in 1888 by Frederick W. Vanderbilt. The next owner of Rough Point was James B. Duke, who left it to his daughter, Doris Duke. At her demise she willed the property to the Newport Restoration Foundation to be maintained and opened as a museum. (Photograph courtesy of the William Bachus Collection)

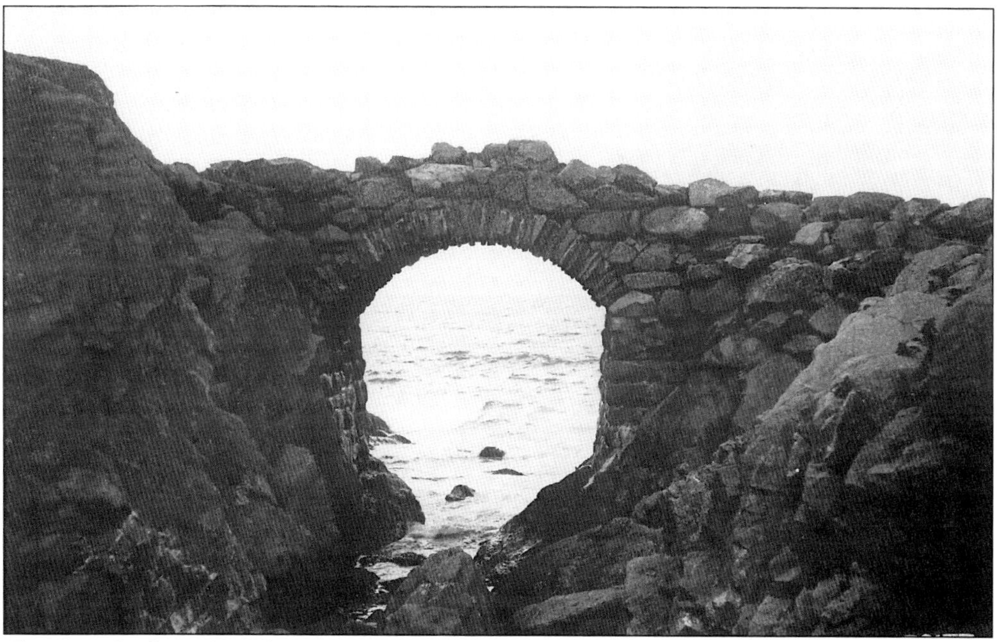

The stone bridge at Rough Point prior to being washed away by the 1938 hurricane.

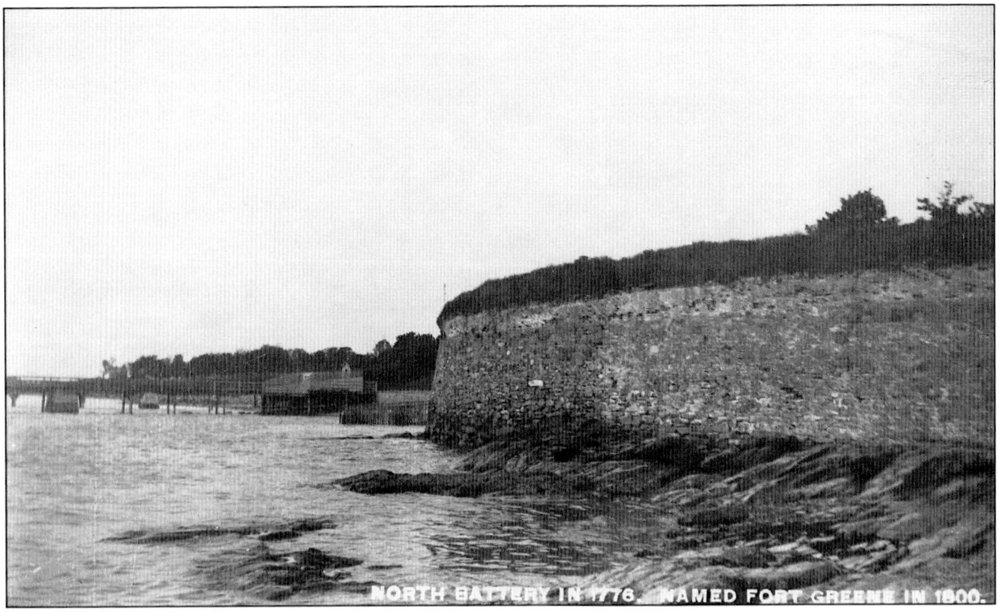

The site of North Battery. Prior to the Revolution there were four houses located here. They were torn down by order of the commanding officer of Rhode Island to erect North Battery. It was an enclosed fort with the entrance on Pine Street and was capable of housing twelve cannon.

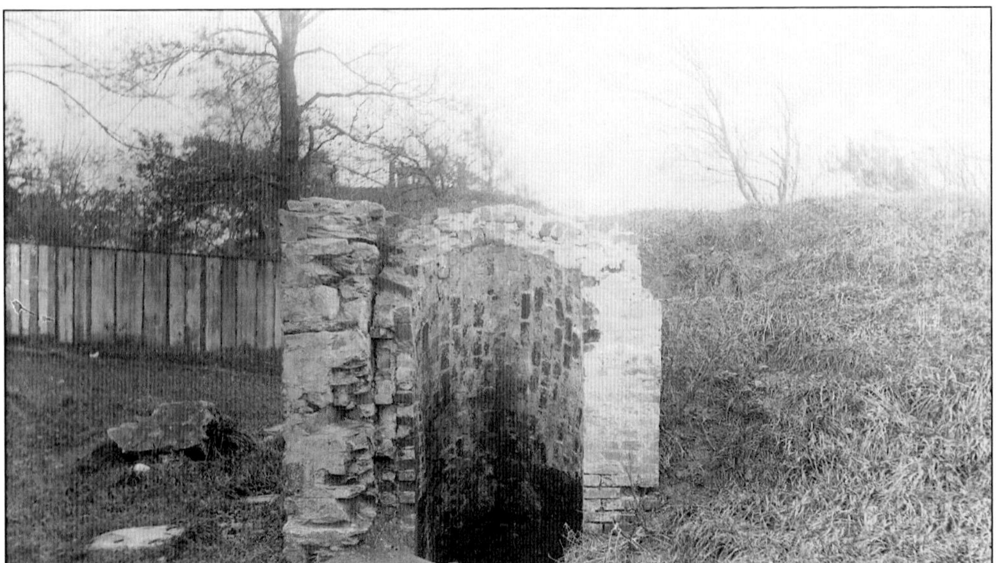

North Battery, renamed Fort Greene in 1798 to honor the great Revolutionary General Nathaniel Greene. In this photograph the entrance to the underground dungeon is shown. It was later filled in to make Battery Park.

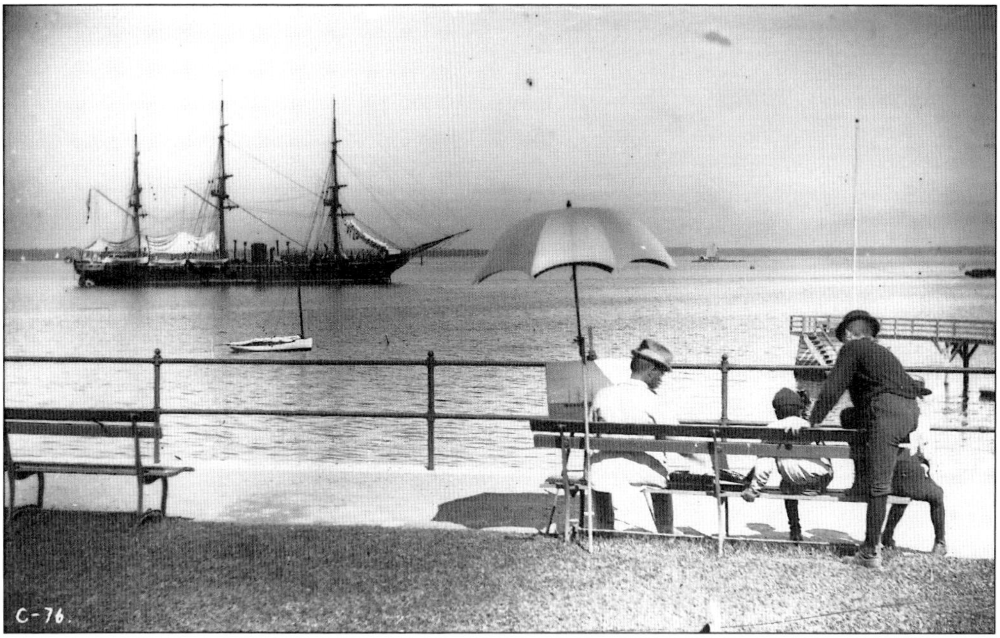

Battery Park on the Point in the 1890s. The artist is Edward Bannister, one of New England's premiere black artists of the 1800s. His subject is a naval training vessel.

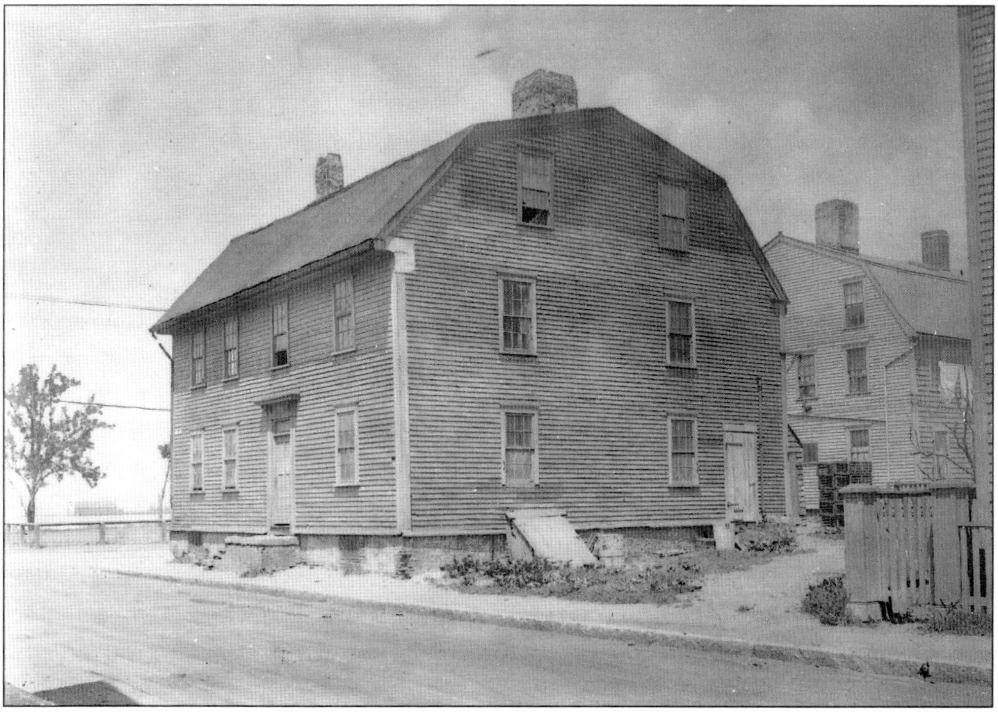

The Simeon Potter House at the corner of Washington and Marsh Streets, built in 1724 by Jacob Dehane. In 1814 the proprietors of Long Wharf started the first free school in this house.

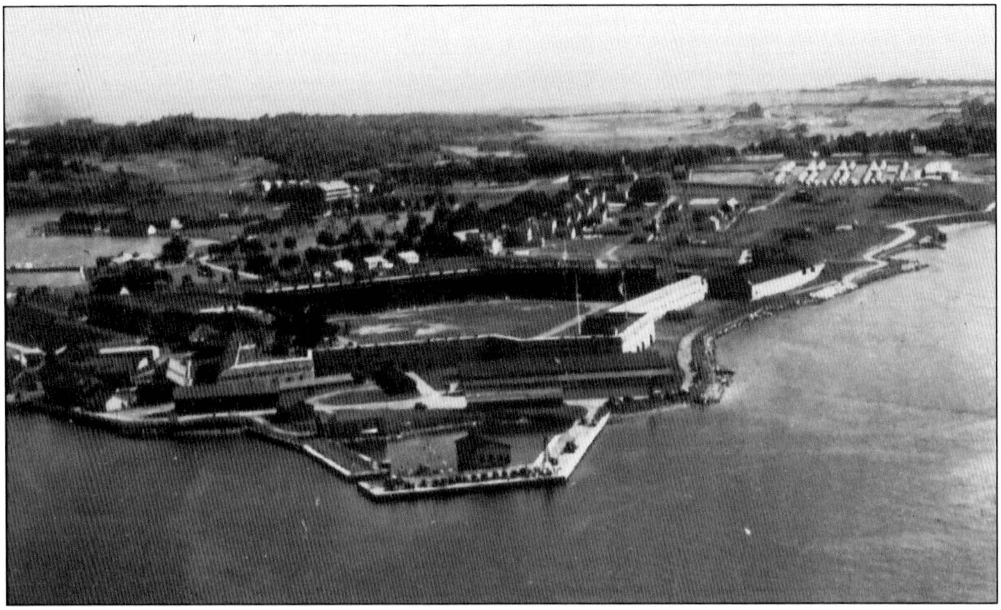

Fort Adams as it appeared in 1937. The site was obtained by the government in 1799 and shortly after a small fortification was built. It was named in honor of President John Adams on July 4, 1799. Between 1824 and 1857 it was enlarged to its present size. In its day it was one of the largest coastal fortifications built.

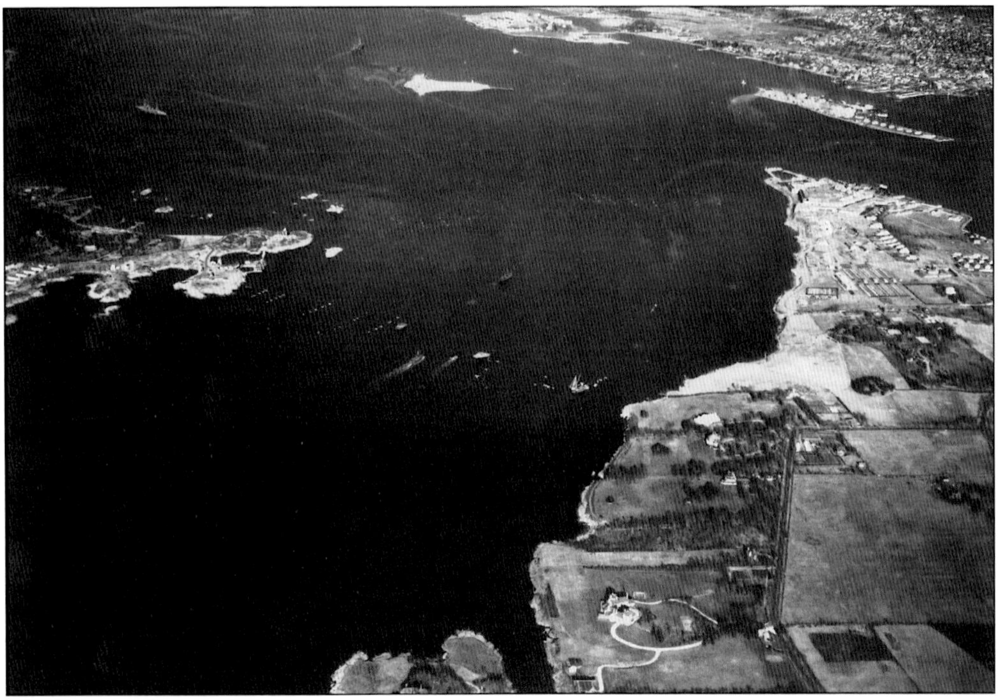

Protection for the bay. In February 1942 an anti-submarine net was stretched across the mouth of Narragansett Bay. The west passage had a continuous loop while the east passage, shown here, employed a gate to allow the passage of ships. The nets were in operation until September 1944. (Photograph courtesy of the Naval War College Archives)

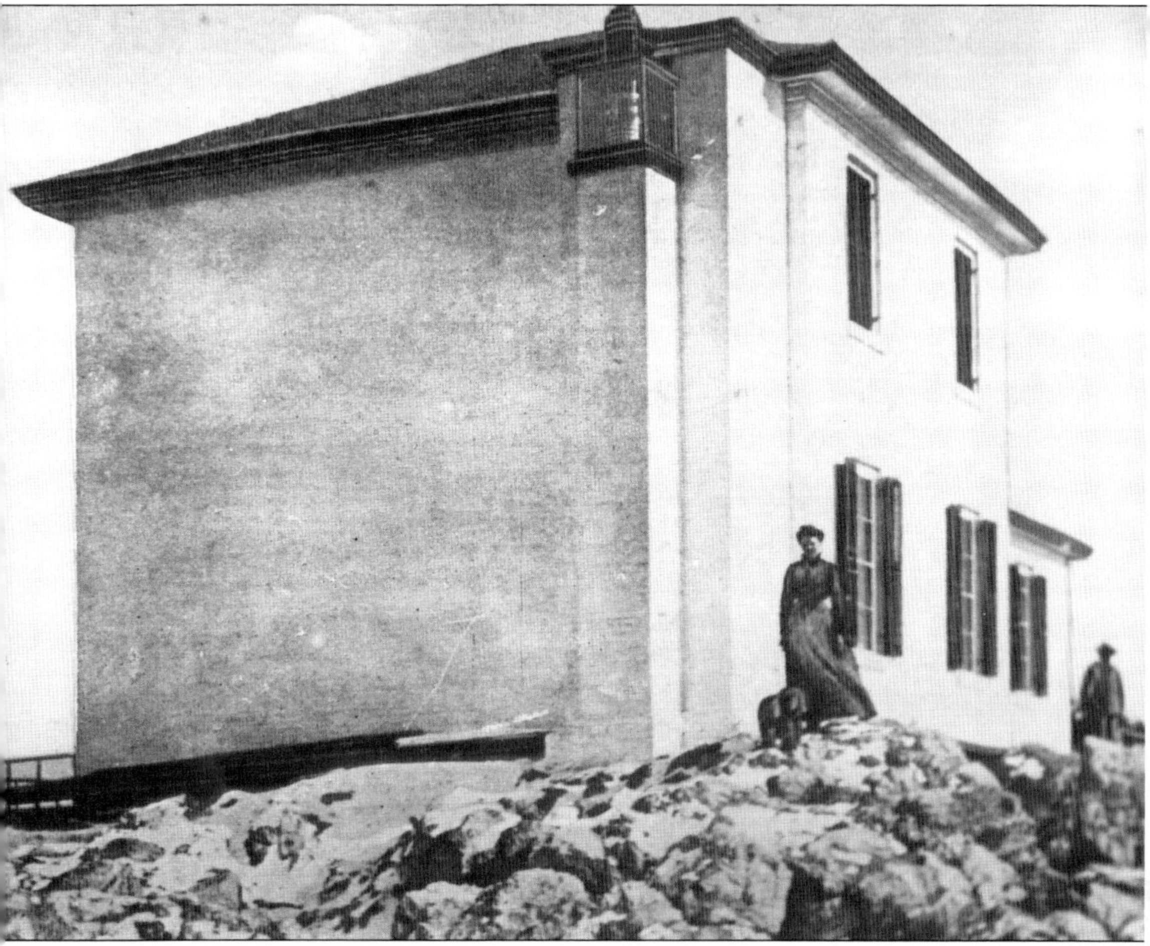

Ida Lewis, born in Newport in 1842. When she was fifteen years old her father was appointed to the position of lighthouse keeper and the family moved to Lime Rock. She succeeded her father and is credited with saving many lives during her tenure as keeper. She was the first woman to receive the Congressional Medal of Honor. In August of 1869 President Ulysses S. Grant was visiting Newport and expressed a desire to meet Ida. On the day that he was leaving from Long Wharf, she rowed over to meet him and the two conversed for a while.

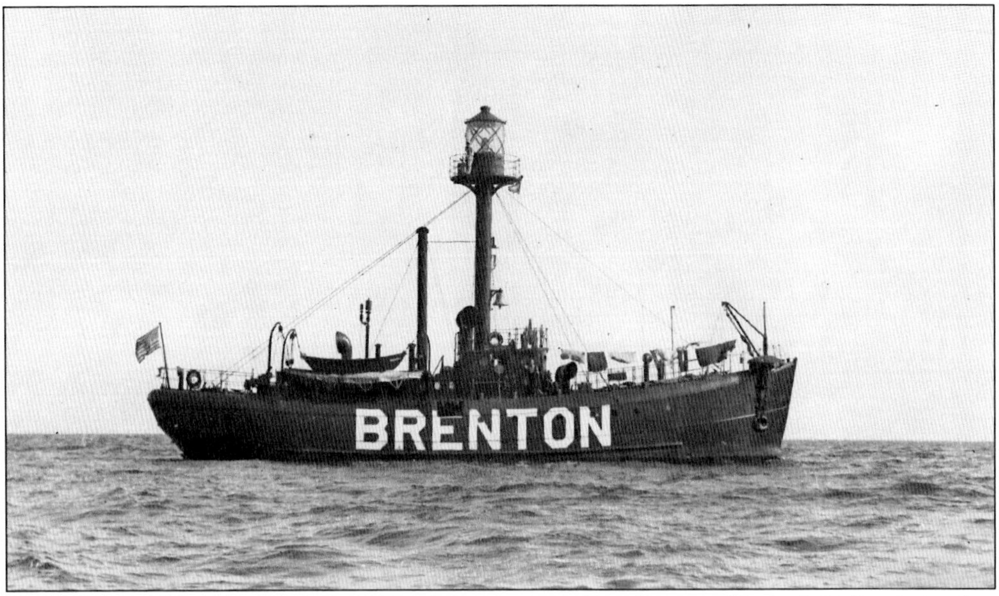

The Brenton Light Ship at the mouth of Narragansett Bay. From 1853 until 1962 a light ship has served on this spot. The first ships were wooden, but were eventually replaced by steel-hulled ships.

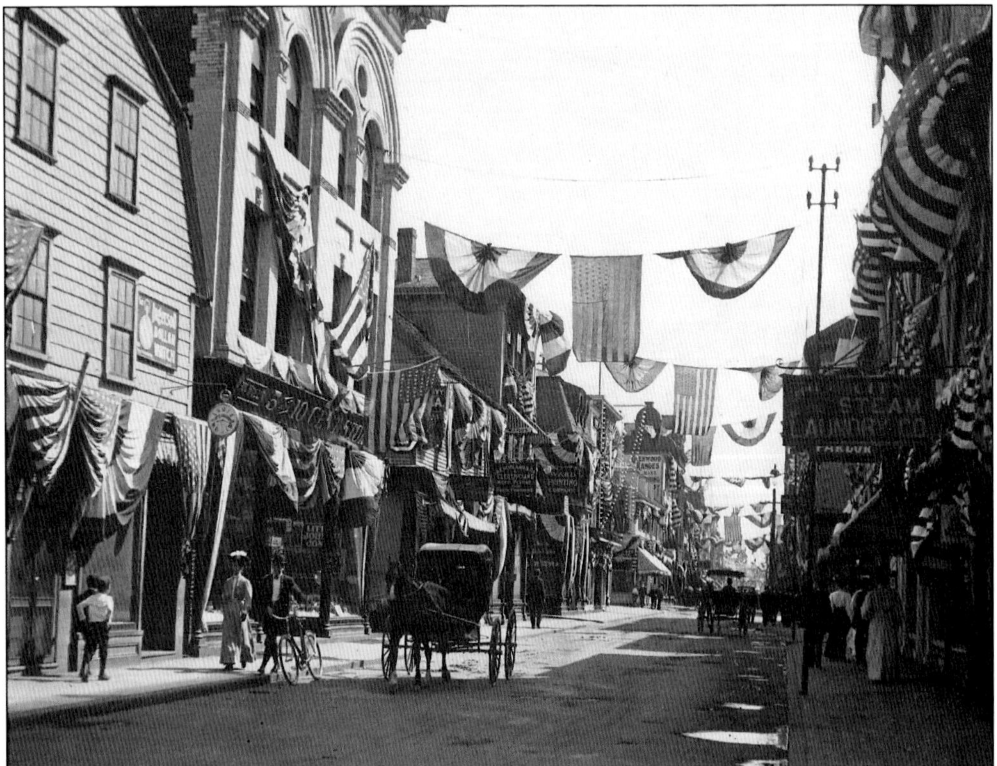

Newport Carnival. In August of 1906 a carnival was held to celebrate the arrival of the Atlantic Fleet. This photograph shows decorations at the corner of Mary and Thames Streets.

Dressed to impress: Carl, Edward, and Gustav Larson in a photograph taken around 1912. The boys grew up on Channing Place. In his adult life, Edward was a ambulance driver for the Navy hospital. (Photograph courtesy of Mike Allen)

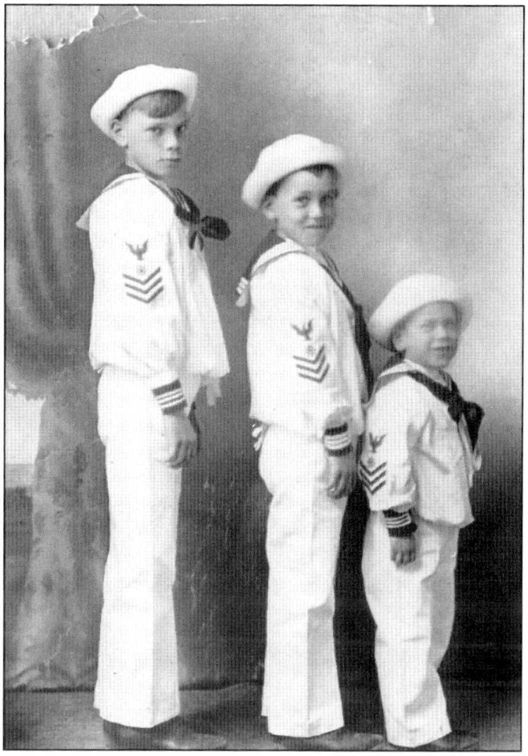

The Commercial House on Park Street. A corner of the Colony House can be seen to the left; the Levi Gale House is to the right. In the mid-1920s, the Commercial House was torn down and the Levi Gale House was moved up Touro Street opposite the Touro Synagogue, making way for the new courthouse.

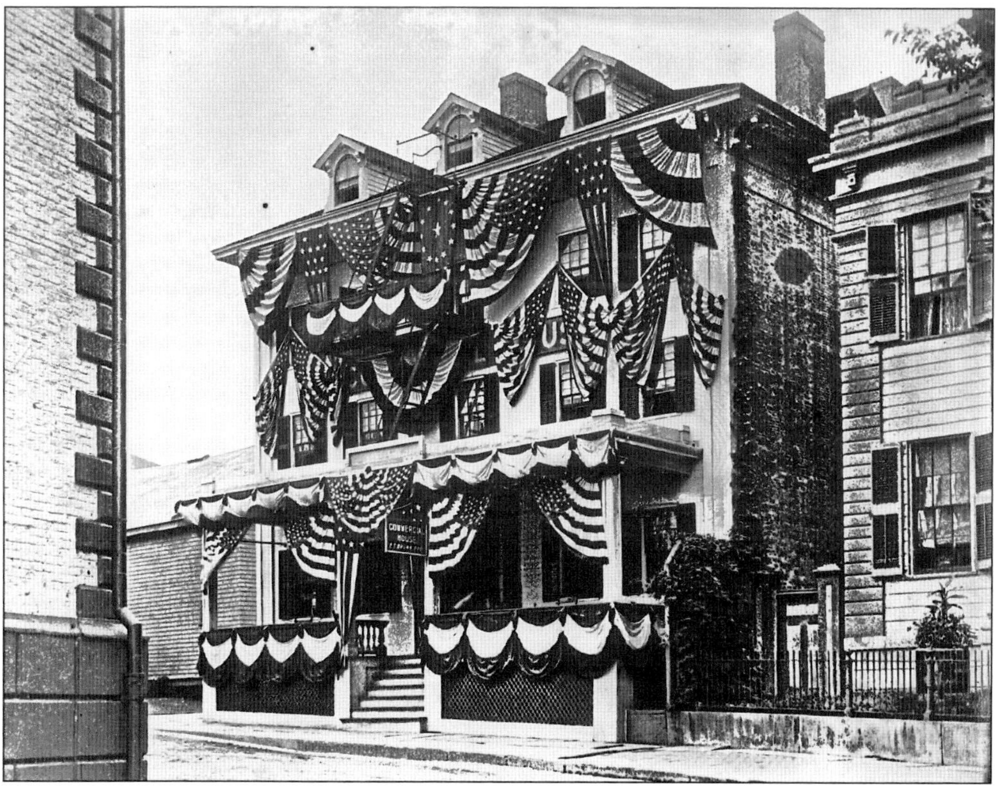

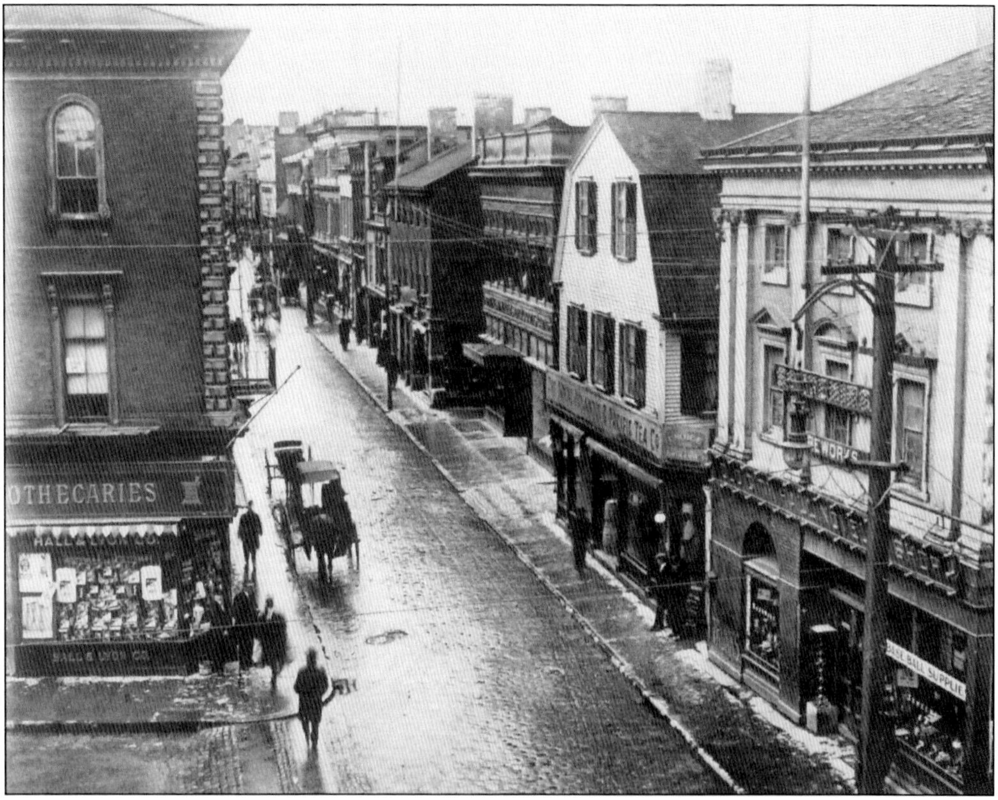

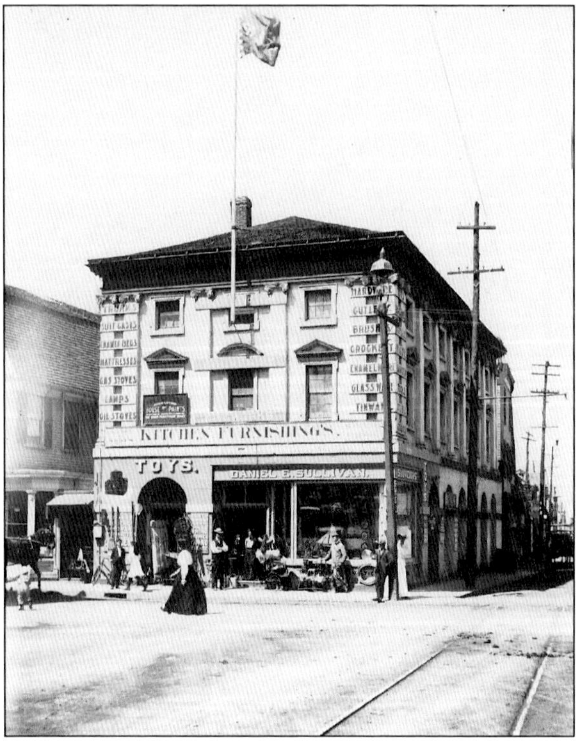

Thames Street at Washington Square looking south in 1913. The Brick Market, built in 1771, is to the right. The gambrel-roofed house next to it is the Erastus Allan House, which was a glass business in the 1860s. (Photograph by Marshall Hall)

The Brick Market. In 1760 the proprietors of Long Wharf set aside land for a market. In 1771 Peter Harrison designed the Brick Market, and it was built shortly after. Over the years it has been a watch house, market, theater, and served as the town hall from 1853 until 1900. It was first restored in 1928 and today, after subsequent restorations, it is the Museum of Newport History, open to the public and maintained by the Newport Historical Society.

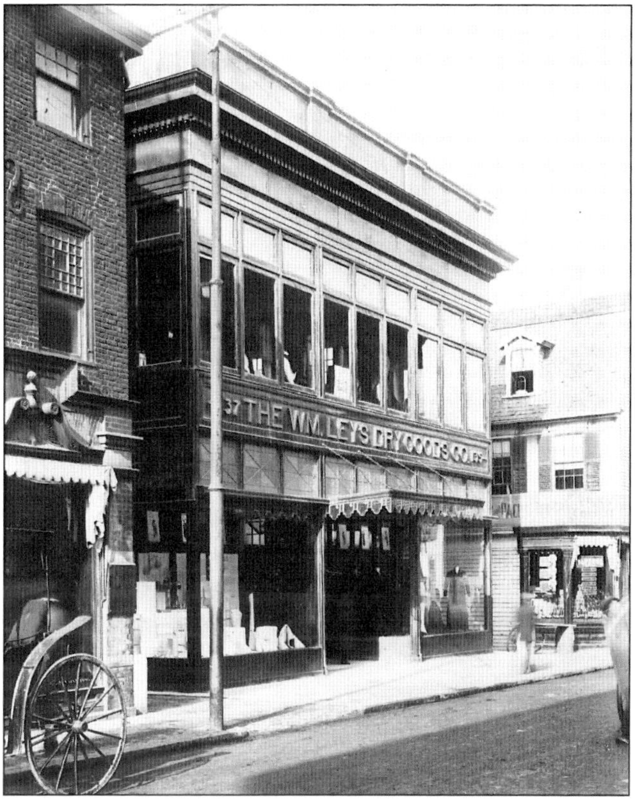

The William Leys Century Store as it was in 1905. Founded in 1796, the store has had several locations, the last being on Long Wharf.

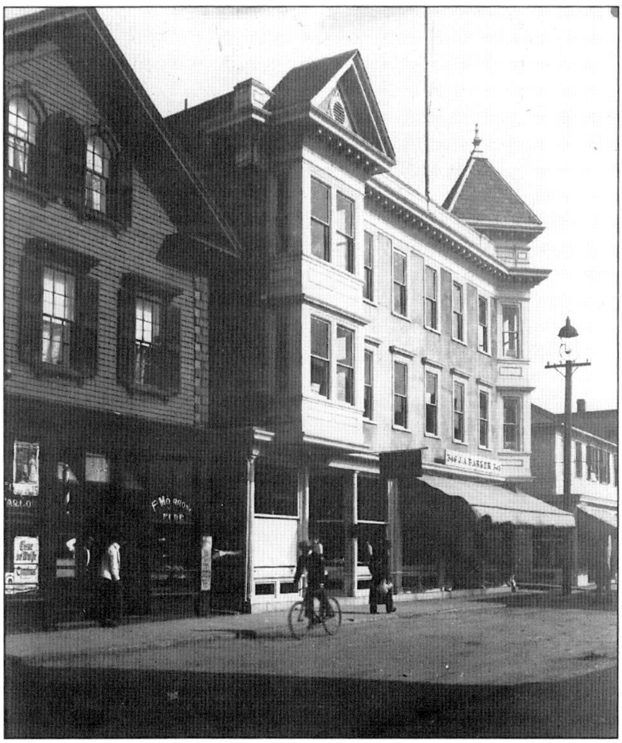

The J.A. Barker Meat Market on Thames Street at the corner of Fair Street. This building, until recently the home of the Ark, is now the Red Parrot Pub.

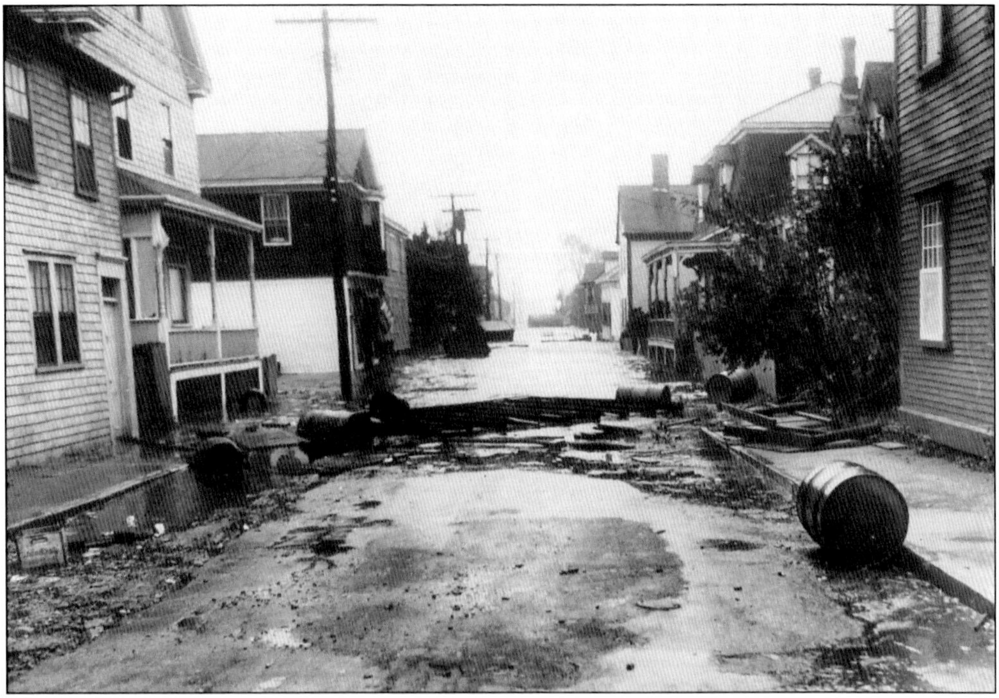

Hurricane Carol flooding Third Street in 1954. By the time this picture was taken, some of the flood water had already receded. The photographer was Ralph Arnold Sr., a very gifted image maker who would reshoot photographs of earlier photographers thereby evidencing the changes in the city. (Photograph courtesy of Ralph Arnold Jr.)

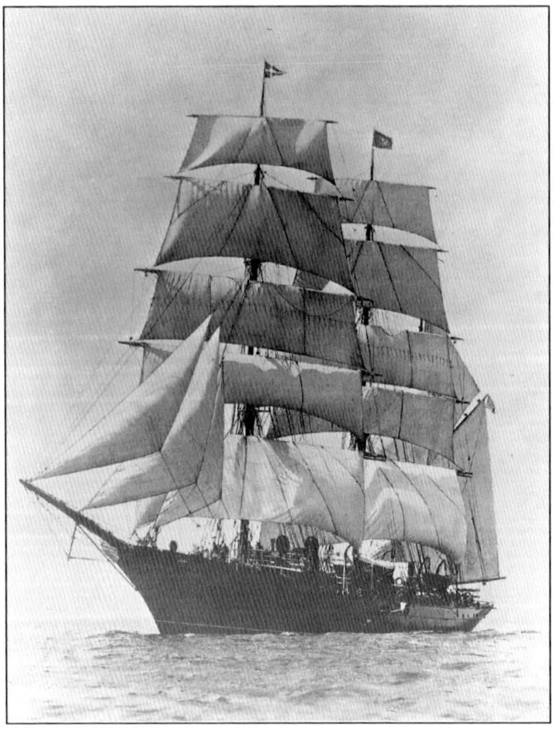

Aloha, the yacht of Arthur Curtis James, photographed in the early 1900s. The ship was 218 feet long and was rigged as a bark with auxiliary power. James was a well-known summer colonist.

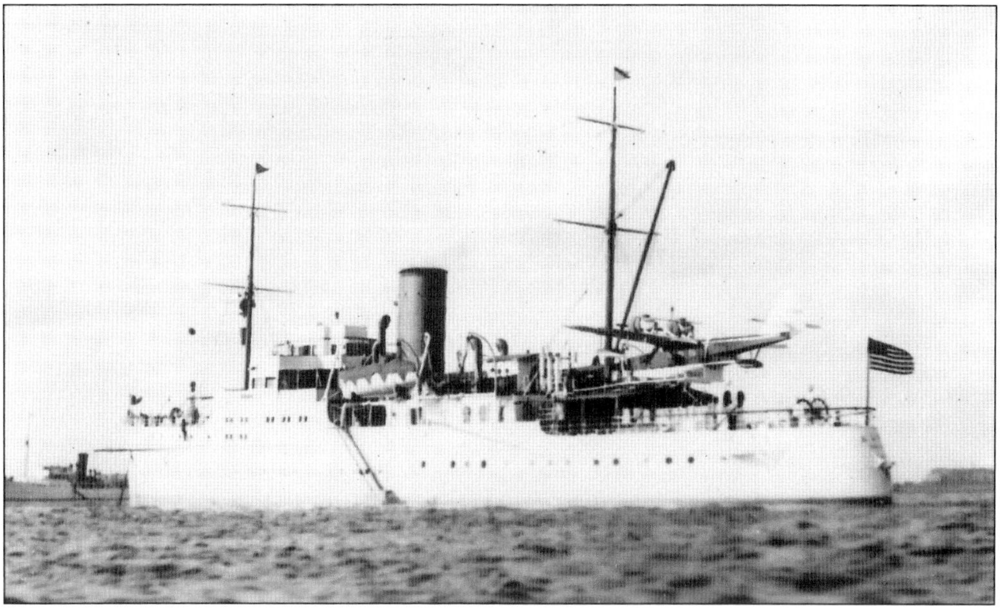

Floating luxury—William K. Vanderbilt's yacht *Alva*. She was a 264-foot steel-hulled vessel that carried a seaplane and an automobile to provide the utmost convenience anywhere she traveled.

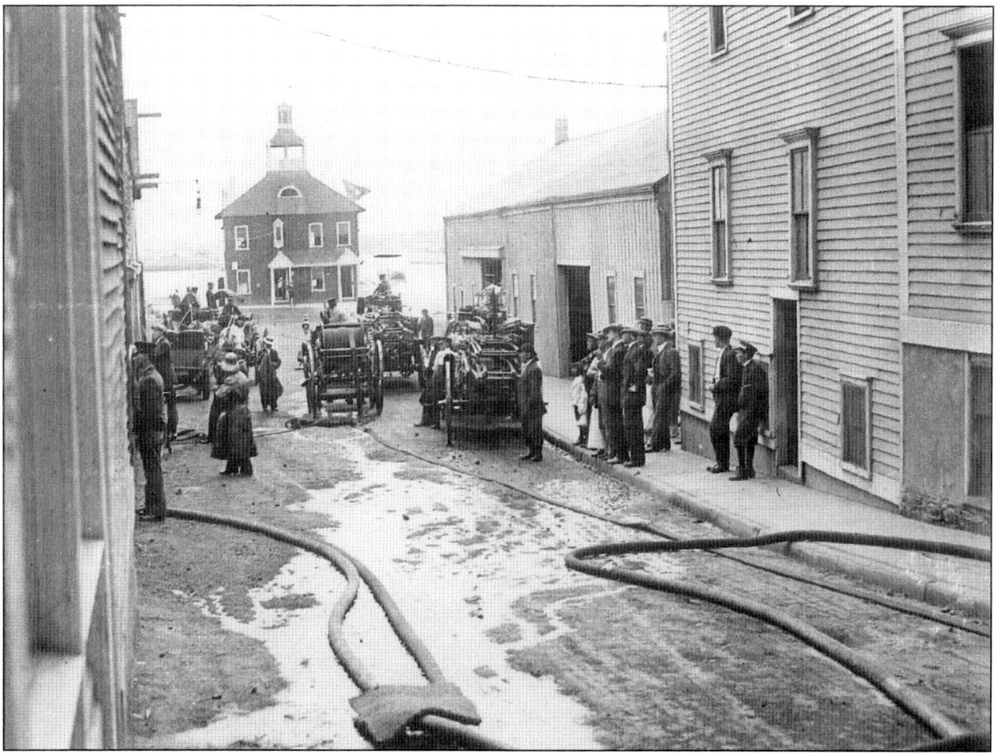

The Newport Fire Department after an alarm on Sayers Wharf in the early part of the century. The New York Yacht Club, organized in New York in 1844, is in the distance. The club opened its Newport doors in 1897.

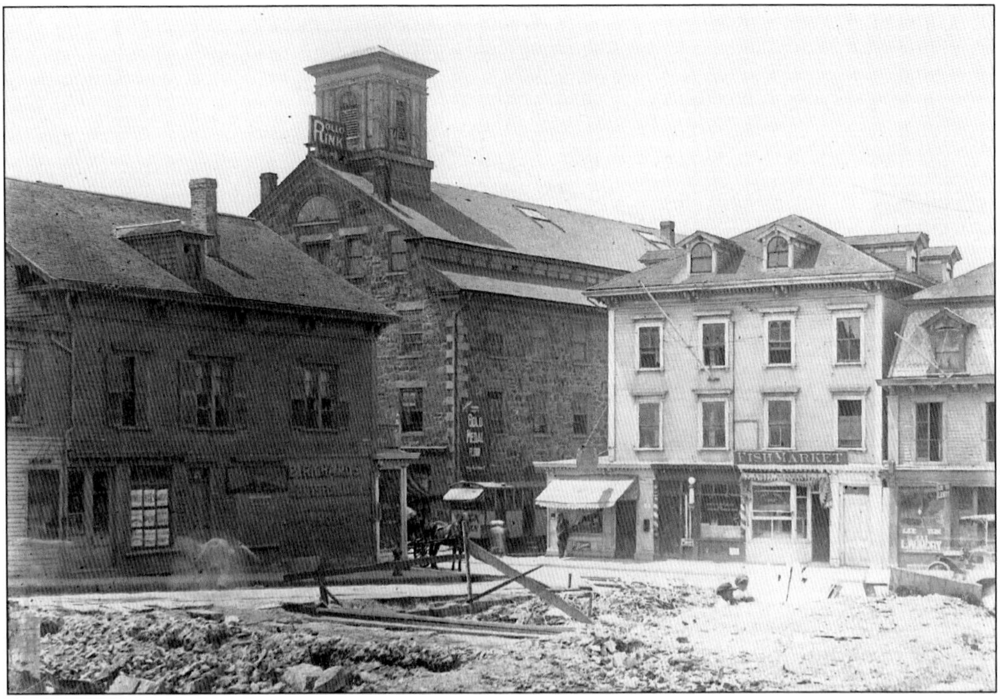

The corner of Cannon and Thames Streets. The old Customs House has been razed to make way for the new post office, built 1916–17. The building with the tower is the Perry Mill, built in 1835. The mill employed over 100 people and had 8,000 spindles operating.

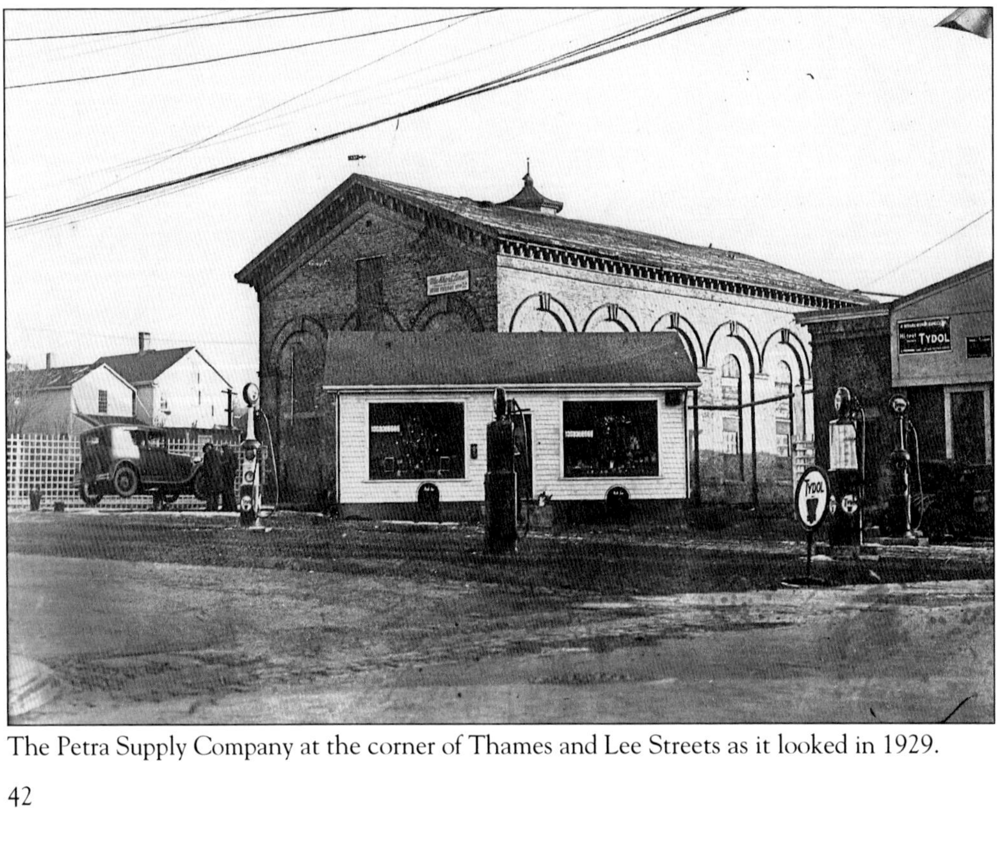

The Petra Supply Company at the corner of Thames and Lee Streets as it looked in 1929.

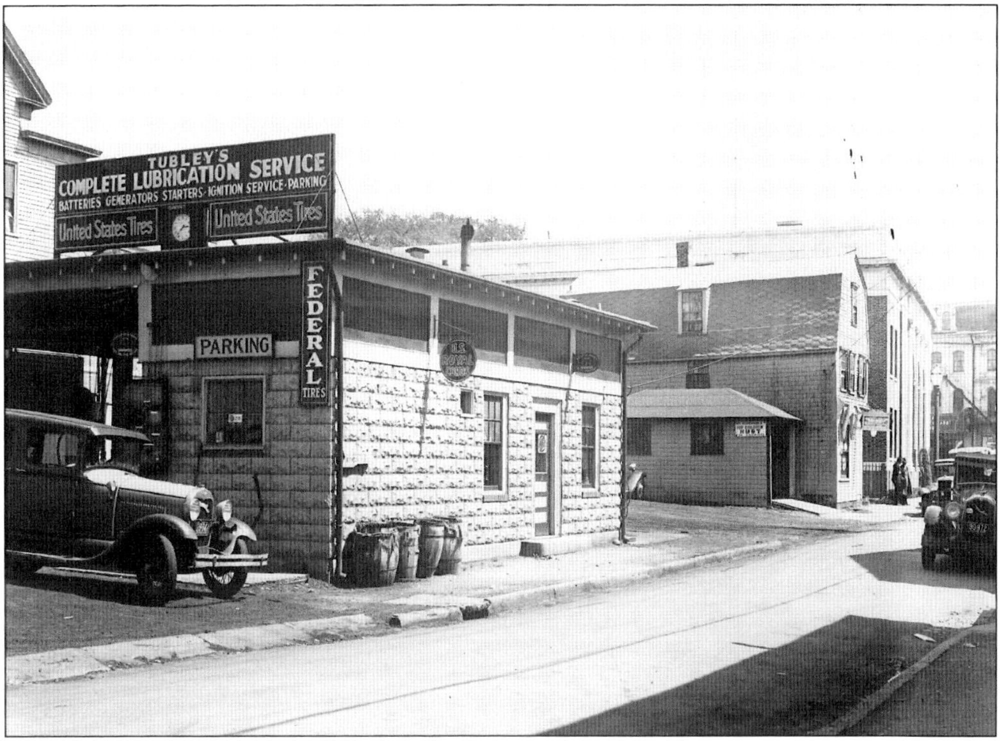

Tubley's service station on Duke Street in 1934.

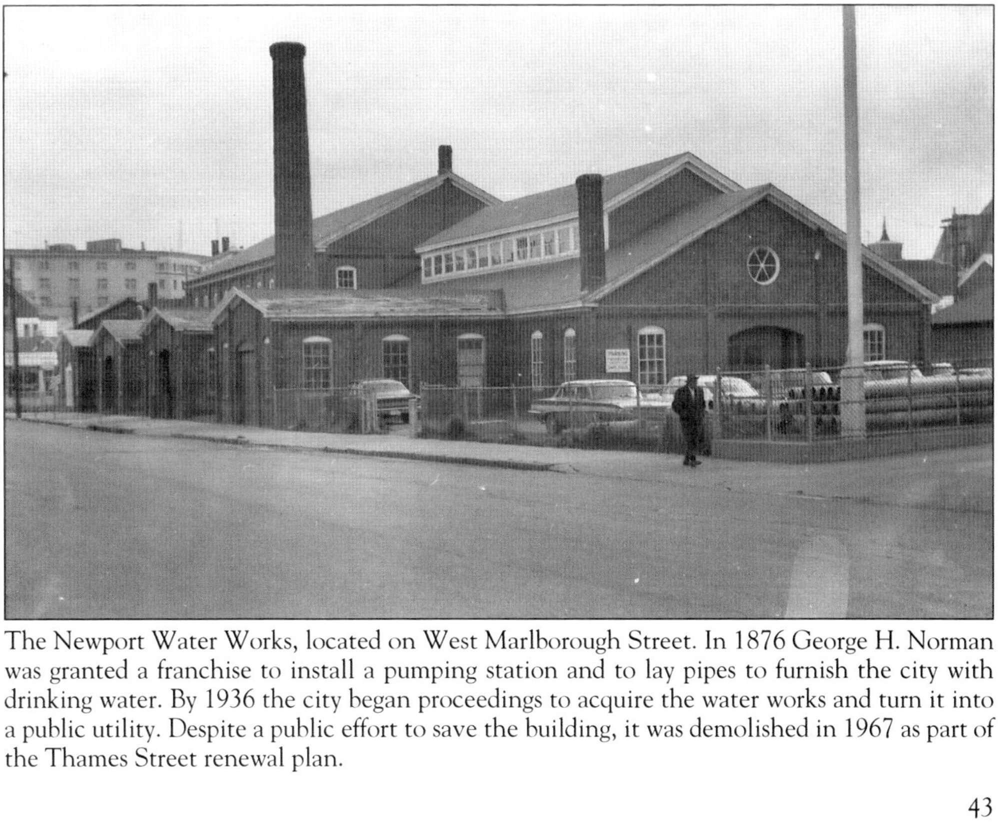

The Newport Water Works, located on West Marlborough Street. In 1876 George H. Norman was granted a franchise to install a pumping station and to lay pipes to furnish the city with drinking water. By 1936 the city began proceedings to acquire the water works and turn it into a public utility. Despite a public effort to save the building, it was demolished in 1967 as part of the Thames Street renewal plan.

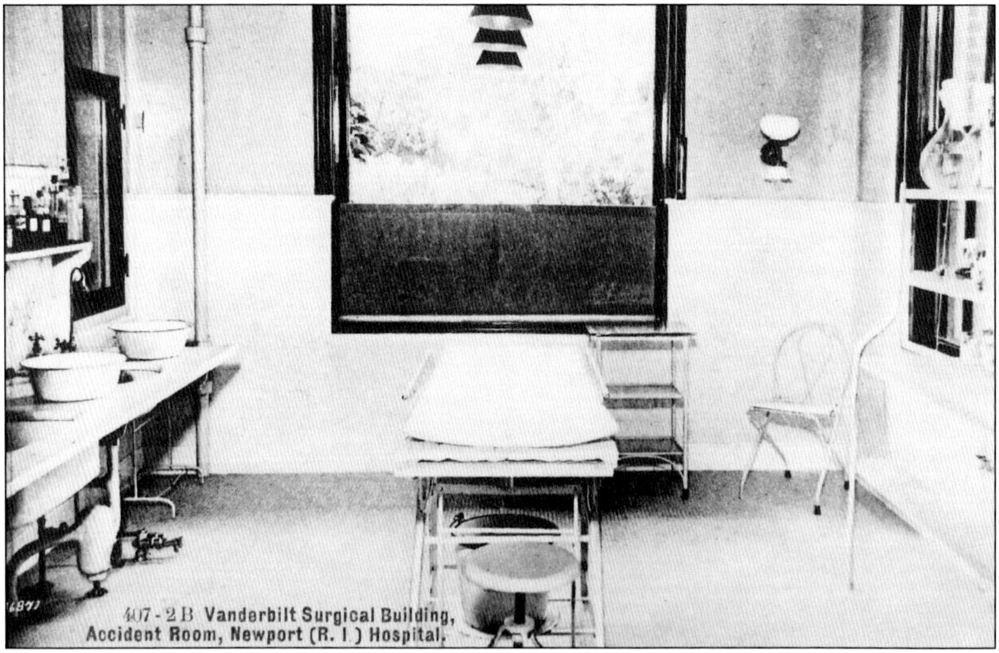

An early 1900s postcard of the accident room in the Vanderbilt Surgical building at Newport Hospital. The hospital was founded in 1873, and the Vanderbilt wing was opened in 1903. In 1923 nurses worked ten-hour days, seven days a week. By 1952 Newport Hospital was the first in the state to implement a forty-hour work week. (Photograph courtesy of Helen Jones)

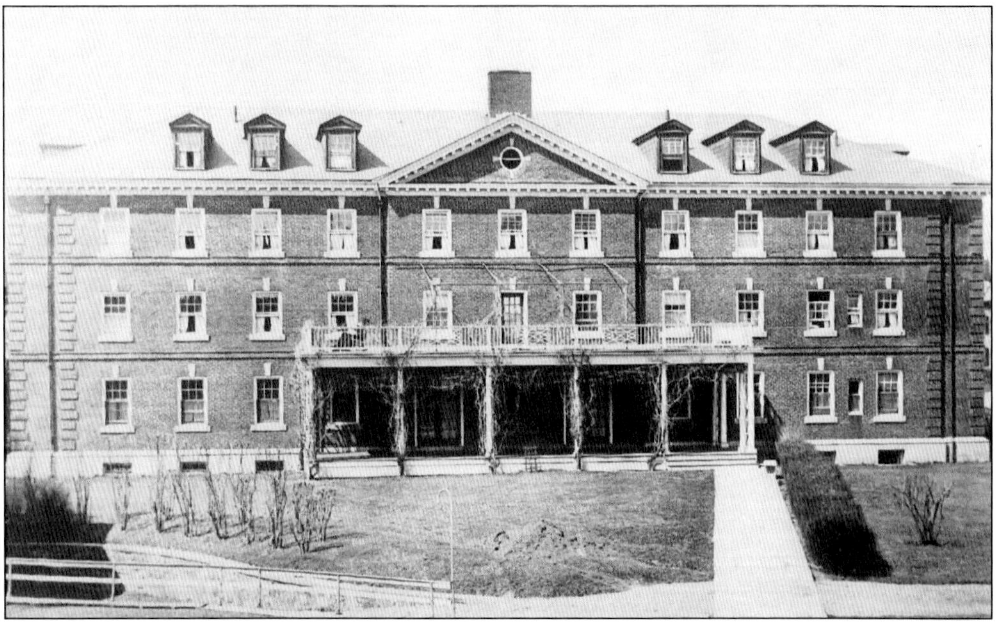
MacLaurin Hall from the rear courtyard before the 1934 expansion which added Gage Hall to the right of this photograph. The Newport Hospital School of Nursing opened in February 1886. The first class consisted of five students and one faculty member, Miss Cornelia Seelye. The namesake of the building, Janet MacLaurin, ran the school from 1908 until 1926. (Photograph courtesy of Helen Jones)

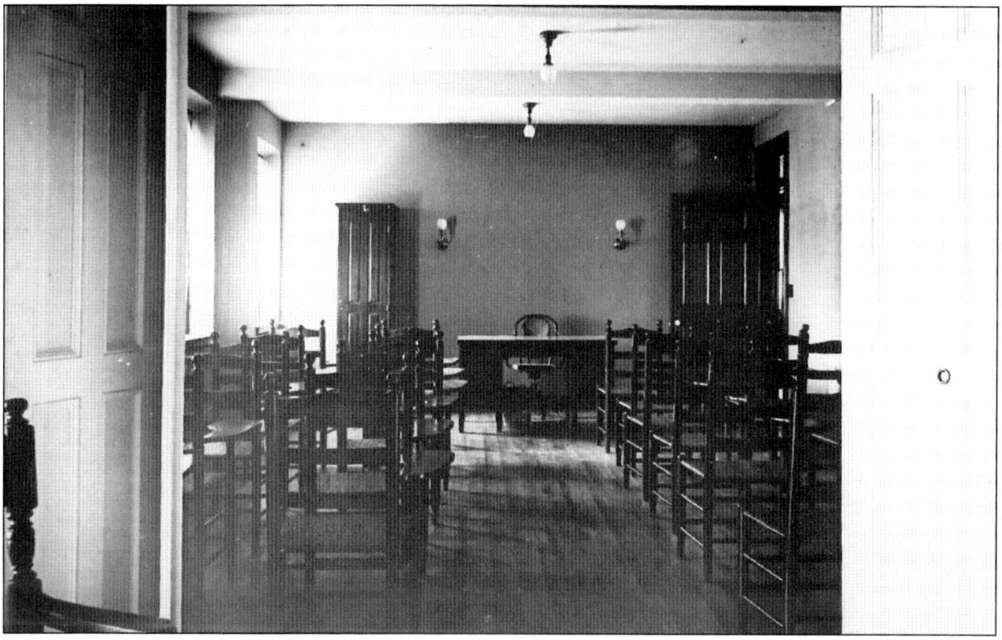

A stark classroom in Gage Hall. In 1903 the nursing program was increased from two to three years and remained that way until the closing of the school. In 1990, upon graduating its 102nd class, the school closed its doors forever, thus ending an era. (Photograph courtesy of Helen Jones)

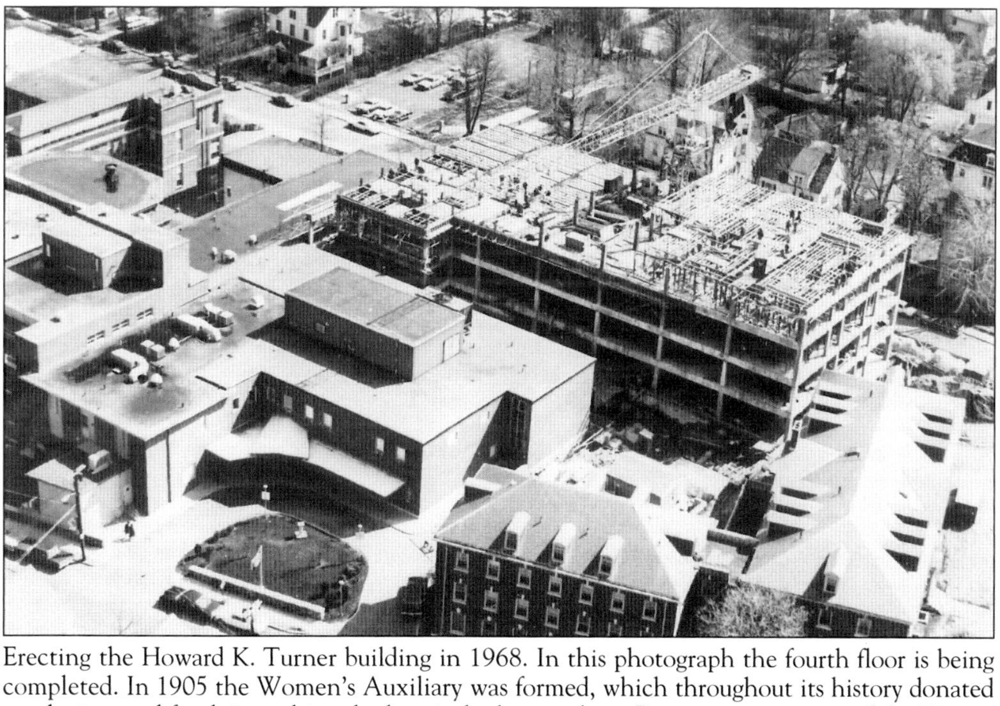

Erecting the Howard K. Turner building in 1968. In this photograph the fourth floor is being completed. In 1905 the Women's Auxiliary was formed, which throughout its history donated much time and funds in making the hospital a better place. During construction of the Turner building, the auxiliary pledged $ 150,000 toward the building fund, exceeding their goal by 144%. (Photograph courtesy of Helen Jones)

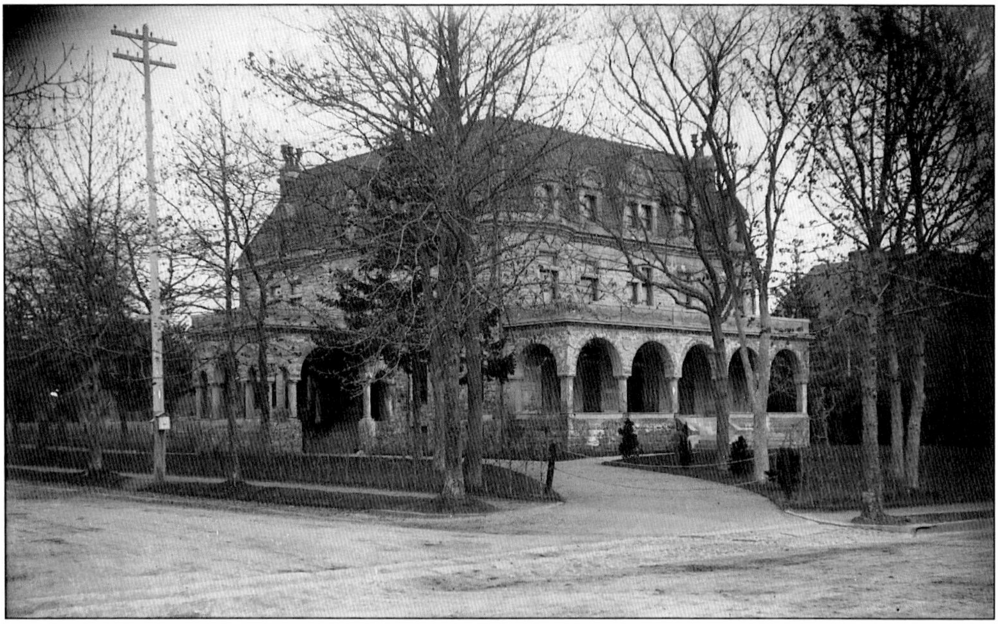

At one time a residence at the corner of Bellevue and Narragansett Avenues, built in 1887 for William Osgood. In 1941 it became Saint Catherines Academy, a Catholic high school for girls. Today it has been renovated and is used as the headquarters for the Newport Preservation Society.

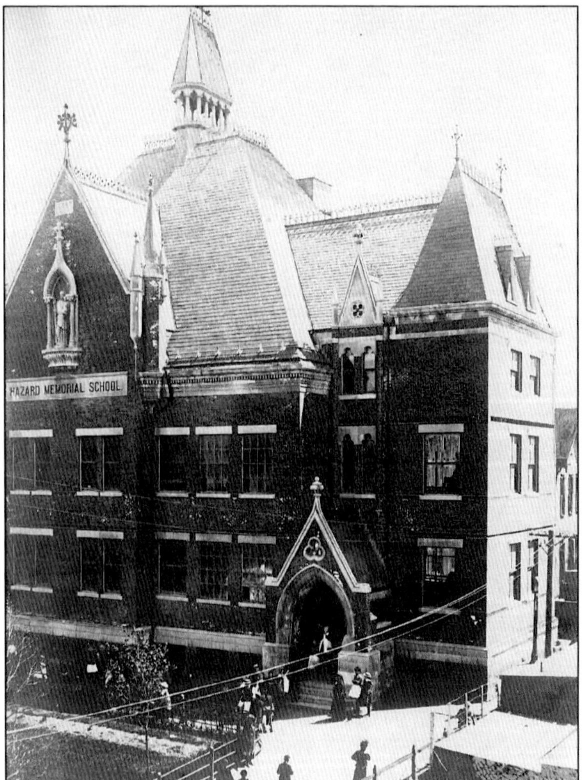

Saint Josephs parochial school, located at what is now the parking lot behind the Jane Pickens Theater. The cornerstone was laid on August 6, 1890, and the following September the school was occupied. The building was a gift from George Babcock Hazard, and when it opened it was staffed by the Sisters of Saint Joseph.

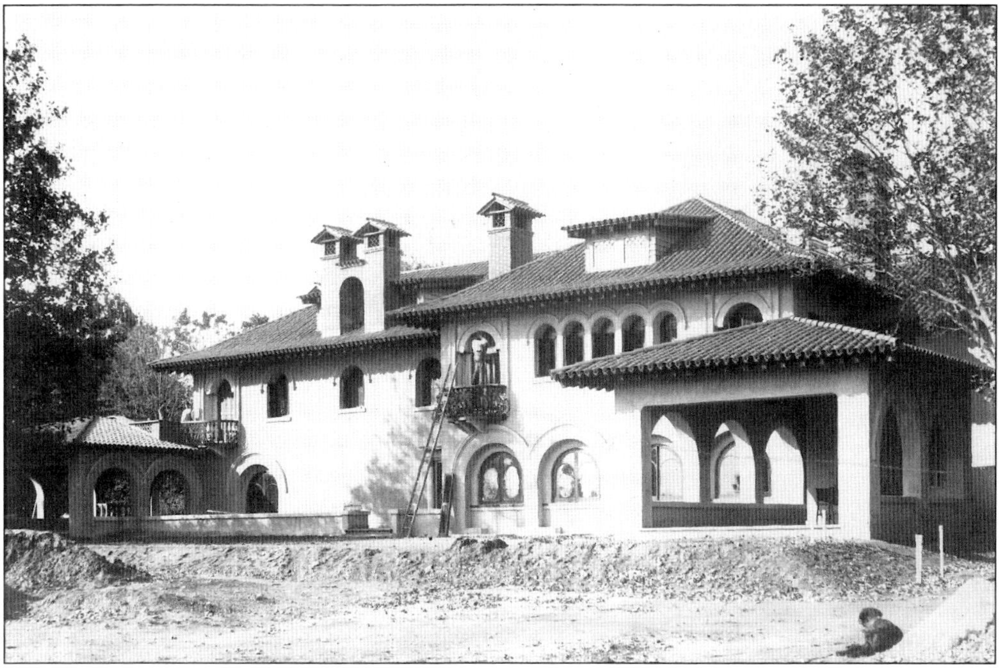

The Ellen Mason House receiving its finishing touches in 1902. In 1938 it became the home of Saint Michaels School on Rhode Island Avenue.

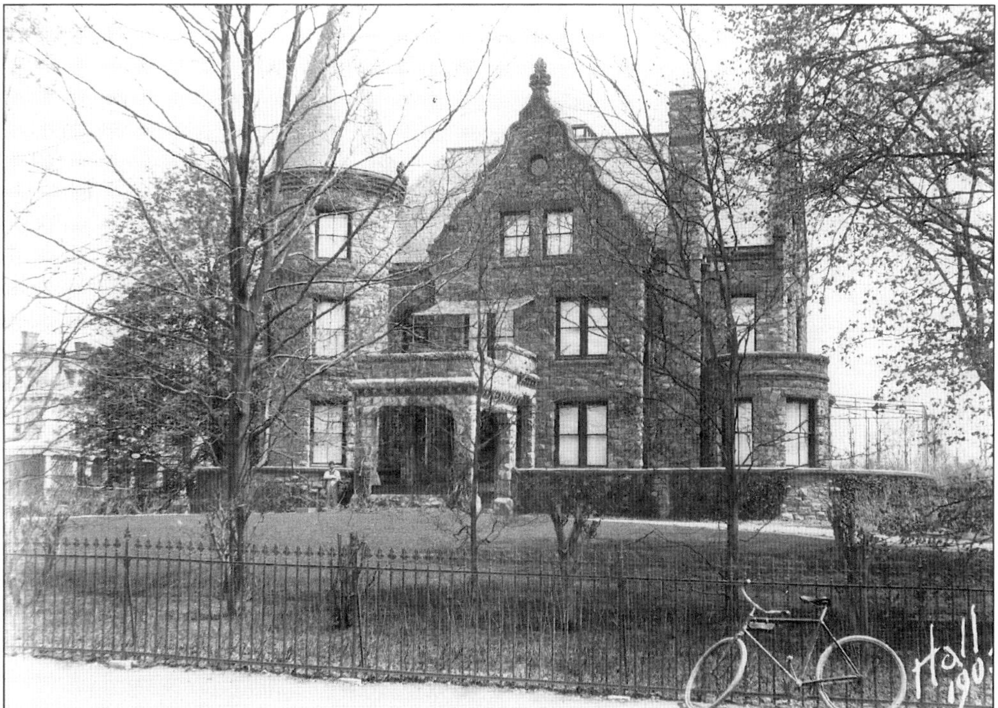

De Lasalle Academy in 1903, built 1882–84 for William Weld, designed by Dudley Newton. In 1924 this building became a Catholic boys high school. Located on Bellevue Avenue, it has since been converted to condominiums.

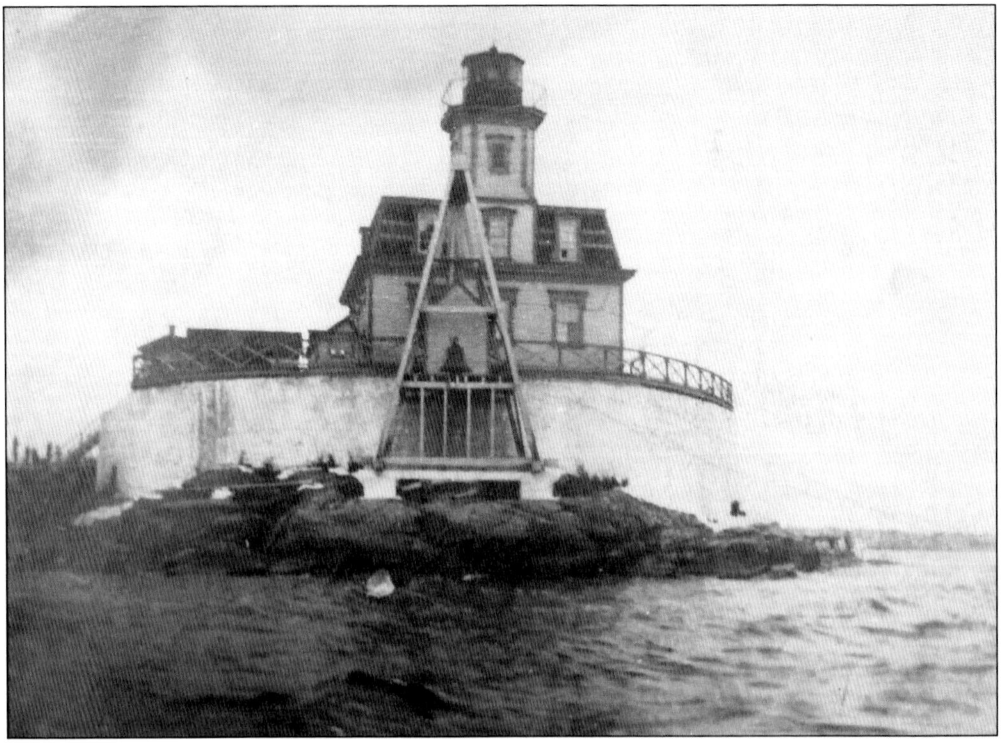

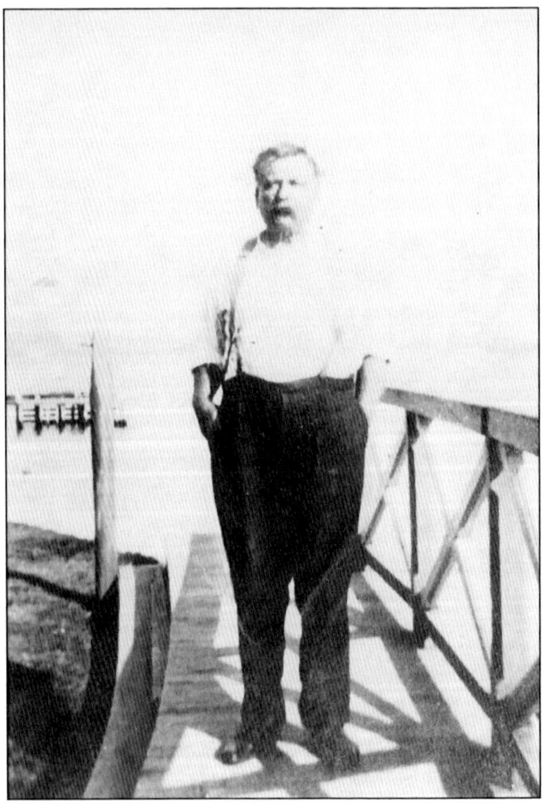

The Rose Island Lighthouse on Rose Island in 1890. The first recorded deed for this land dates to February 1659, when it was sold to Benedict Arnold of Newport. In 1798 to 1800 Fort Hamilton was constructed. The present lighthouse was lit in 1870. The "A" frame that once housed a fog bell can be seen here. (Photograph courtesy of Rose Island Lighthouse foundation)

Keeper of the light. Charles S. Curtis held the record for the longest tenure, serving from 1887 until 1910. During his service he earned two medals for saving lives. (Photograph courtesy of Rose Island Lighthouse Foundation)

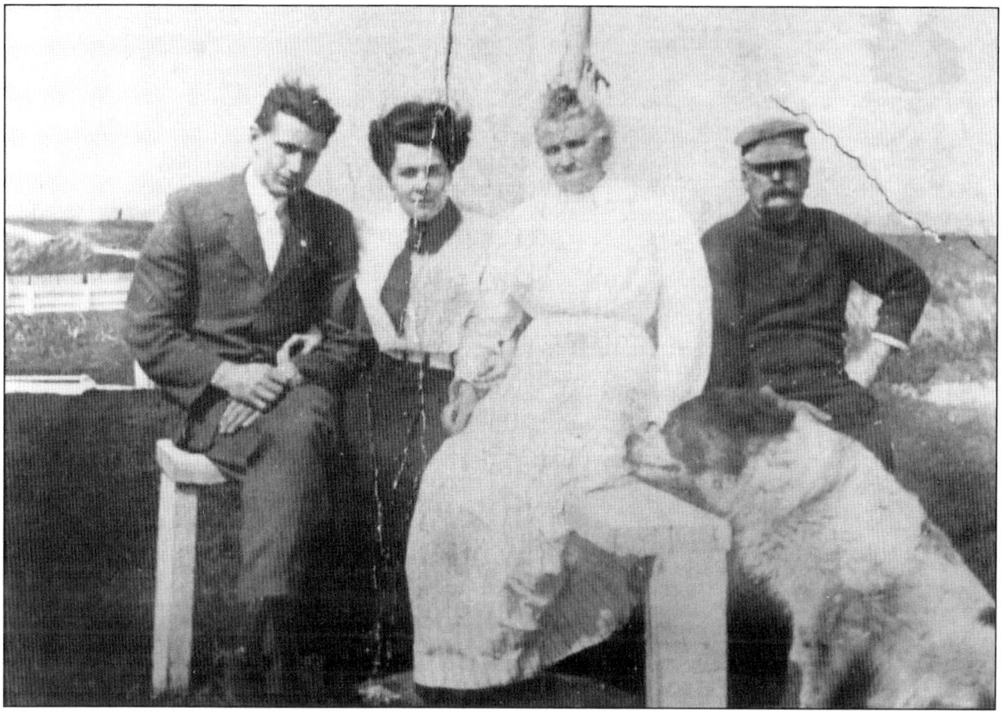

The Curtis family at the dock on Rose Island at the turn of the century. (Photograph courtesy of Rose Island Lighthouse Foundation)

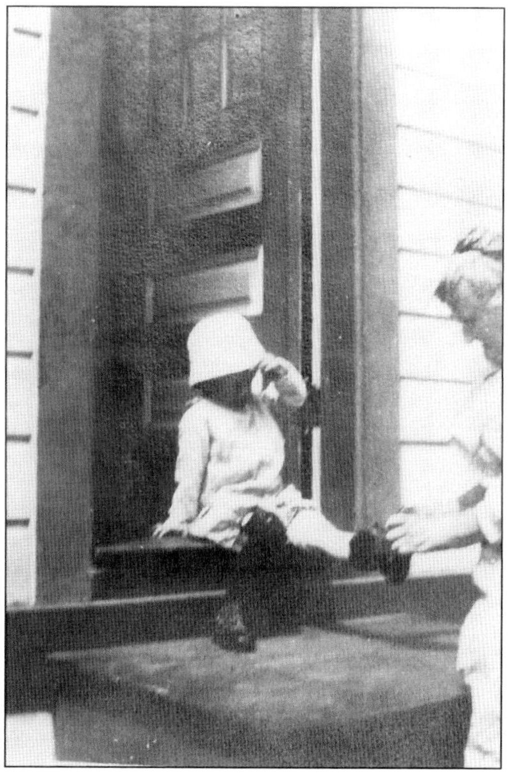

Wanton Chase in 1910 with his grandmother, Christina Curtis, in the doorway of the lighthouse. (Photograph courtesy of Rose Island Lighthouse Foundation)

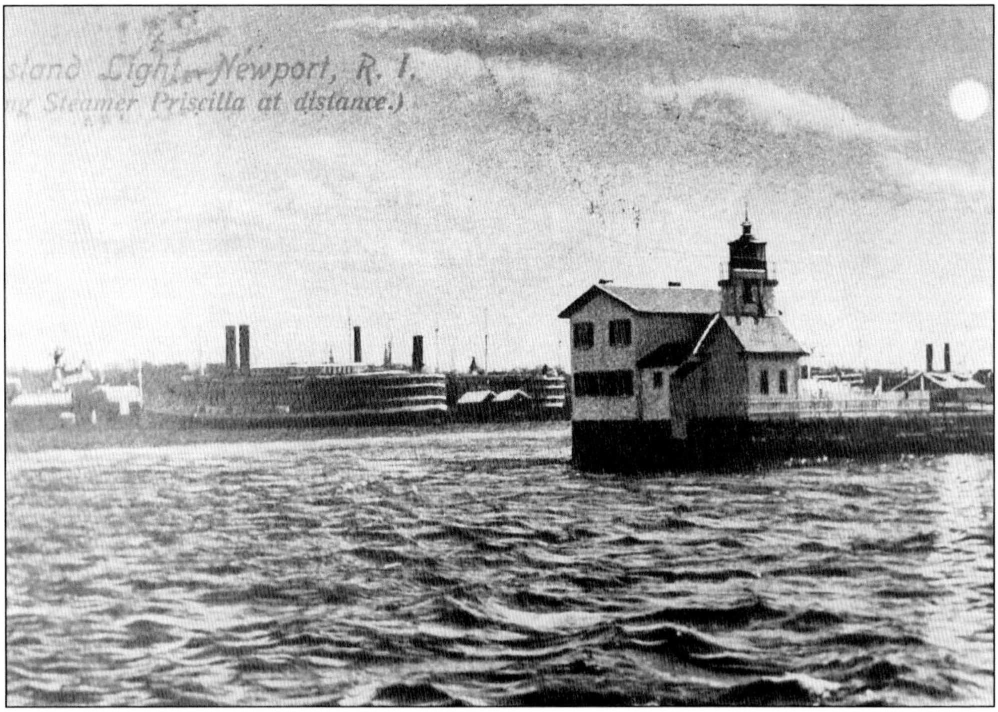

The Goat Island Lighthouse, built in 1842 at the north end of Goat Island. The steamship *Priscilla* can be seen in the distance, docked at Long Wharf. She went into service for the Fall River Line in 1894, and could accommodate 1,400 passengers and 800 tons of freight. In 1937 she, along with the *Plymouth*, the *Providence*, and the *Commonwealth*, was taken out of service and scrapped.

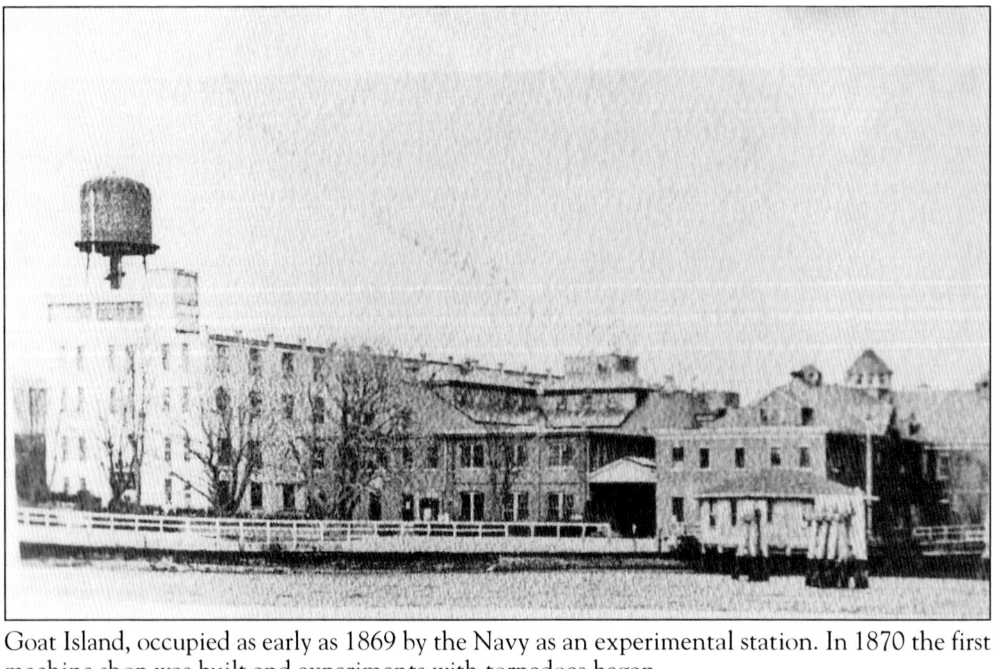

Goat Island, occupied as early as 1869 by the Navy as an experimental station. In 1870 the first machine shop was built and experiments with torpedoes began.

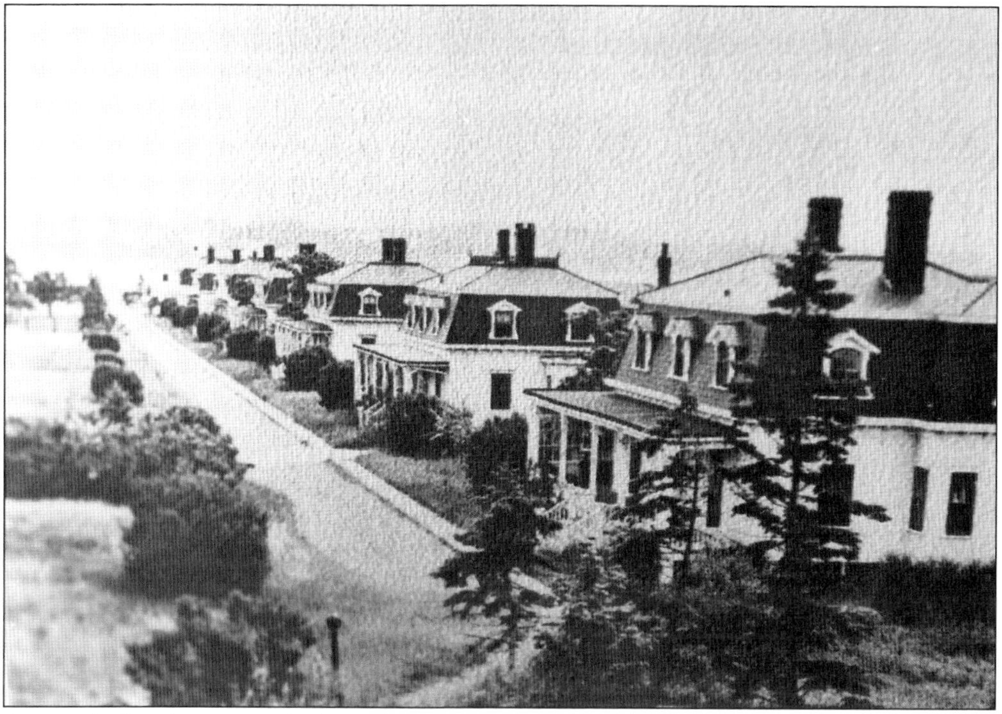

A row of officer's cottages, built on the southern end of Goat Island in 1874.

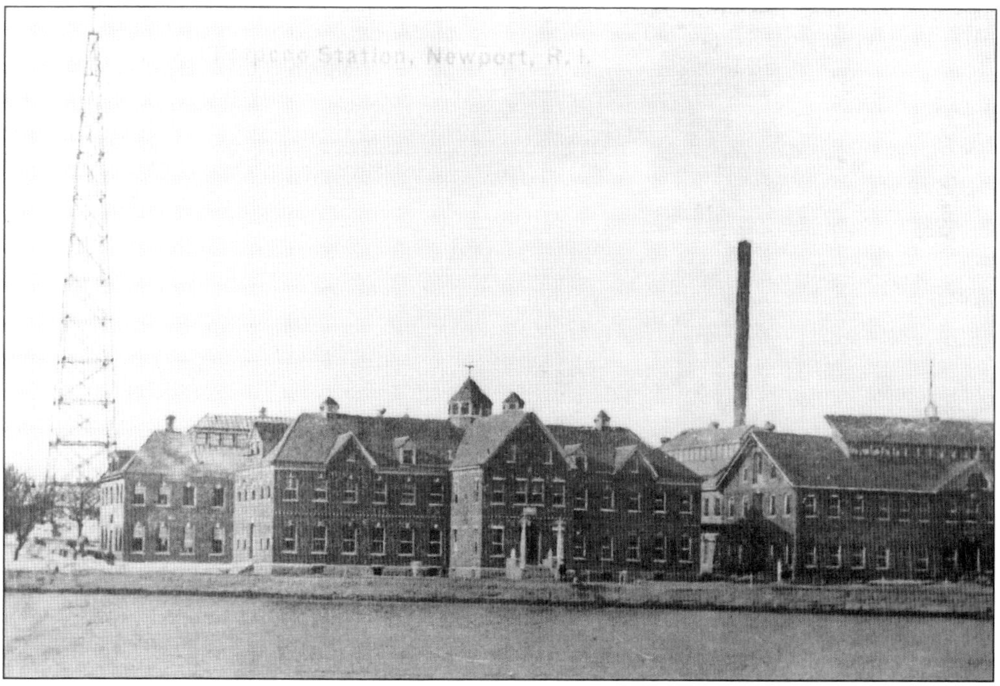

Torpedo station, Goat Island. In 1886 a time ball was constructed at the torpedo station and connected to the Naval Observatory in Washington, D.C. Every day at noon the ball would drop and a whistle would sound allowing the people of Newport to check their timepieces.

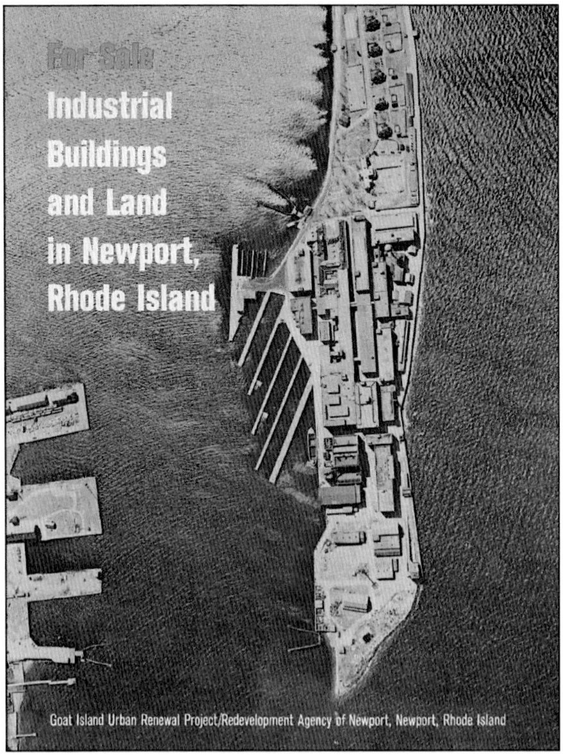

Newport for sale. In the 1960s urban renewal forever changed the face of the city. This picture is the cover for a brochure in which Goat Island is being offered for private development.

Long Wharf tradition. This picture shows the Narragansett Cafe when it was at the top of Long Wharf, closer to Thames Street. The building was erected in 1936 and torn down in 1967 as part of the Brick Market development project. A new building was put up in 1967, farther down on the wharf, that to this day is home to the Narragansett Cafe.

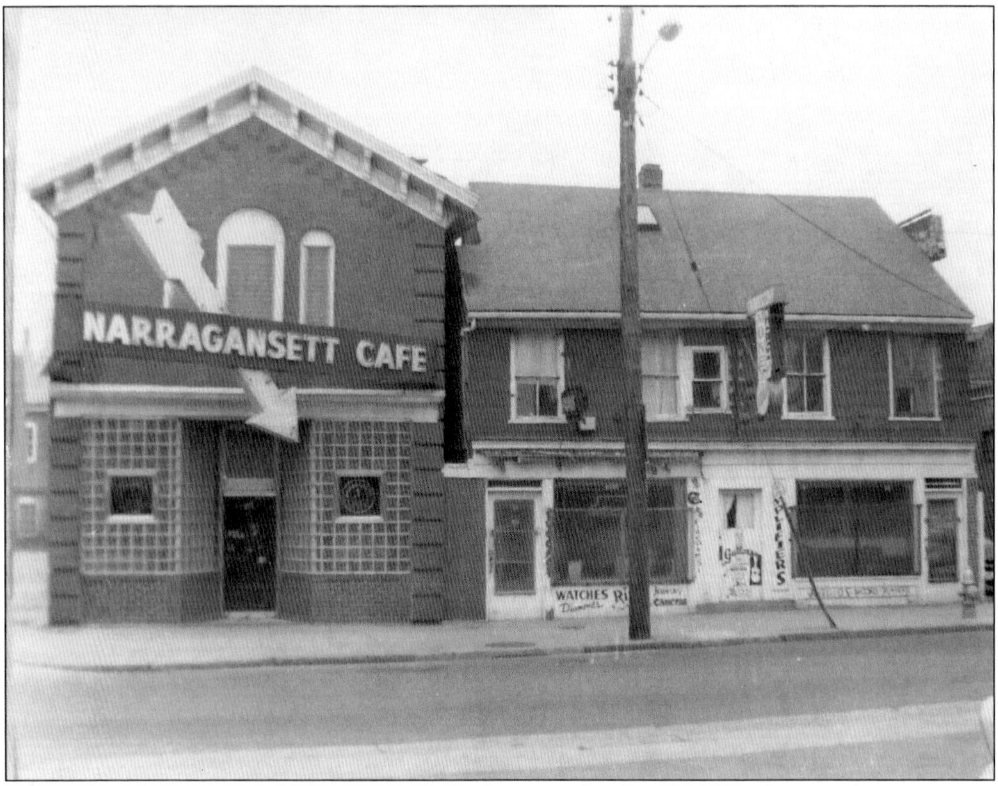

Two

Coasters Harbor Island

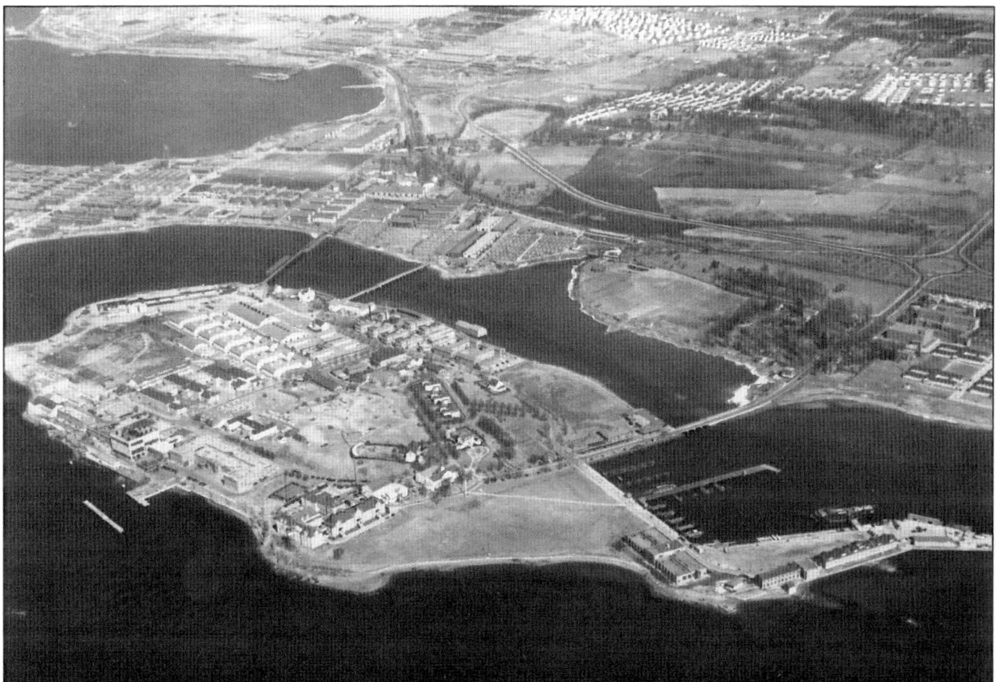

Coasters Harbor Island, today home to the War College, a museum, and various officer training schools. In April of 1639, Nicholas Easton and his two sons left Pocassett Settlement to explore the southern part of Aquidneck Island. They landed on a small island and the next day named it Coasters Harbor Island. It was purchased from the Native Americans in 1654; in the deed it is referred to as Woonachaset. In 1881 the Navy acquired the land and two years later the Naval War College was opened by Commodore Stephen Luce. (Courtesy of the Naval War College Archives)

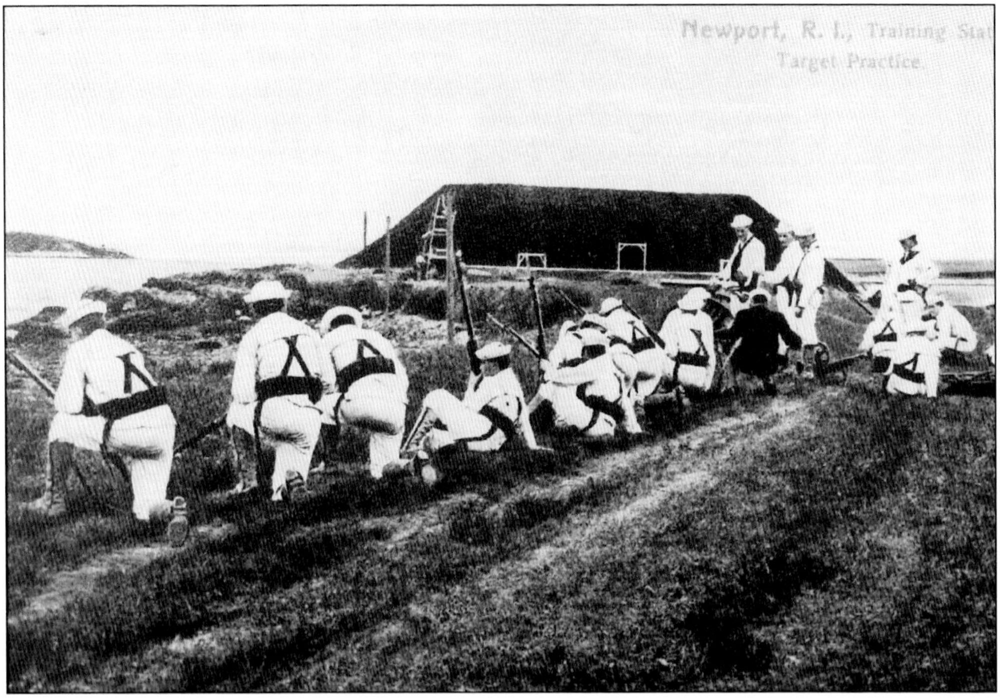

Target practice for cadets at the Newport Naval Training Station around the turn of the century.

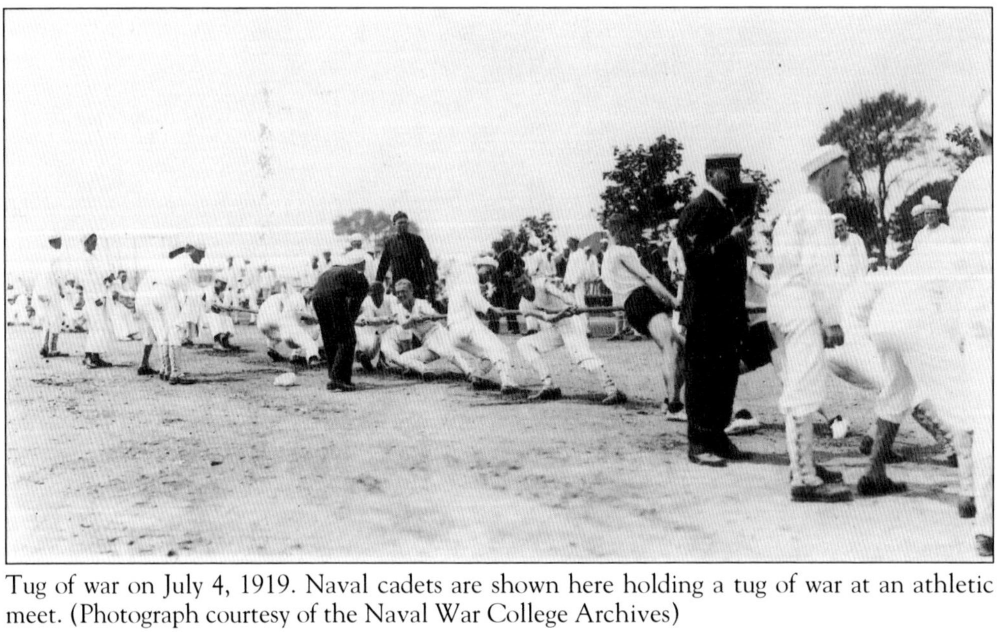
Tug of war on July 4, 1919. Naval cadets are shown here holding a tug of war at an athletic meet. (Photograph courtesy of the Naval War College Archives)

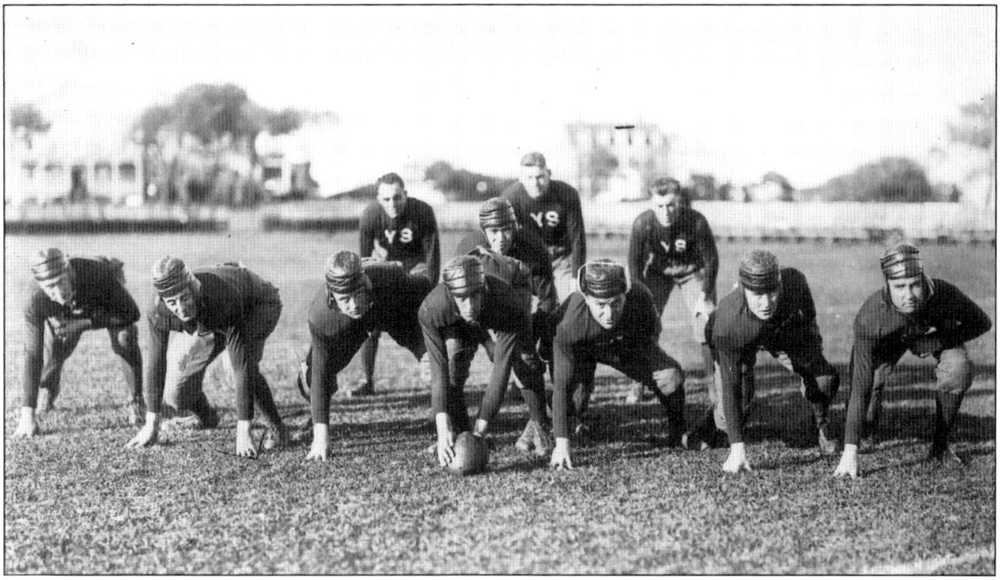

The Yeoman school football team at the Naval Training Station on October 4, 1918. (Photograph courtesy of the Naval War College Archives)

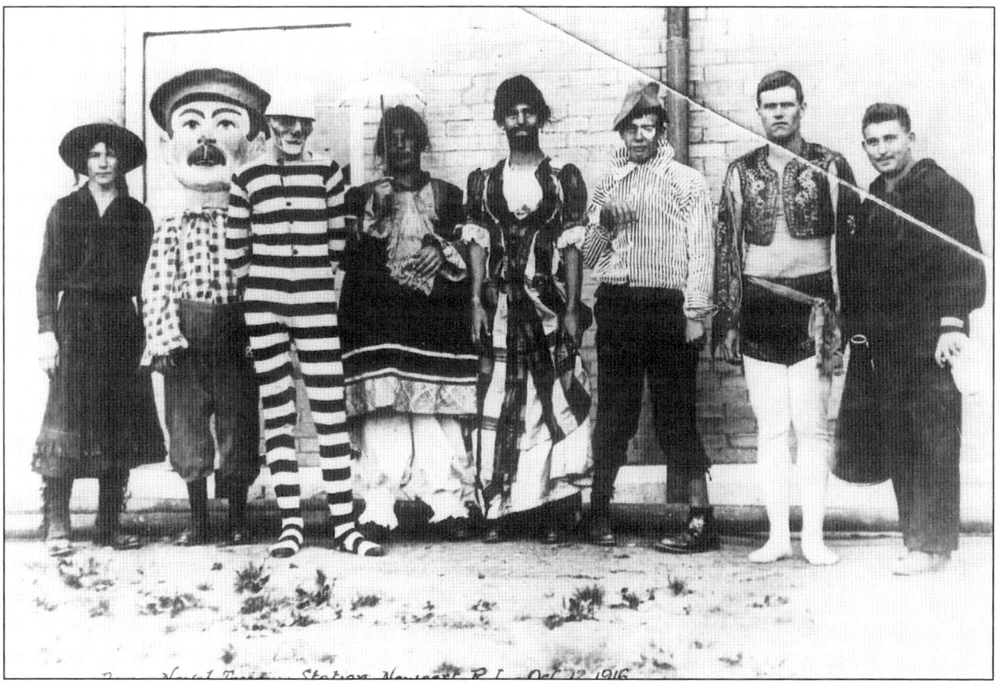

Naval cadets in costume to celebrate Circus Day in October 1916. This photograph was taken at the Naval Training Station. (Photograph courtesy of the Naval War College Archives)

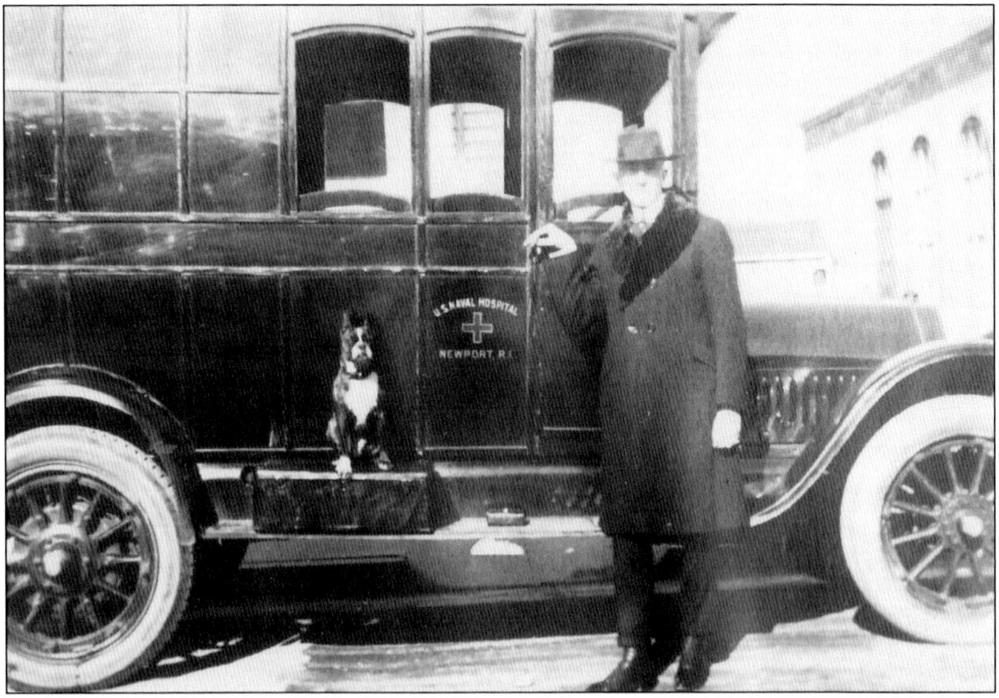

A Navy ambulance with a driver and man's best friend in the 1920s. The Naval Hospital opened its doors in 1913. (Photograph courtesy of Mike Allen)

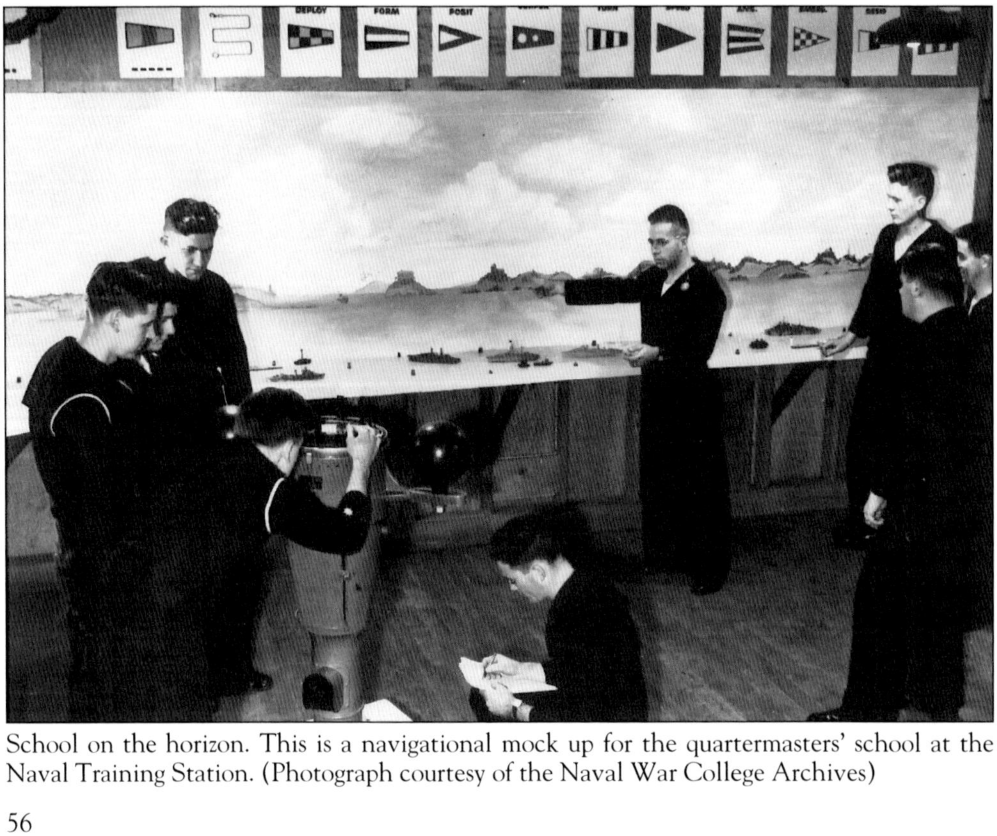

School on the horizon. This is a navigational mock up for the quartermasters' school at the Naval Training Station. (Photograph courtesy of the Naval War College Archives)

Ike and Mamie before a tour of Coasters Harbor Island. On September 4, 1957, the *Daily News* headline read "President wildly cheered here on vacations 'auspicious' start." The President and Mrs. Eisenhower had arrived in Newport for the start of a three week vacation. (Photograph courtesy of the Naval War College Archives)

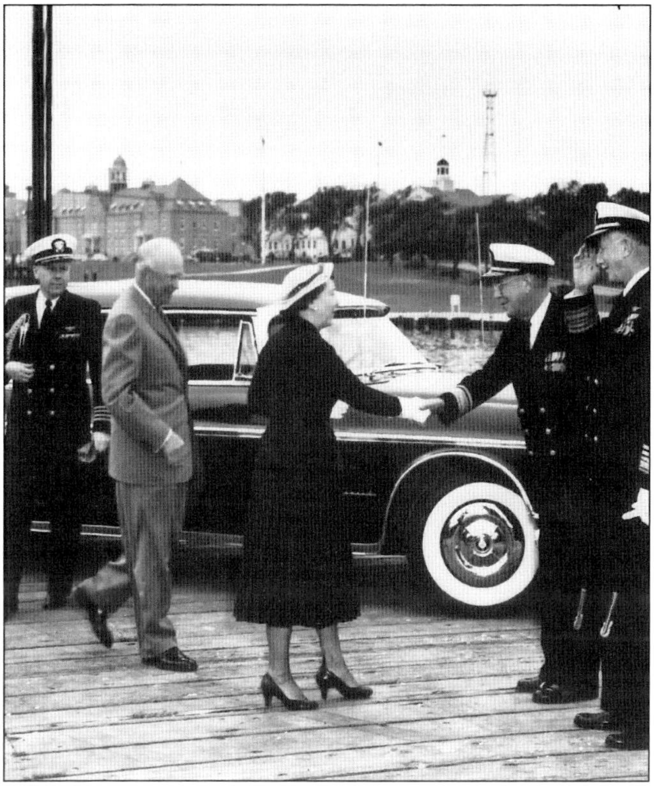

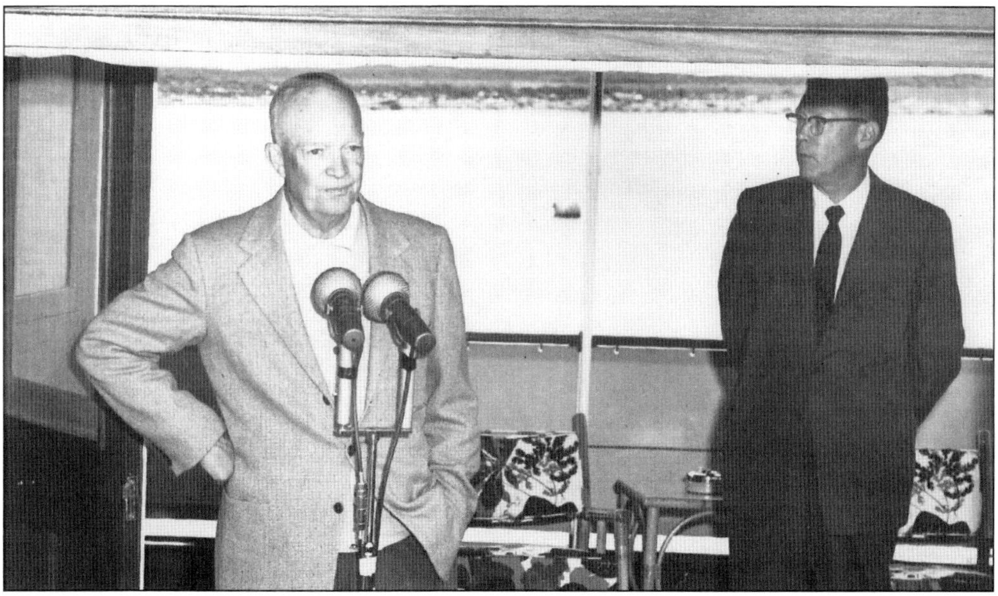

President Eisenhower on the admiral's barge during his 1957 visit. The Victorian cottage at Fort Adams served as the summer Whitehouse in 1957, 1958, and again in 1960. (Photograph courtesy of the Naval War College Archives)

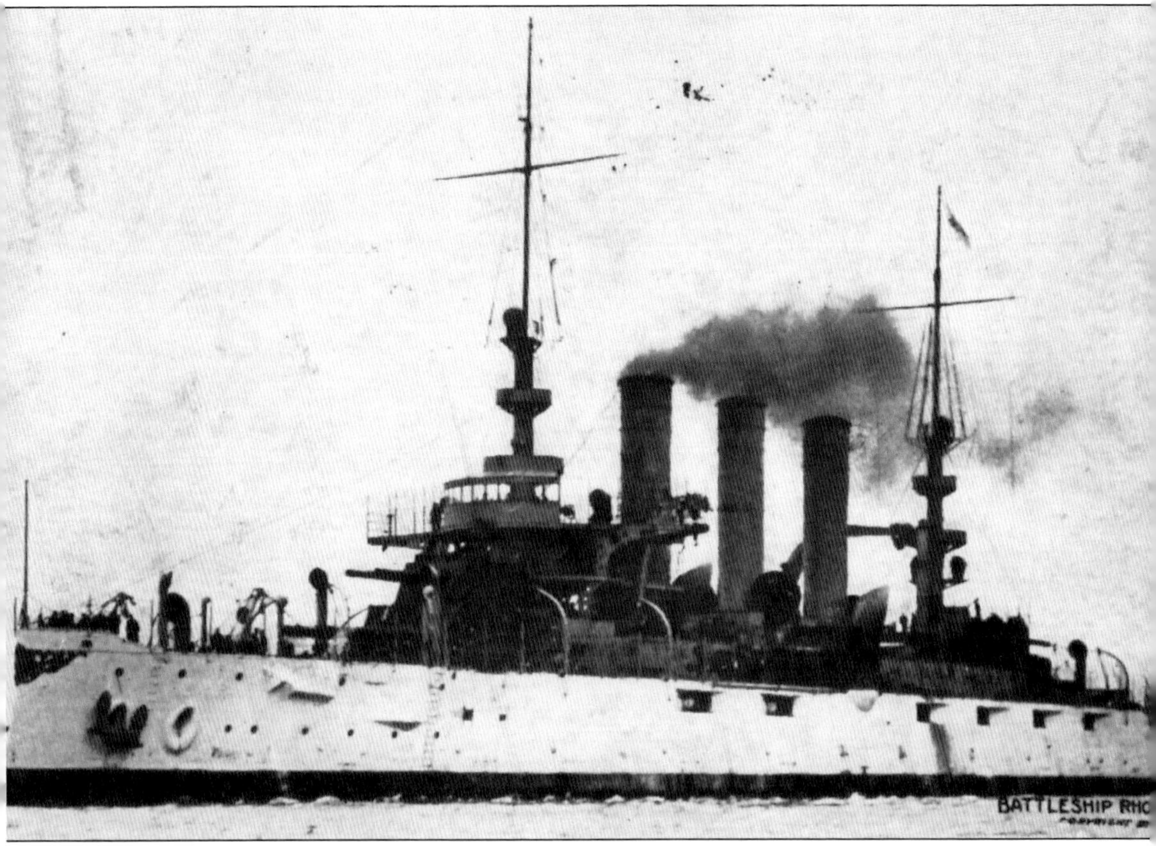

Our two Rhode Islands. The first ship to bear the name Rhode Island was a wooden side-wheel steamer built in 1860. She served in the Navy until decommissioned in November 1867. The second ship (pictured here) was launched on May 17, 1904, in Quincy, Massachusetts. It was one of five Virginia-class ships. After an extensive shakedown and acceptance trials, the ships first assignment was to the Division 2, Atlantic Fleet, stationed at Guantanomo Bay, Cuba. The ship served in the Atlantic Fleet until May 1916, when she was placed in reduced commission at Boston Navy Yard. She was again commissioned as a support vessel for World War I and was active until rendered incapable of any further warlike service on October 4, 1923, in accordance with the Washington Treaty limiting naval armaments. She was sold on November 1, 1923, for scrap.

Three

Middletown

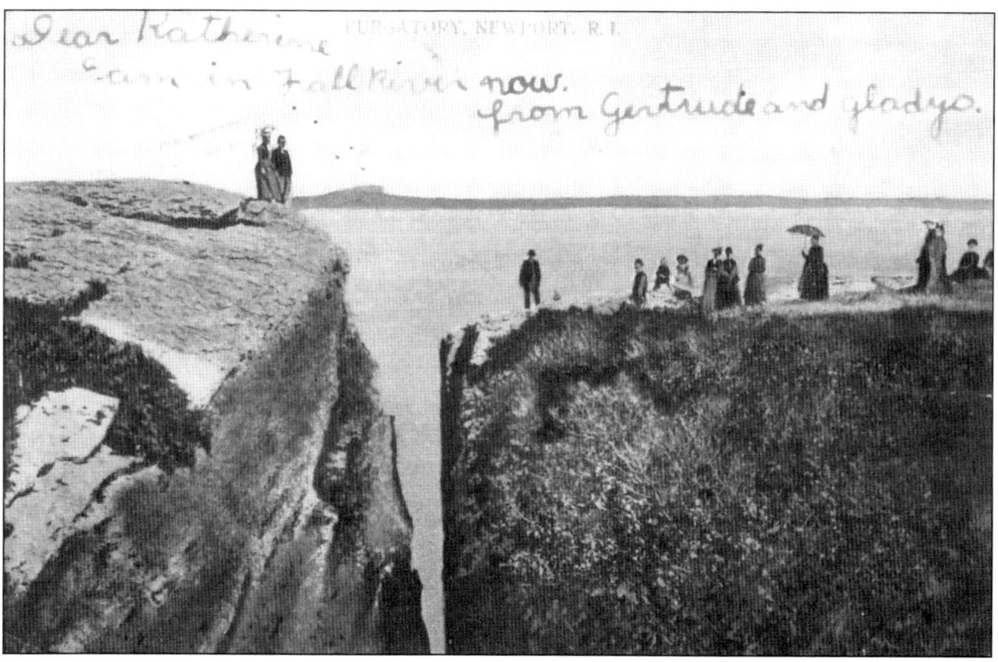

Purgatory Chasm in Middletown. This postcard is labeled Newport. Through the years, many events that occurred in Portsmouth and Middletown were attributed to Newport. The chasm was formed over the last 10,000 to 12,000 years, after the last glacial melt.

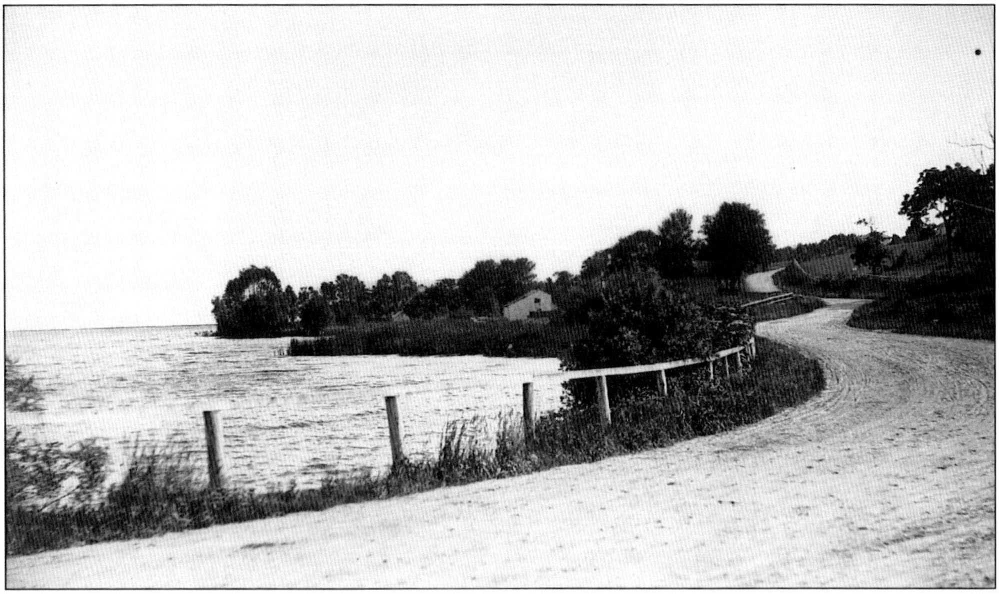

The head of Eastons Pond at Green End Avenue in 1890.

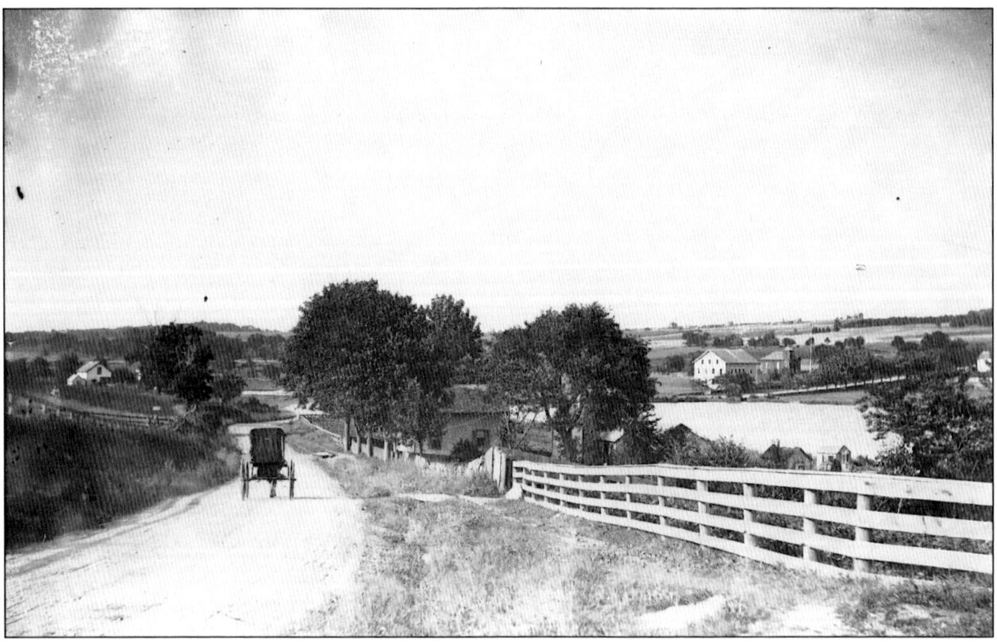

Another view of Green End Avenue looking north.

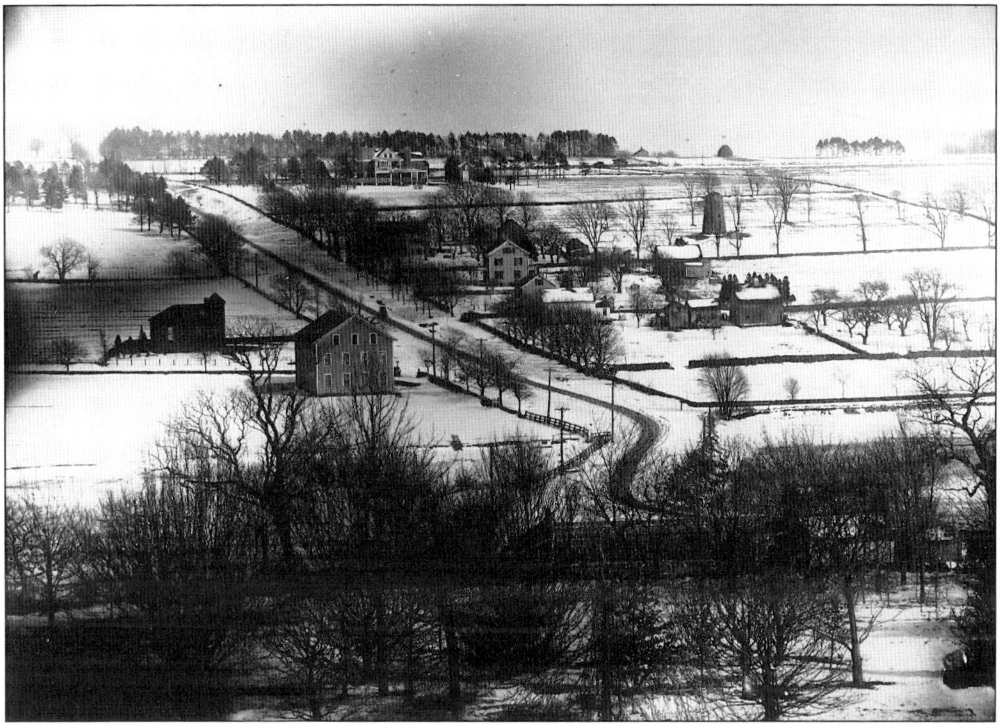

Honeyman Hill with a light dusting of snow in February 1904. The dark building to the left is the Witherbee School, built in 1892. The Harkness windmill is still standing although her arms are no longer present. The Jethro Peckham homestead, seen below the mill, was built in 1870.

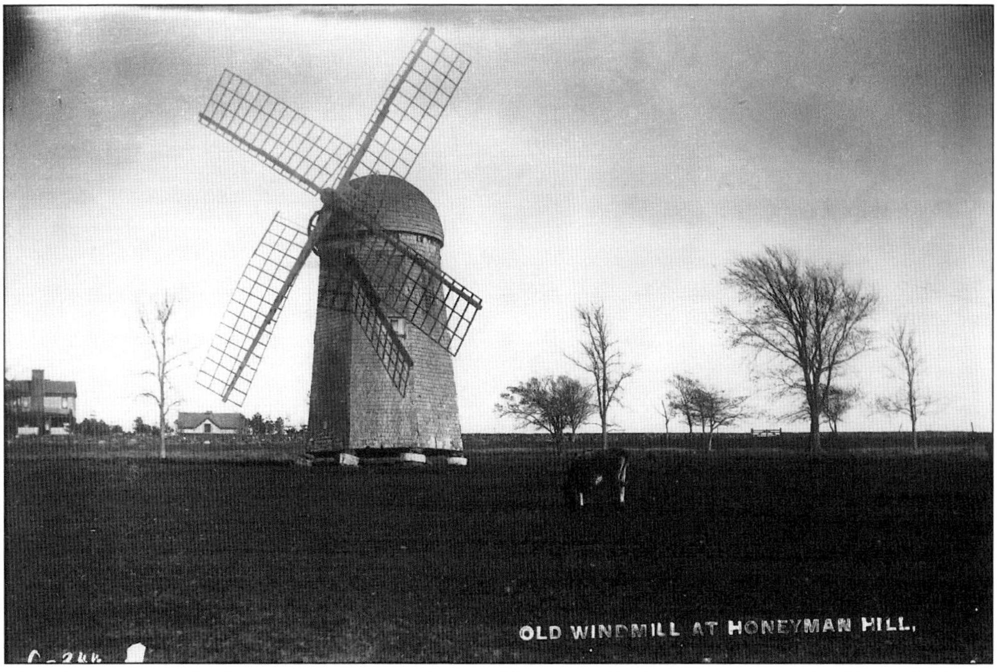

The Harkness windmill in 1890. It originally stood between Catherine Street and Old Beach Road.

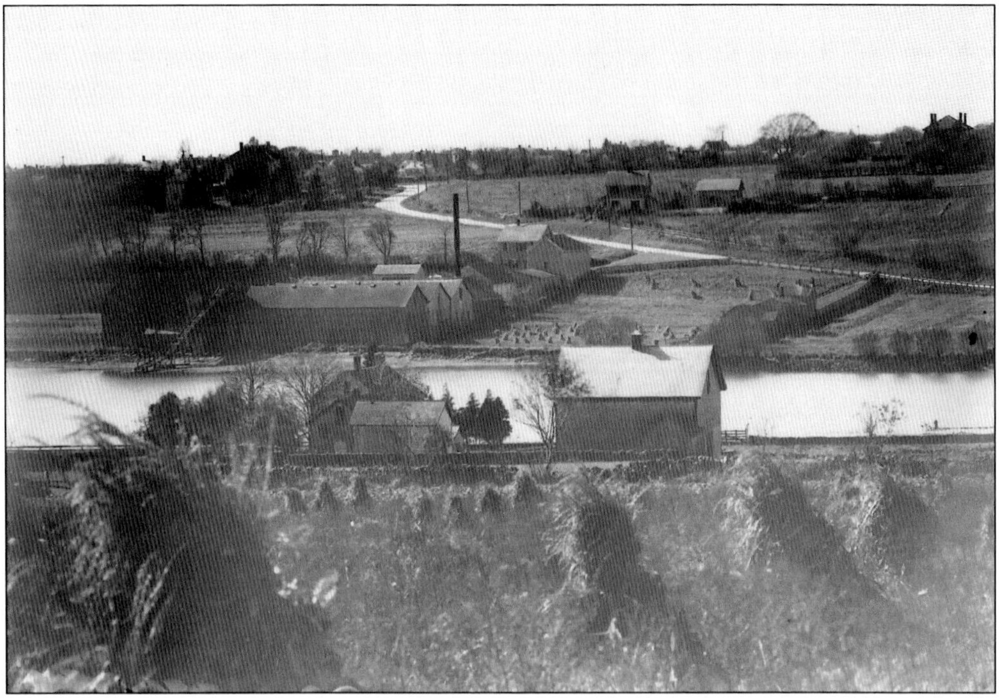

Ice houses at Eastons Pond. Ice cutting was done by the Arctic Ice Company and the Newport Ice Company at Eastons Pond and Lily Pond. About 275 men were employed during the cold months. Over 35,000 tons of ice could be harvested in a season.

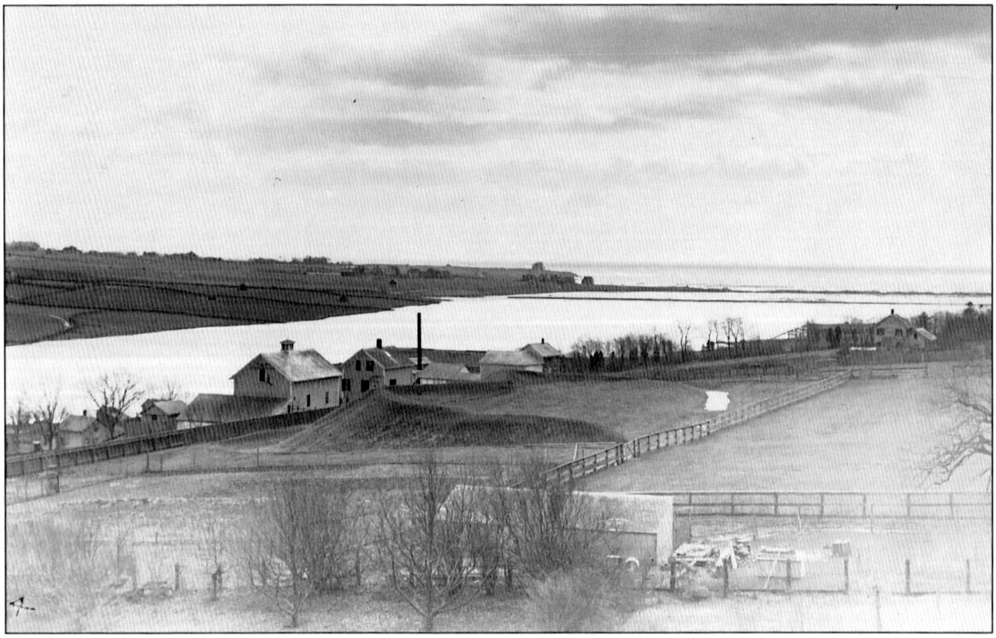

Redoubt De Saintange. Referred to for years as Green End Fort or Cards Redoubt, it has recently been correctly identified in an article printed in the bulletin of the Newport Historical Society. This was part of a line of defense built by the British in 1777 and 1778 to defend Newport.

The building of Saint Georges gothic chapel. The groundbreaking took place on April 23, 1924, Saint Georges Day. It was designed by Ralph Adams Cram and was a gift from alumnus John Nicholas Brown.

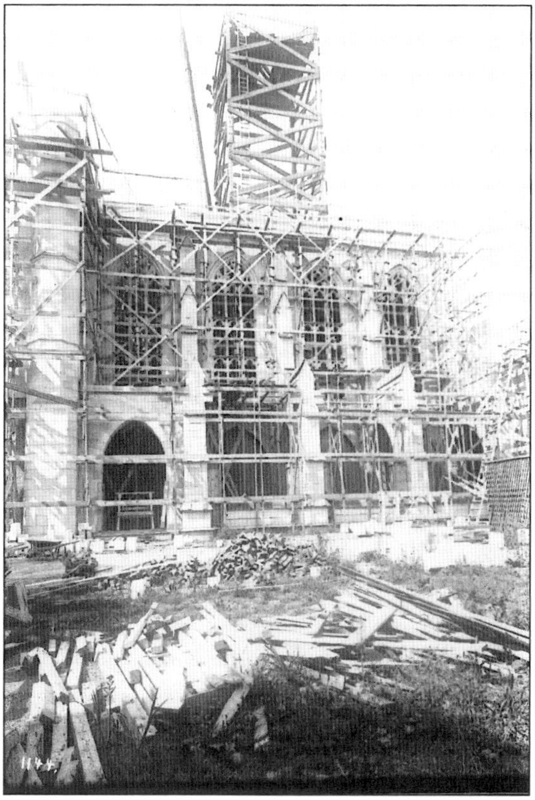

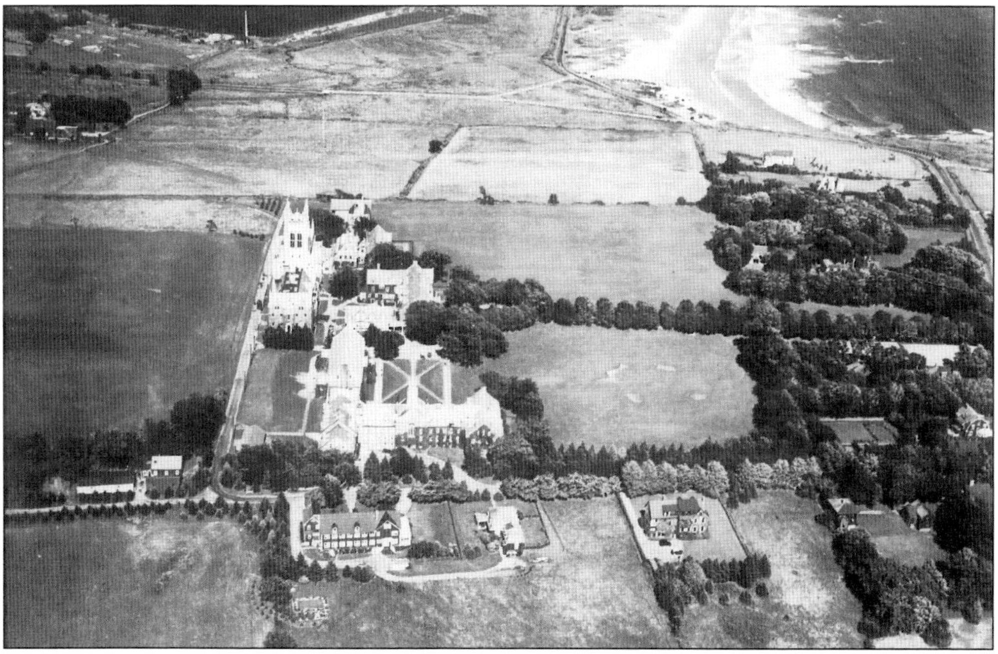

Saint Georges School, founded in 1896 by Reverend John Diman. This aerial view was taken in 1937. Sachuest Beach, or Second Beach, is in the distance. (Photograph by H.H. Harris, courtesy of the William Bachus Collection)

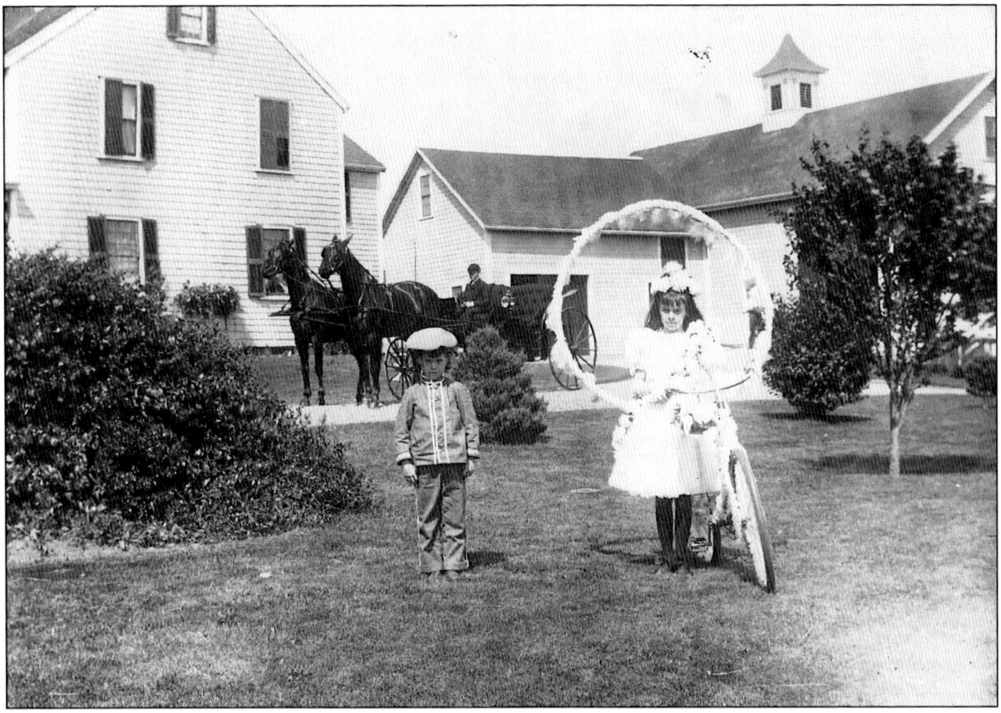

May Day. Members of the Brown family pose in front of their home. The house dates to the mid-1800s.

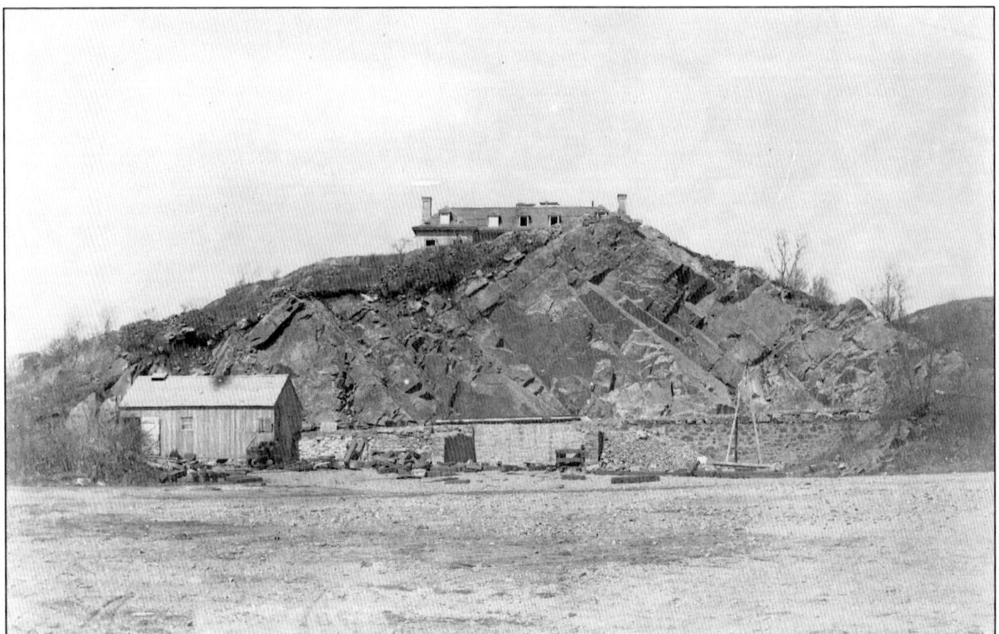

The Cottons, then the Peckham Brothers, Quarry, at 220 Paradise Avenue. Purchased in March 1844, it was incorporated in May of 1905. Over the years it has also been known as Paradise Rocks.

The Wyatt Mill near Four Corners in the 1890s. Built in 1750 in Bristol, the mill was moved in the late 1700s to Fall River, then Tiverton, and finally Newport. By 1797 it was in Middletown near Mitchels Lane and East Main Road. In 1855 Sam Wyatt bought the mill and moved it to Wyatt Road. The mill continued to operate until 1923, when it was purchased by Colonel E.H. Green and moved once more, this time to South Dartmouth, Massachusetts, to be used as a guest house. (Photograph by P.H. Caswell)

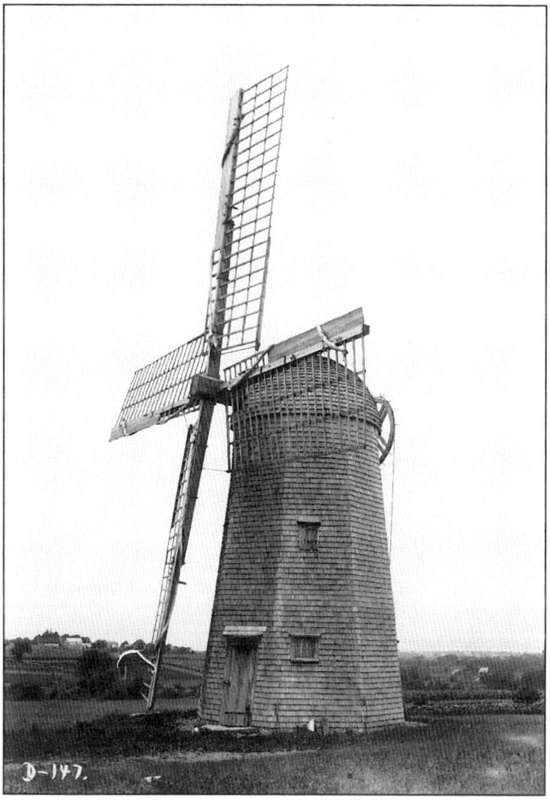

The Coggeshall Farmhouse. The earliest recorded documentation of this house is 1725, although it is believed that the house could have been built as early as the late 1600s. The Coggeshall family settled in what is now Middletown sometime before 1700, and the farm is still owned by Coggeshall descendants, who continue to work the land.

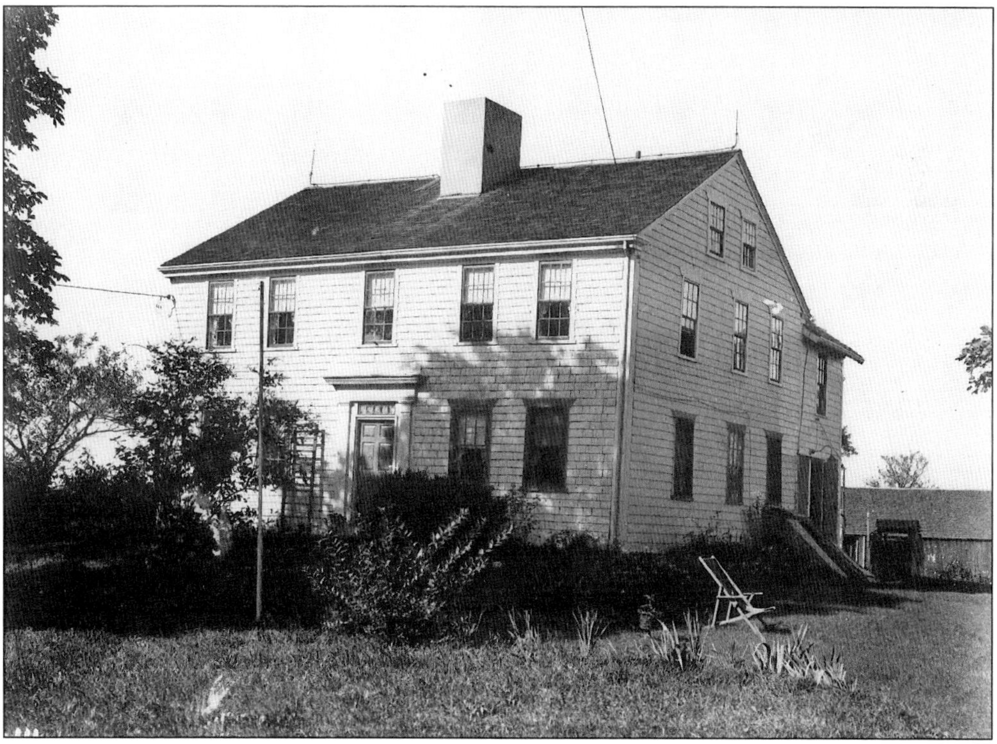

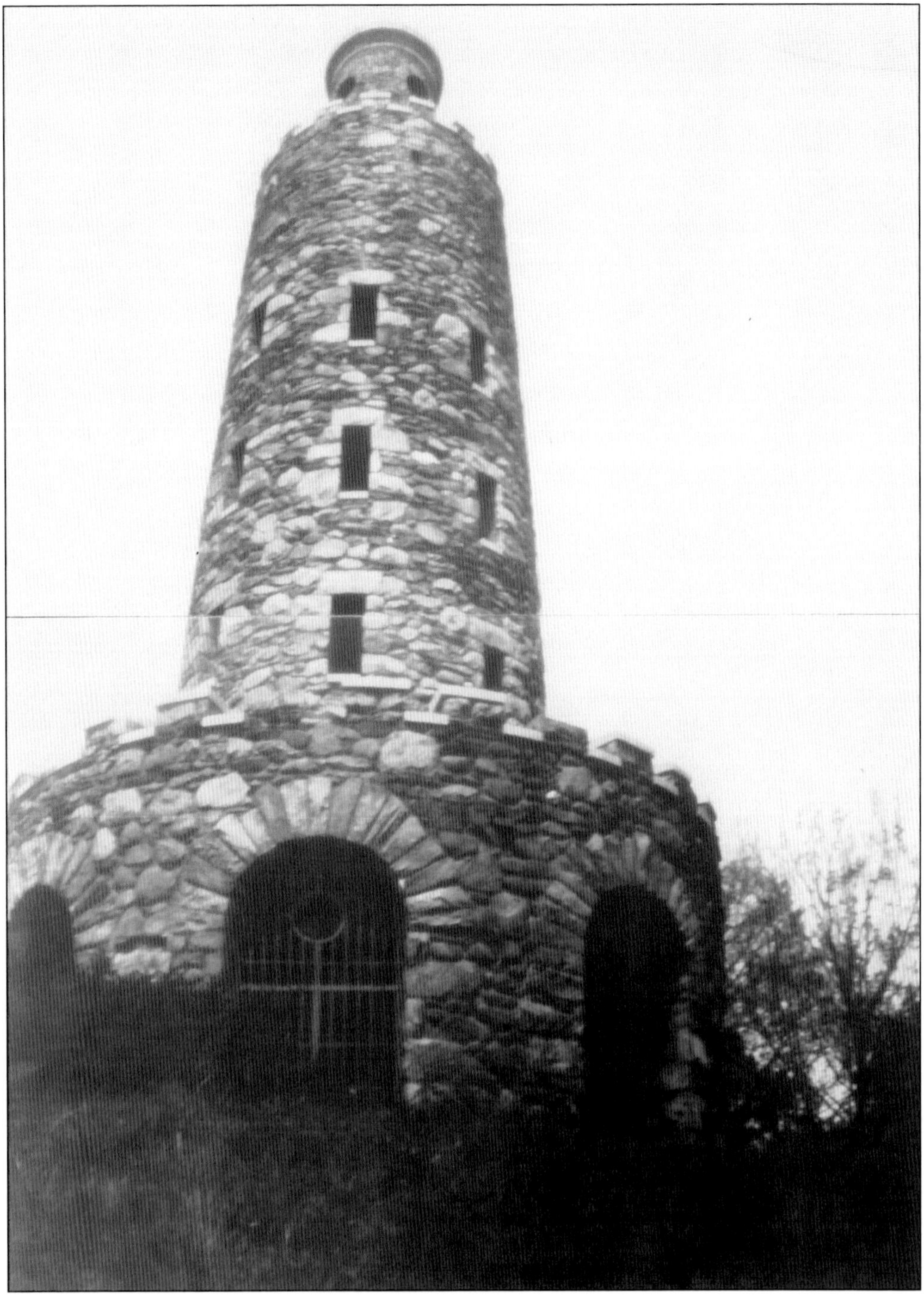

The Miantonomi Monument on Tonomy Hill at the Newport/Middletown line. In the 1920s the city obtained full possession of the hill and a memorial to veterans of World War I was erected. It stands 90 feet tall and was constructed over a powder magazine built by the British when they fortified the hill during the occupation of Newport. (Pinhole image by Rob Lewis, 1988)

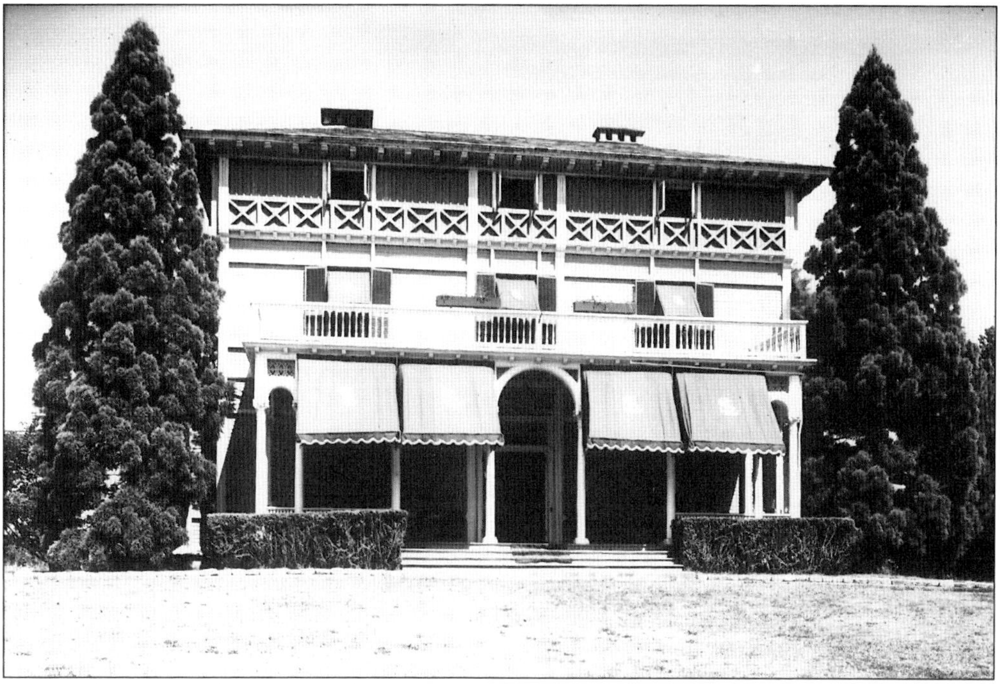

Shadow Lawn on Miantonomi Avenue. The Hamilton Hoppin House was built in 1856, in the stick style. It was designed by Richard Upjohn, and has a series of external embellishments which mirror the structural components of the frame.

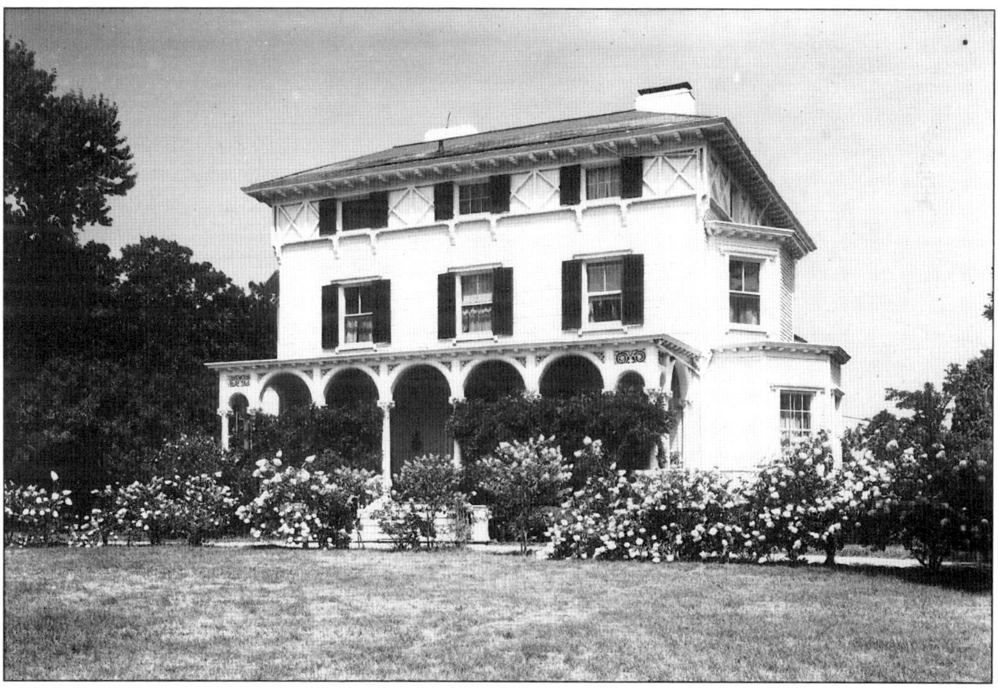

The Alexander Van Rensselaer House. Built in 1860, a short time after the Hamilton Hoppin House, it mimicked the style of Upjohn. During the 1940s Admiral Kalbfus resided in the house.

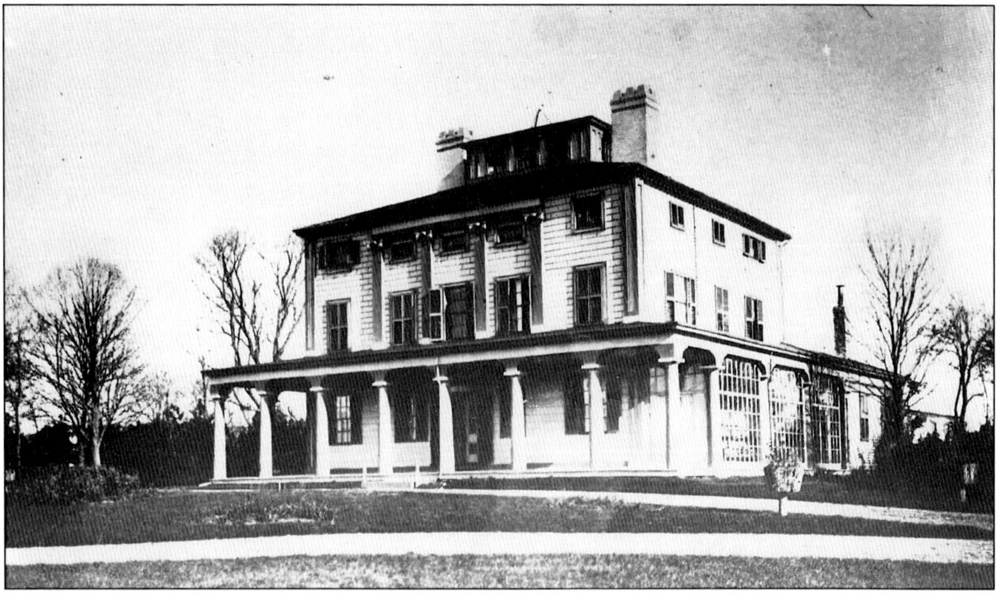

The home of British customs collector Charles Dudley. This house, located about 200 yards north of One Mile Corner on the east side of West Main Road, was built in 1750 to a Peter Harrison design. It was demolished in 1952.

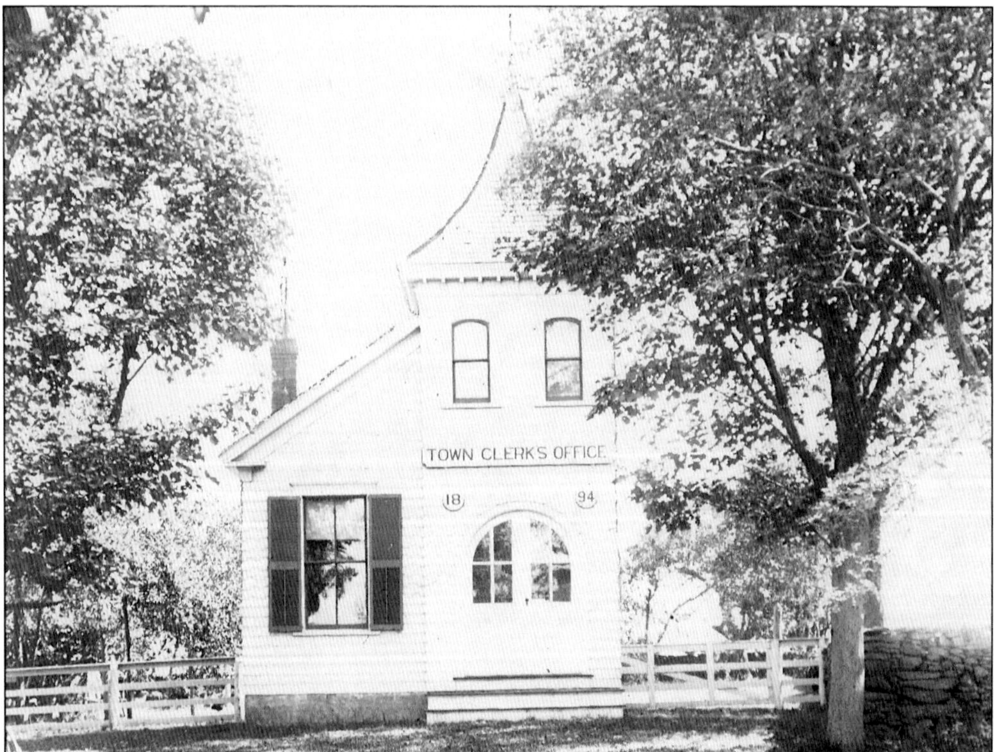

The Middletown Clerks Office, built in 1894 on West Main Road. The building is located next to 1777 West Main Road, where the town clerk resided. The structure stands today, minus the tower peak, in use as a private residence.

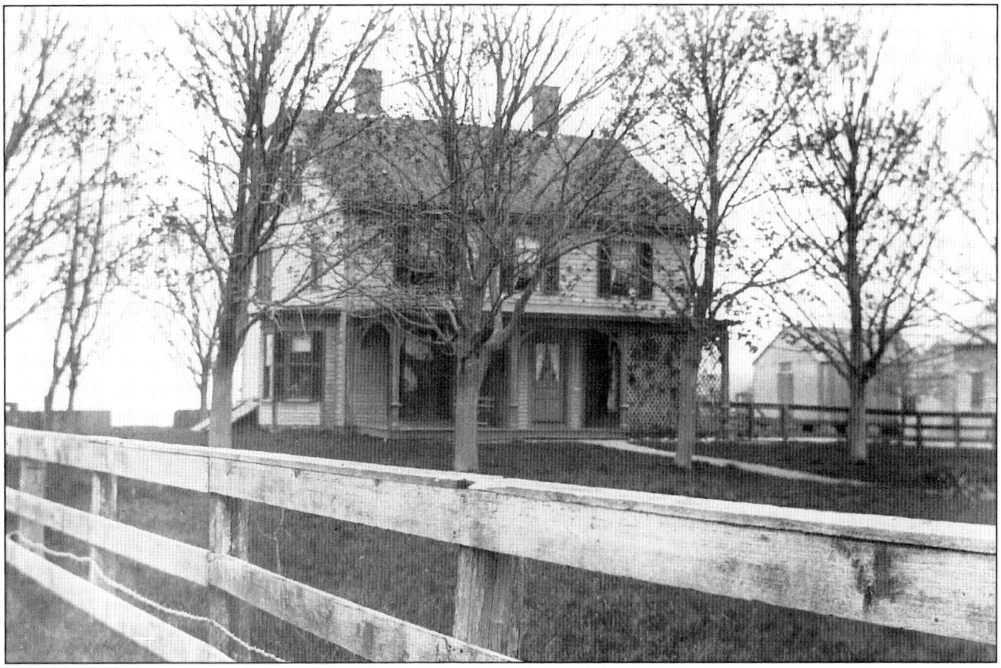

The home place on Chases Lane. This farmhouse was built in 1854 on Chase Farm. It is one of three houses that were built by members of the Chase family in the mid-1800s.

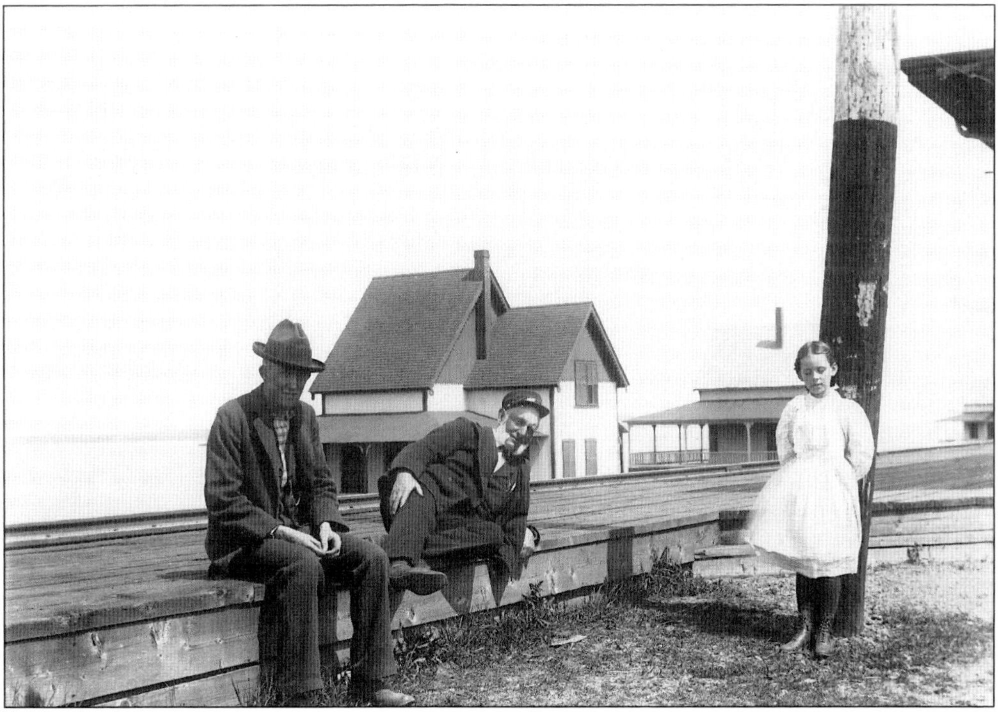

Mr. Brown, Mr. White (the station manager), and another White family member. In the background the Middletown railroad station that was at the bottom of Greene Lane can be seen.

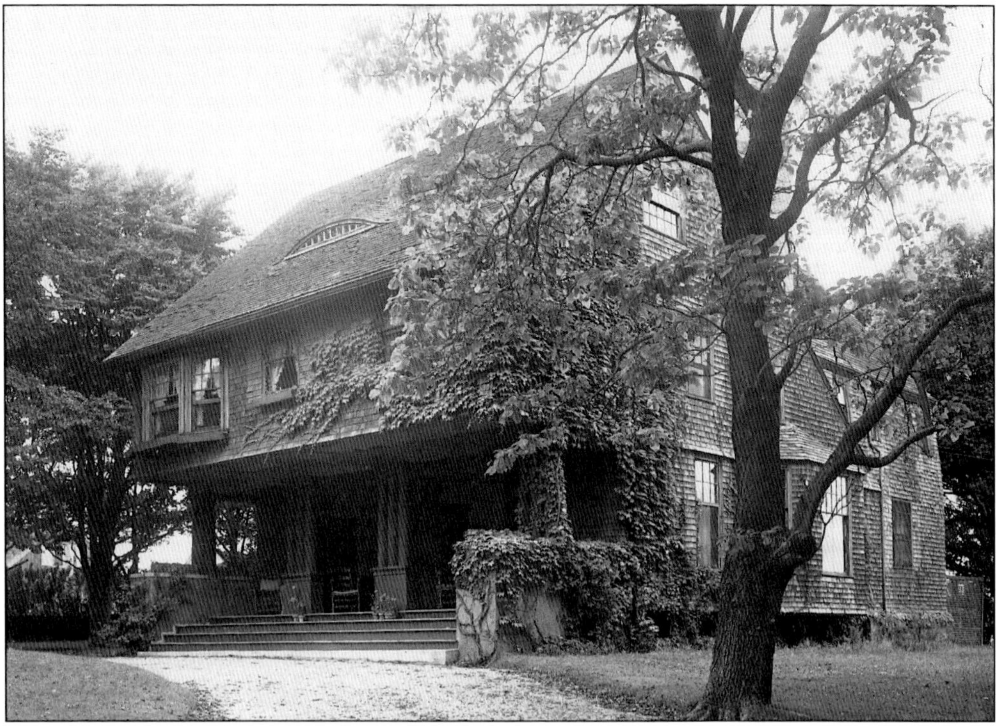

The Conover House on Indian Avenue as it appeared in the 1940s. It was built in 1888 by Clarence S. Luce from Boston.

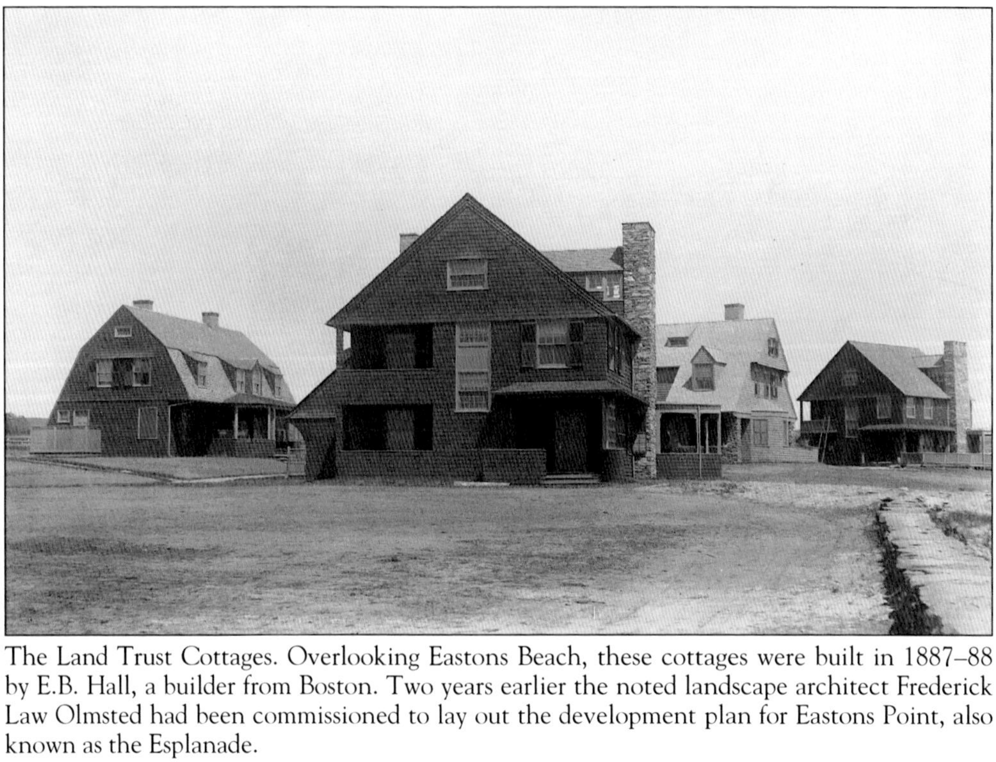

The Land Trust Cottages. Overlooking Eastons Beach, these cottages were built in 1887–88 by E.B. Hall, a builder from Boston. Two years earlier the noted landscape architect Frederick Law Olmsted had been commissioned to lay out the development plan for Eastons Point, also known as the Esplanade.

Jethro Peckham, born in November 1821. Peckham held various town offices and from 1861 until 1866 he served in the state senate. He was a farmer during his early life, but later became a housewright. He died in December 1887 (see p. 61).

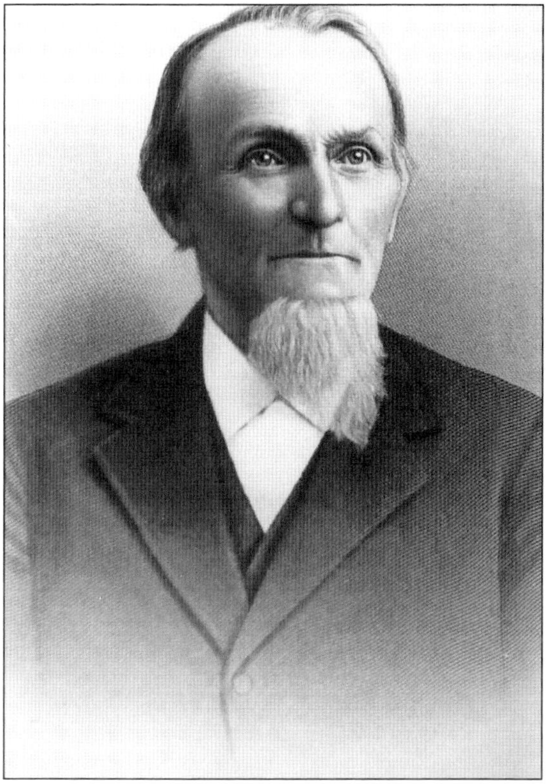

Saint Columba's Chapel on Indian Avenue in 1884. This church, formerly known as the Berkley Memorial Chapel, contains a memorial window for Mary Devlin, the wife of Edwin Booth (see p. 77).

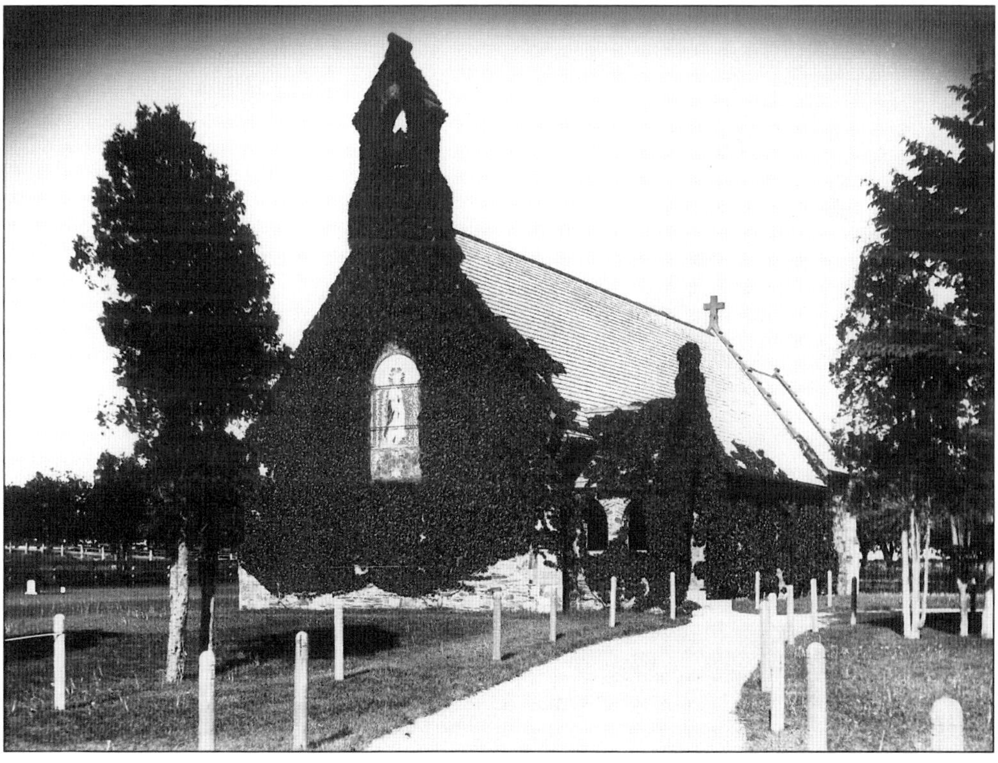

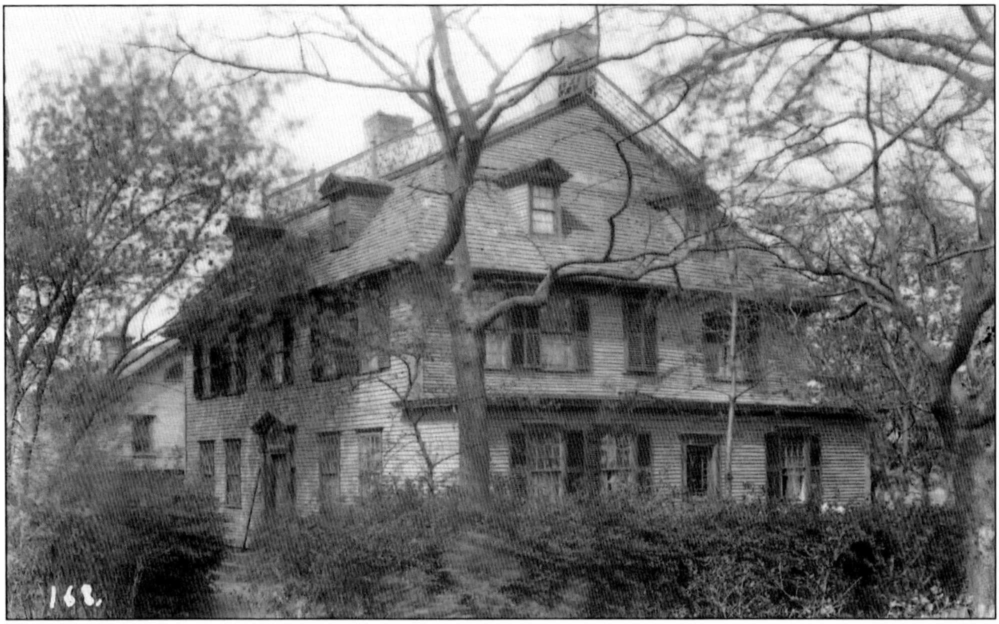

William Redwood's country house at 317 West Main Road. The house is an early Georgian structure built by Deputy Governor Joseph Whipple in 1745. Redwood, a successful merchant, acquired the house in 1755. It was later occupied by Quaker minister David Buffum. Today the house has been moved 125 feet north and is being restored by Stop Over Services of Newport County.

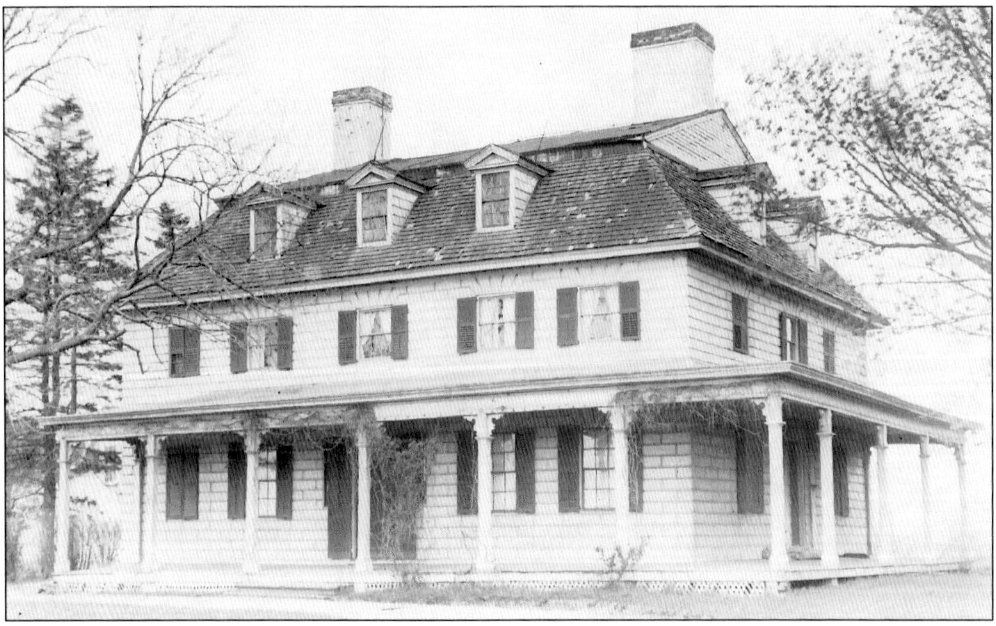

The John Bannister House at West Main Road, located slightly north of One Mile Corner. Built by Bannister in the 1750s, the porch was a later addition. Bannister, a British sympathizer, left town during the Revolution and the house was occupied by Colonel George Irish. In 1952 the house was dismantled and parts of it were rebuilt in Delaware for the Duponts Winterthur Museum.

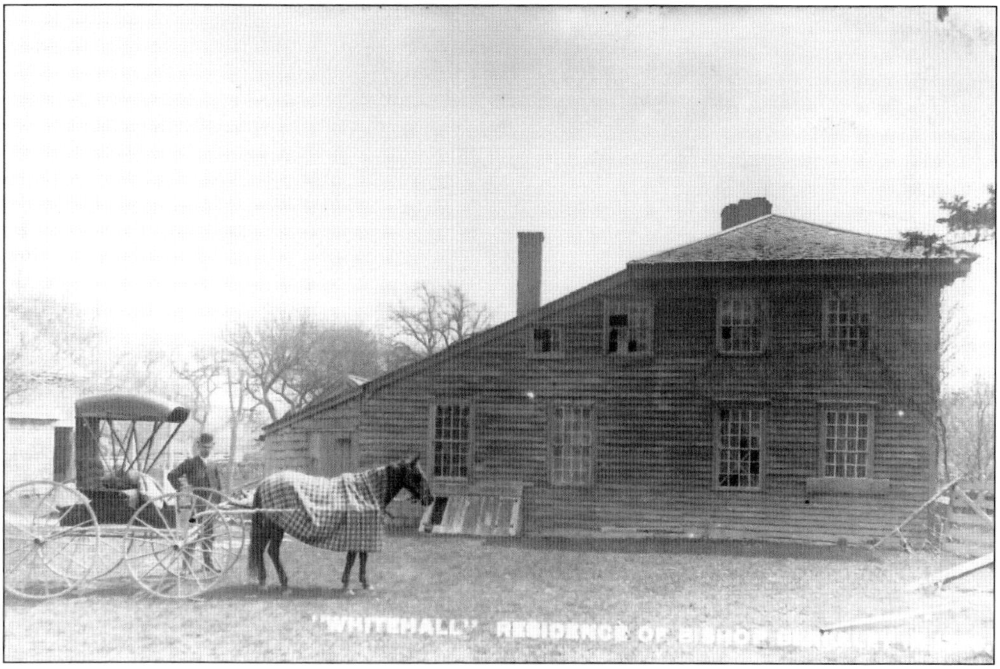

Whitehall, the Middletown residence of Dean Berkley from 1729 to 1732. When he left to go back to England he gave the house and grounds to Yale University. Since 1899 it has been maintained by the Colonial Dames of Rhode Island. Today it is restored and open for tours.

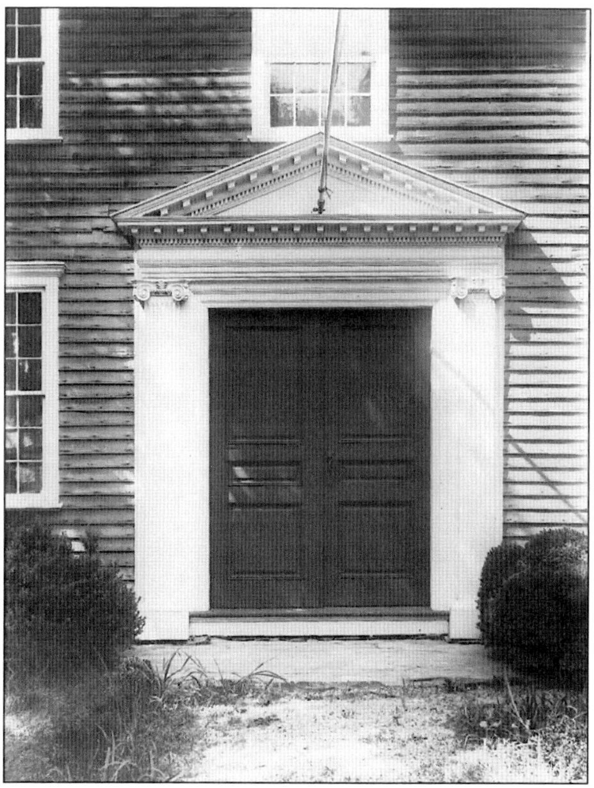

The front door and pediment of Whitehall. Only the door on the right is functional, the second door being added for symmetry. In 1730 Dean Berkley helped found the Newport Literary and Philosophical Society, which in turn founded the Redwood Library.

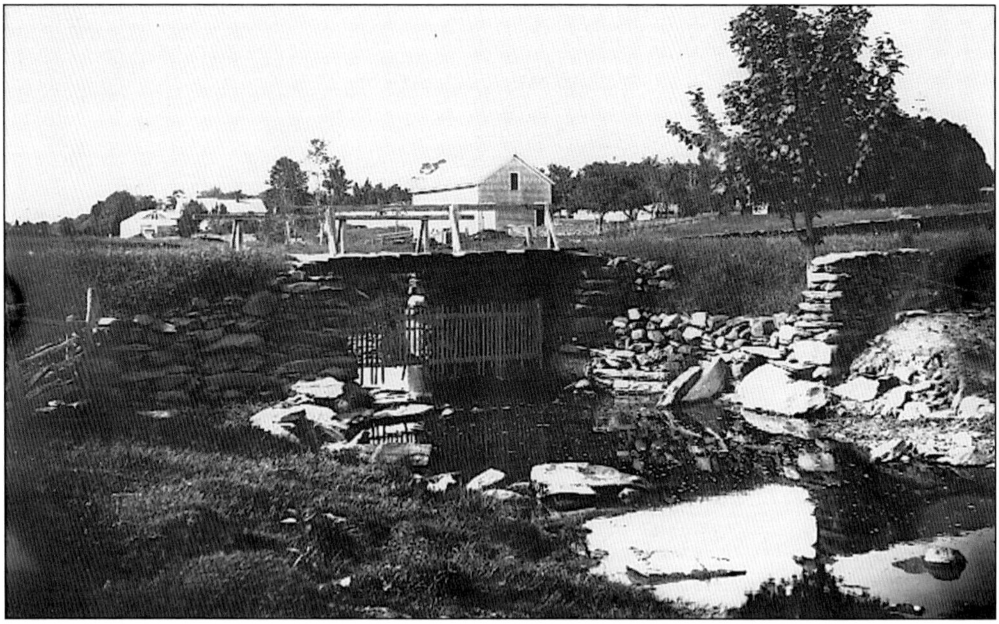

A foot bridge over Stoney Brook where it runs along Paradise Avenue in Middletown in the late 1800s.

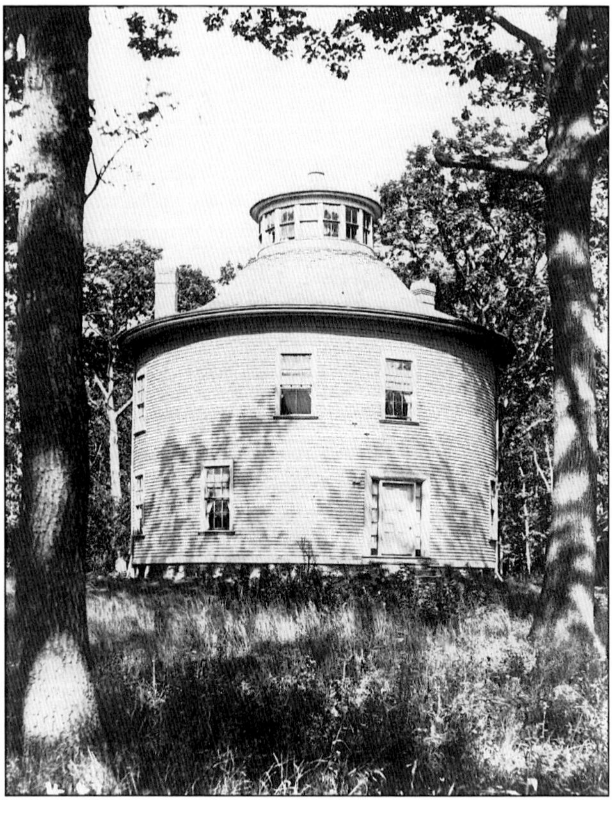

The Round House, built about 1840 by Joseph Southwick, a shipwright, at Southwicks Grove on Forrest Avenue. The story goes that Southwick was laughed at when he boasted that he could build a round house, so he proceeded to build one. The house stood until this century, when it was destroyed by fire. After World War II Southwicks Grove was converted into the Newport Air Park, and in 1960, it was purchased by the state to be used as a state airport.

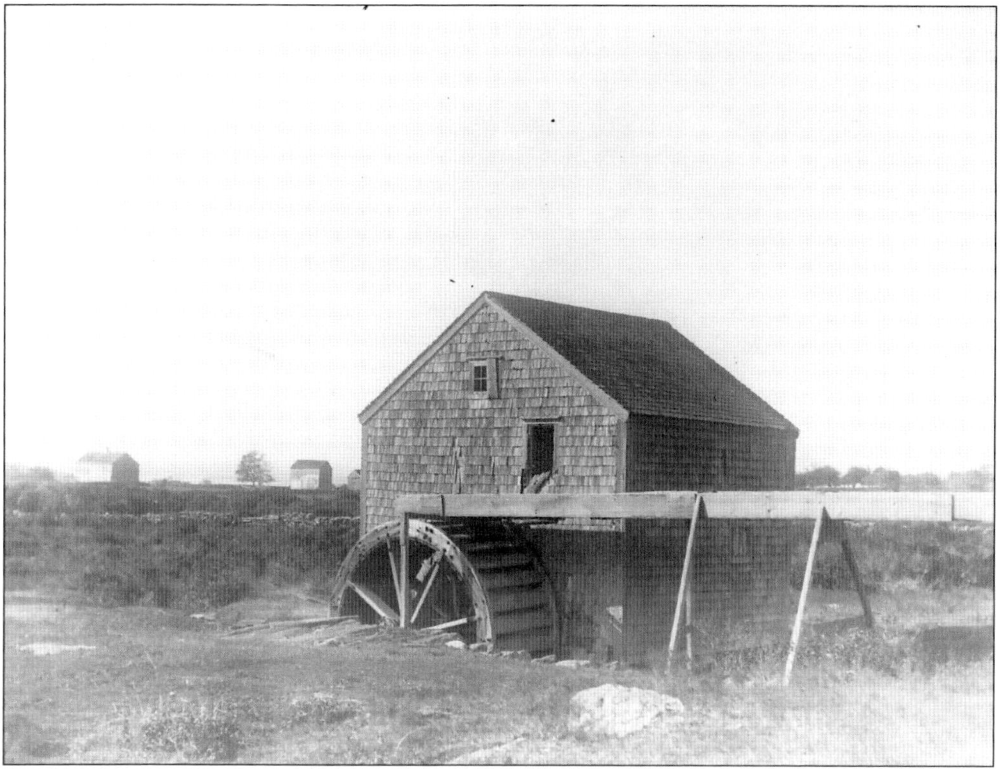
A mill on Wapping Road in the late 1800s. As early as 1640 water power was being harnessed for sawing lumber and, to a lesser extent, milling grain.

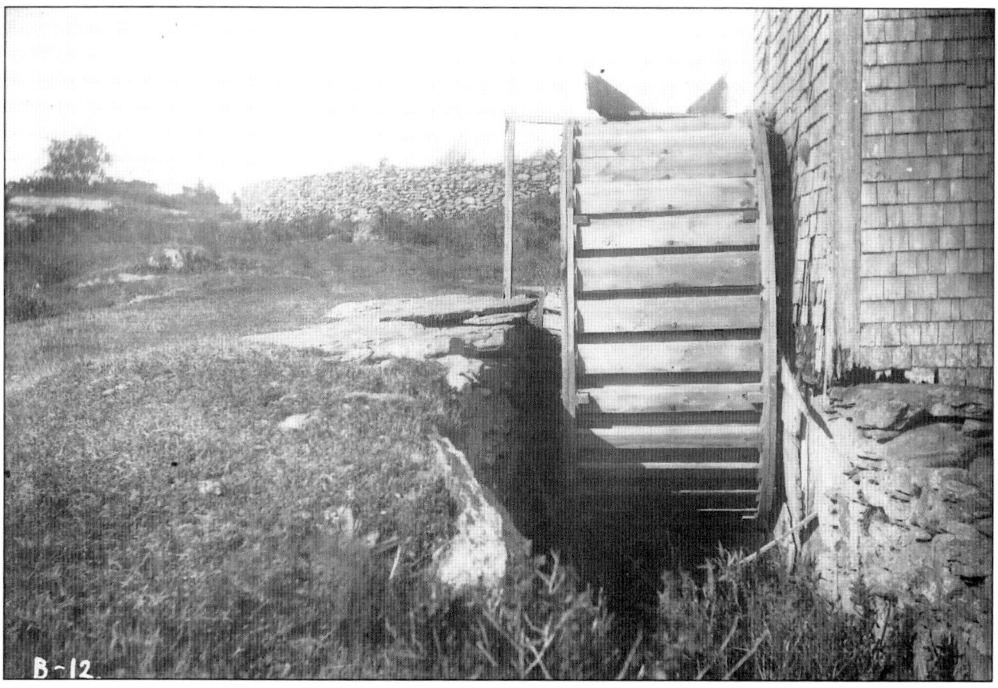

A close up of the waterwheel, showing the water luge and the spillway.

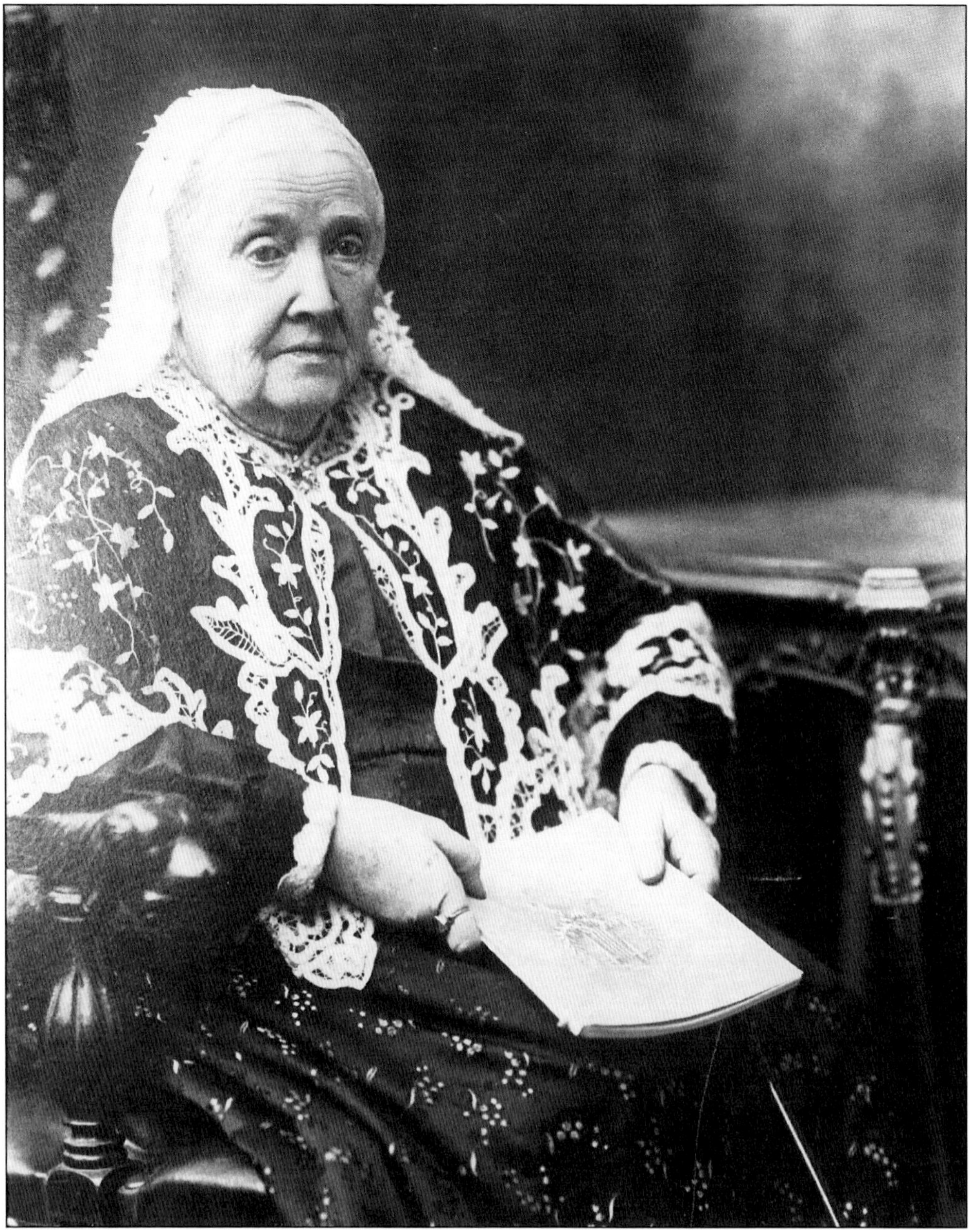

Julia Ward Howe (1819–1910), wife of humanitarian Samuel Gridley Howe. After marrying Samuel Howe in 1843, Julia Howe edited the Boston *Commonwealth*, an antislavery paper. In February 1862 she wrote the "Battle Hymn of the Republic," from which she achieved great popularity. From 1868 on she was associated with the movement for women's emancipation. In 1872 she was a delegate on the World Prison Reform Congress which met in London, and in that same year she founded the World Peace Association. Her estate was located on Union Street and still stands today.

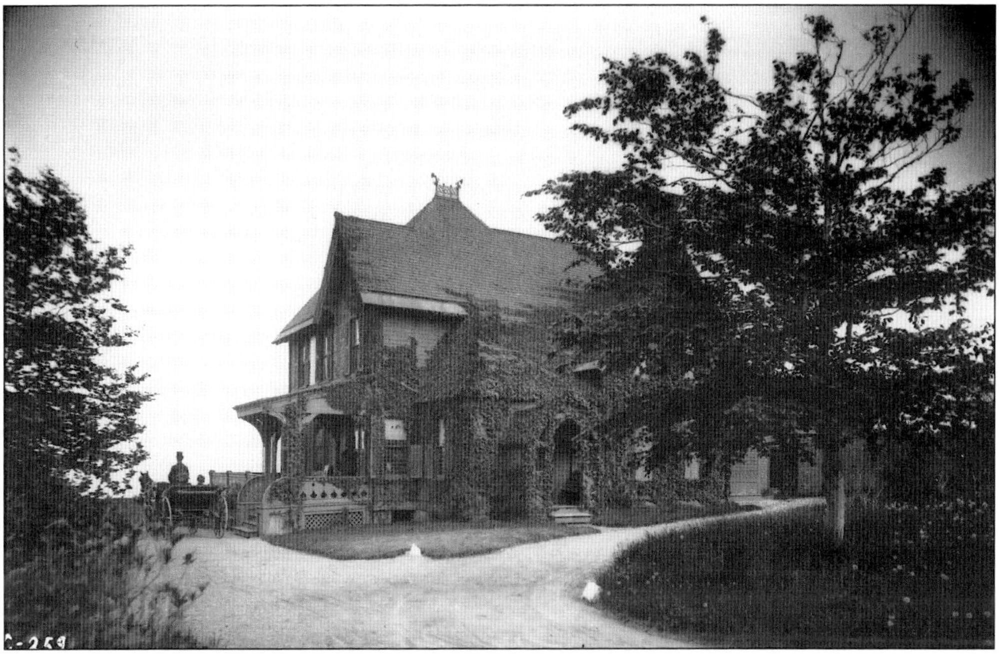

Boothden on Indian Avenue in the late 1800s. This was the home of Edwin Booth, probably the first great American actor. His brother, John Wilkes Booth, assassinated President Lincoln in 1865.

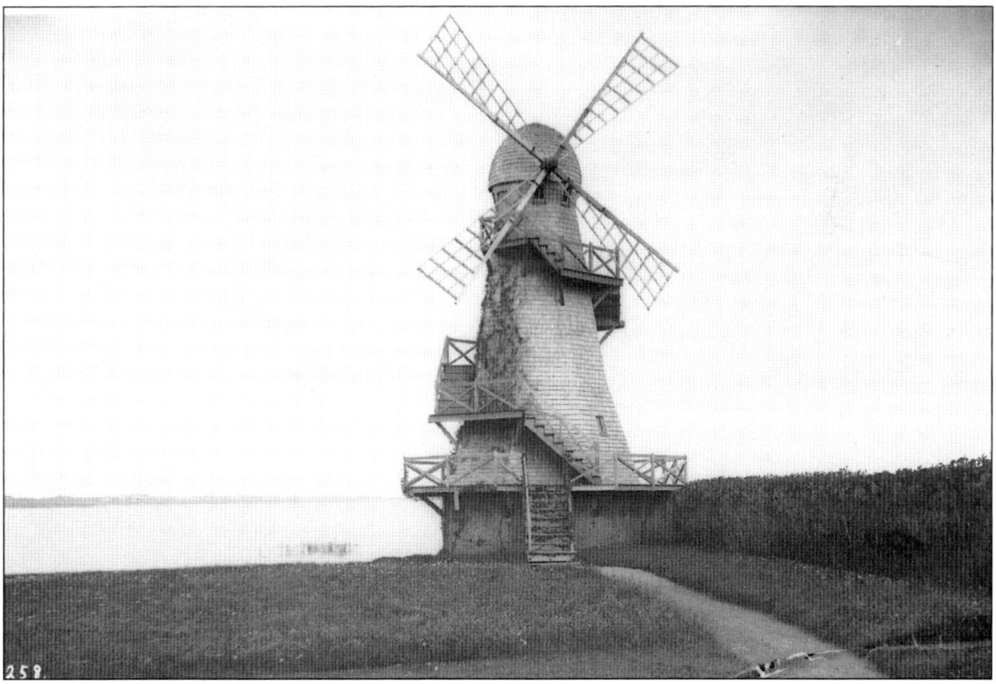

The Normandy-style windmill near the water at Boothden. This mill, originally built to be used as a hen house, sometimes doubled as a lighthouse; Booth's daughter would light a lantern at the top when her father was sailing at night or in the fog.

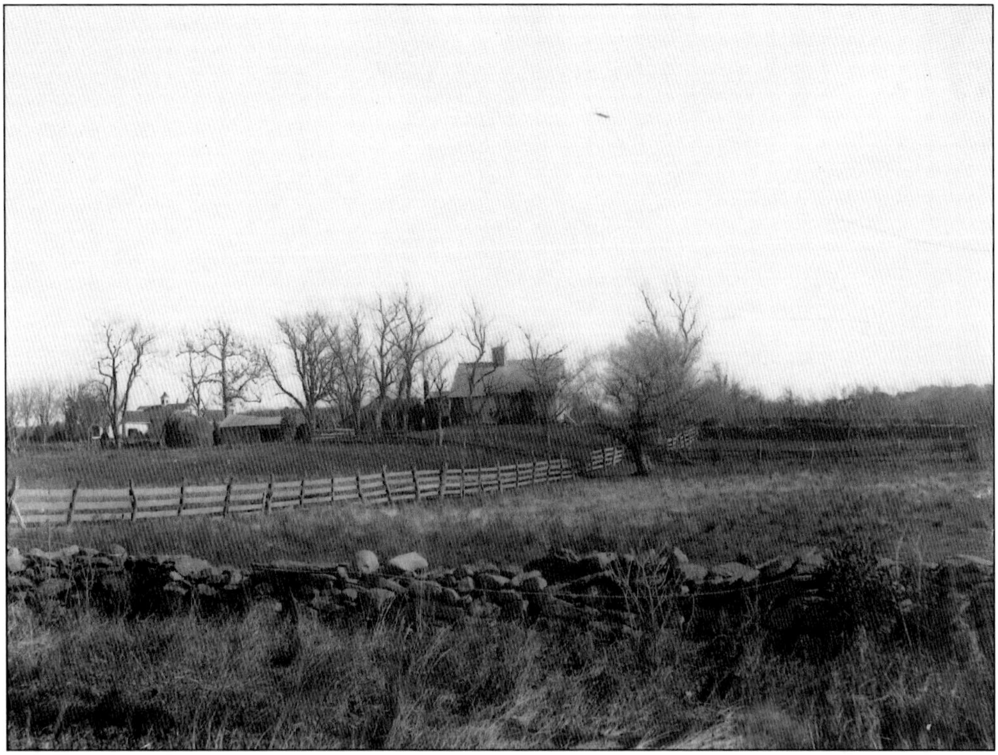

The Joseph Anthony House and outbuildings on West Main Road, built in the mid-1800s.

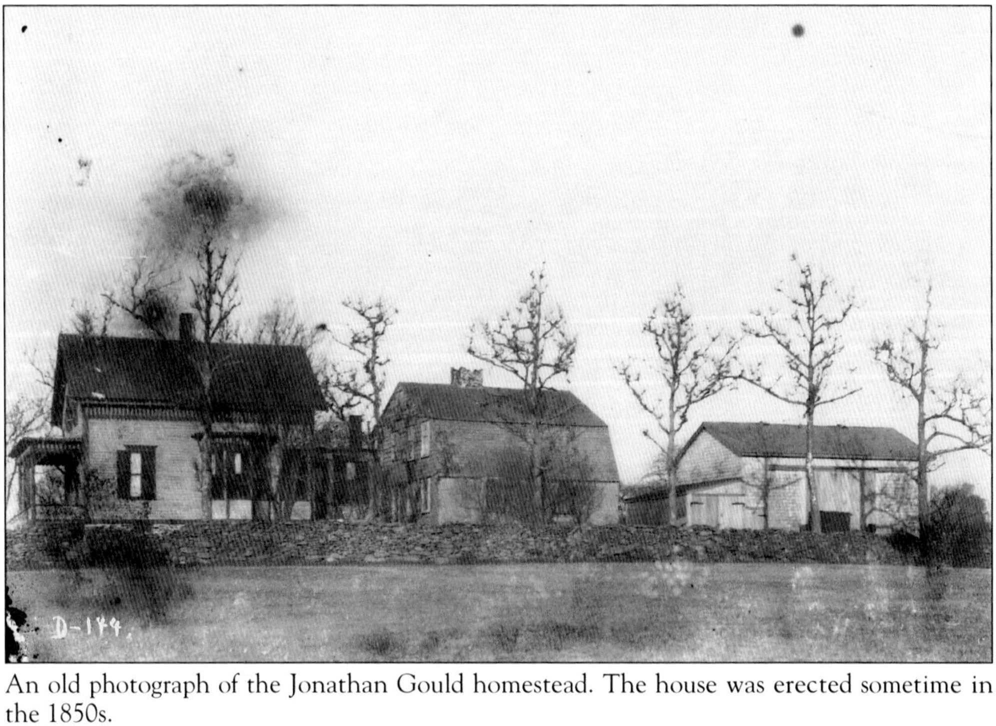

An old photograph of the Jonathan Gould homestead. The house was erected sometime in the 1850s.

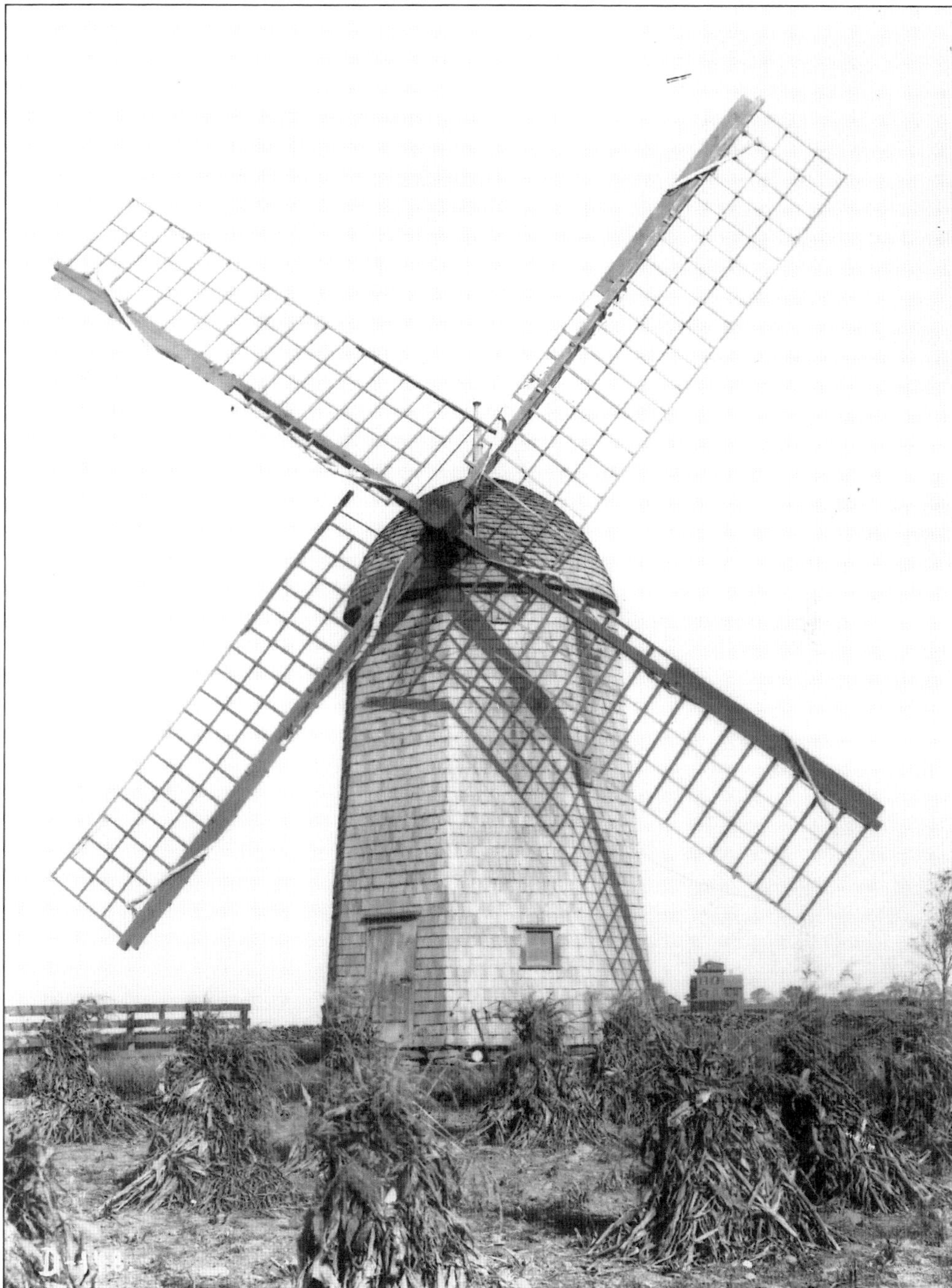

The Thomas Gould/Joseph Anthony mill off West Main Road. In 1840 it was located near Gould Street off Broadway in Newport, but it was later moved to a location near Saint Georges Church on Rhode Island Avenue. In 1864 it was purchased by Joseph Anthony and moved off West Main Road in Middletown. It was consumed by fire on May 5, 1910.

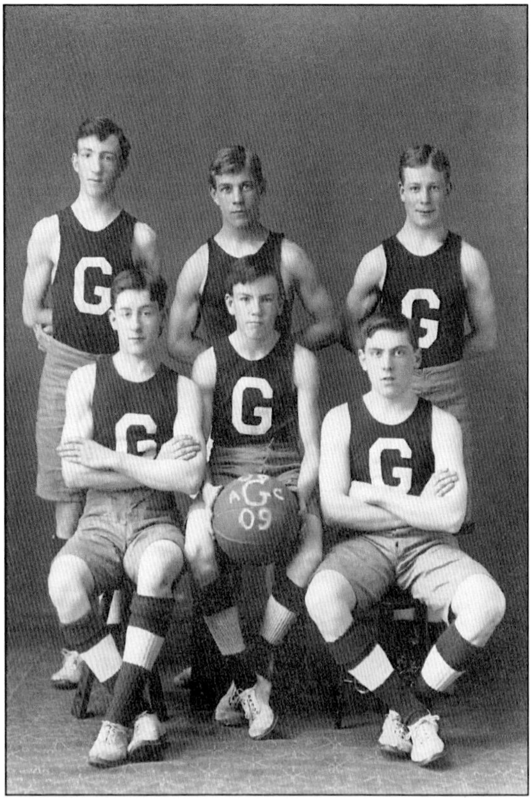

Team players—the Galahad Athletic Club in 1909. In the back, on the right-hand side, is Leland Holt from Middletown. (Photograph courtesy of the Peter H. Sherman family)

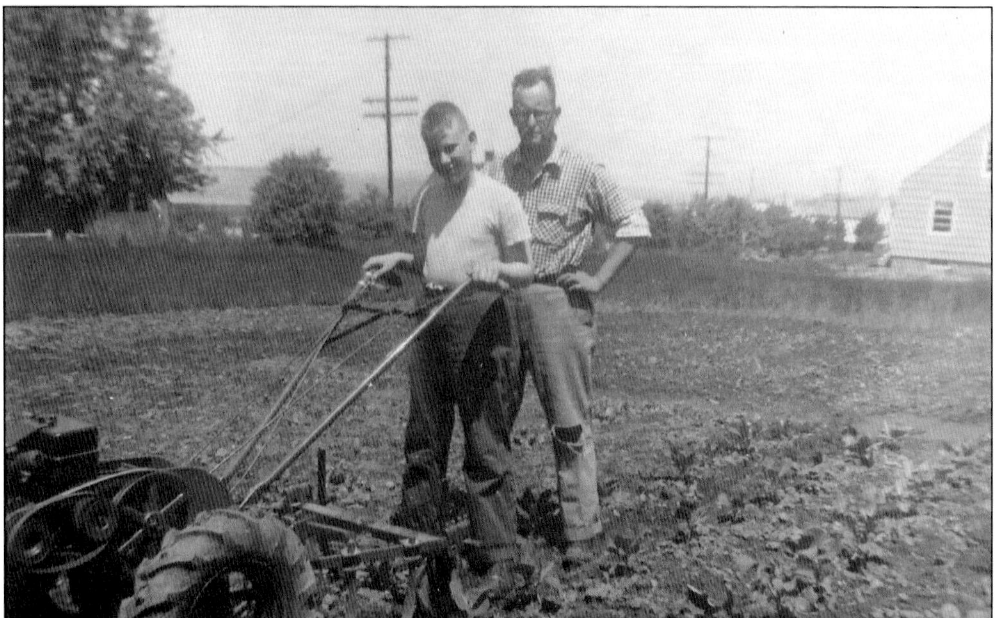

David Sherman with his dad, Alton P. Sherman Jr., in the early 1950s. The location is the corner of Maple Avenue and Sherman Lane, where for years the Sherman family kept a vegetable garden. (Photograph courtesy of the Peter H. Sherman family)

Four

Portsmouth

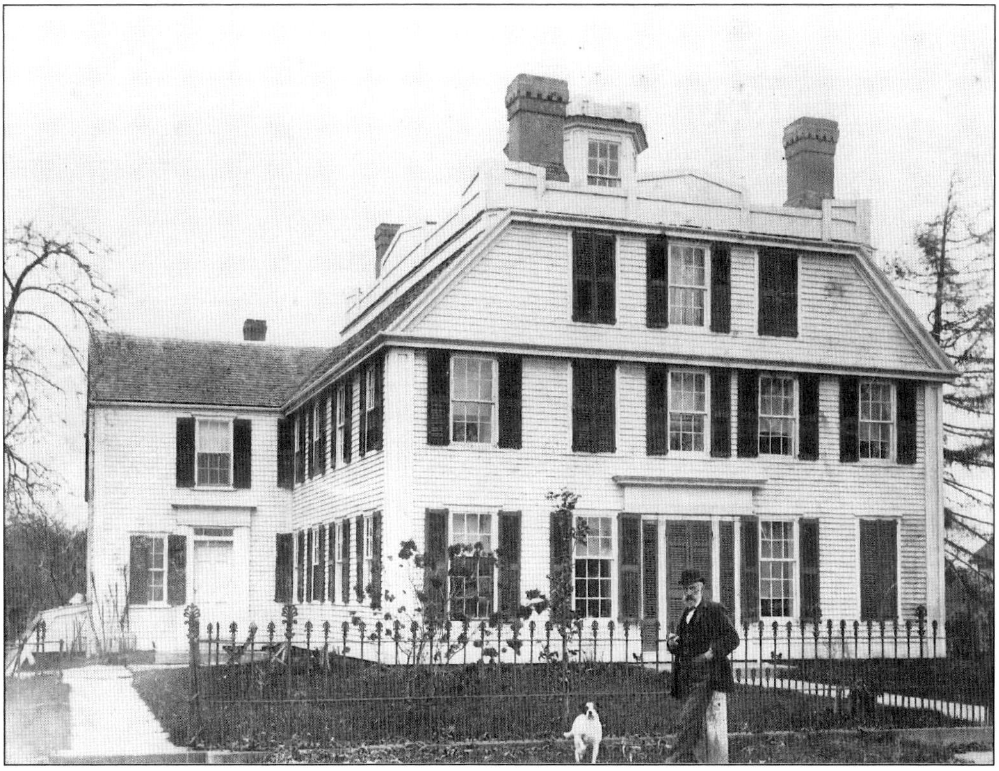

The Chase House at 2492 East Main Road, built in the late 1700s. John Chase lived in the house from 1876 until 1911, and at one time served as Portsmouth's state representative. This photograph dates to the 1890s (see p. 85).

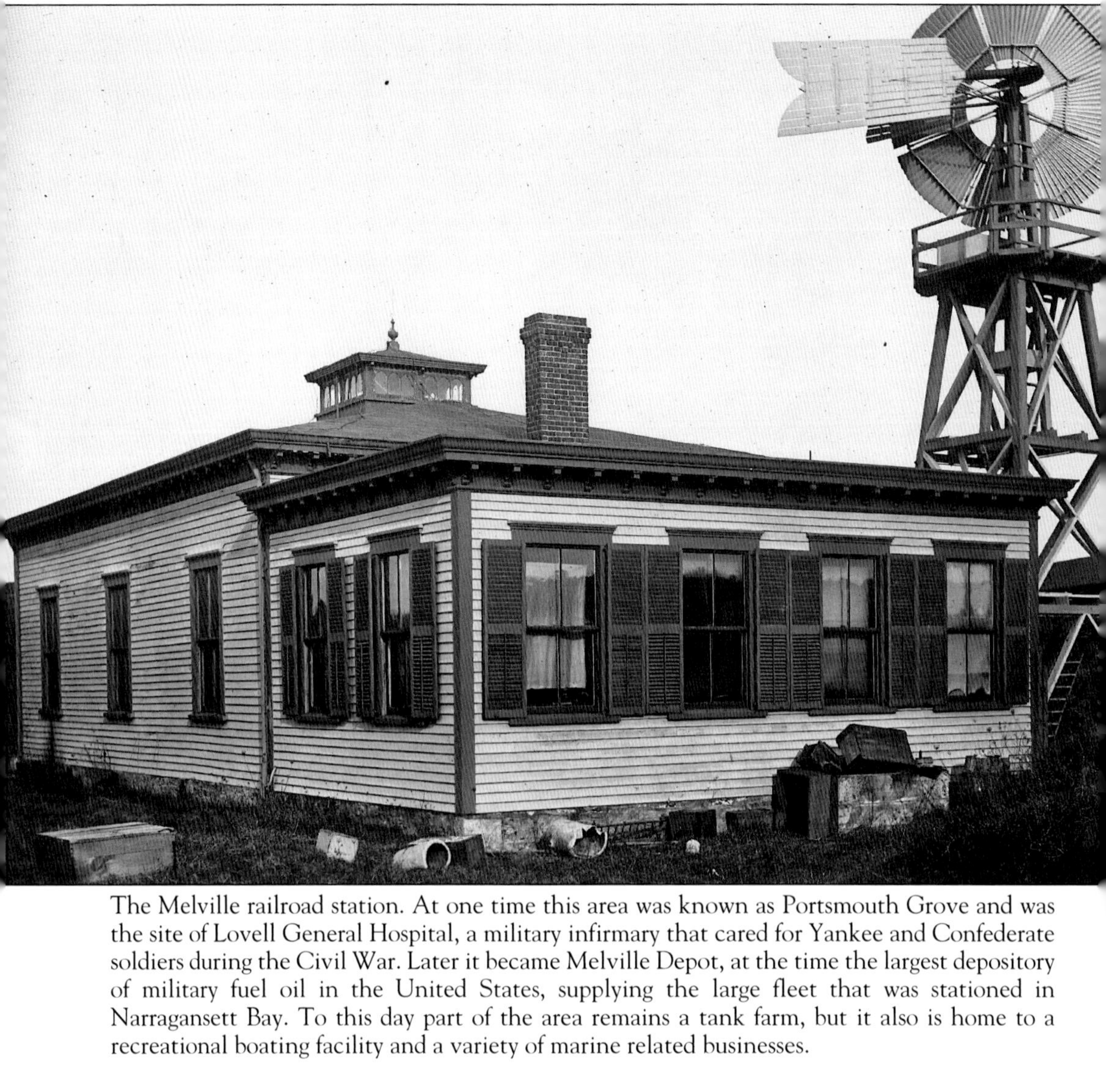

The Melville railroad station. At one time this area was known as Portsmouth Grove and was the site of Lovell General Hospital, a military infirmary that cared for Yankee and Confederate soldiers during the Civil War. Later it became Melville Depot, at the time the largest depository of military fuel oil in the United States, supplying the large fleet that was stationed in Narragansett Bay. To this day part of the area remains a tank farm, but it also is home to a recreational boating facility and a variety of marine related businesses.

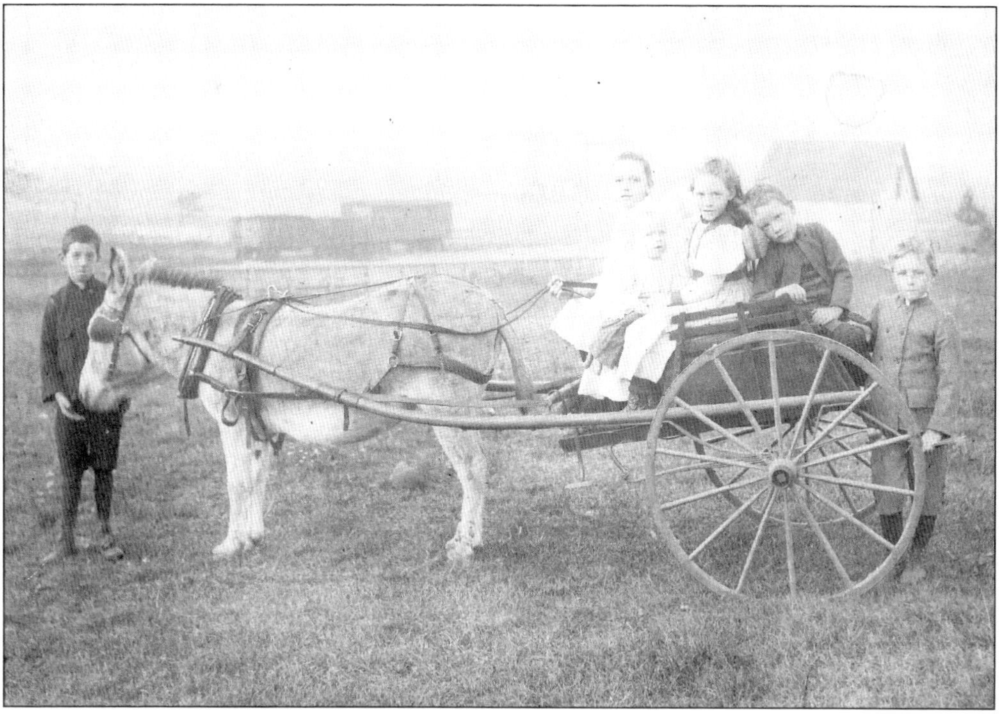

The family of Benjamin and Annie Hall in 1905. (Photograph courtesy of Lorraine Davol)

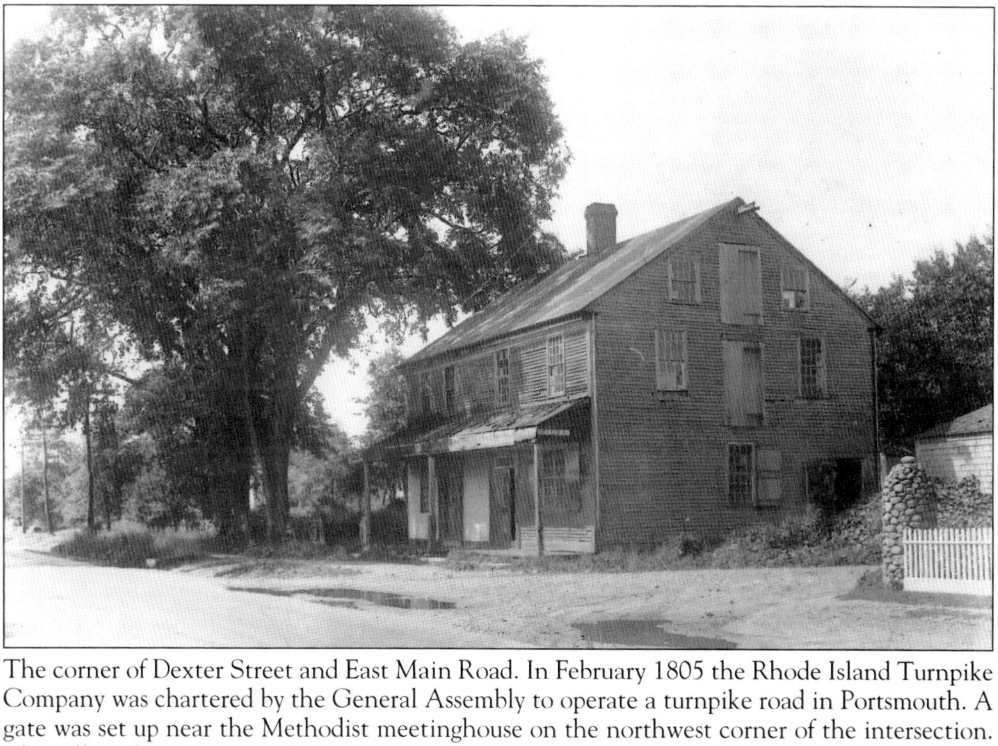

The corner of Dexter Street and East Main Road. In February 1805 the Rhode Island Turnpike Company was chartered by the General Assembly to operate a turnpike road in Portsmouth. A gate was set up near the Methodist meetinghouse on the northwest corner of the intersection. The toll road was open until November 1864, when the town accepted the turnpike as a public road and the tollgate was abandoned.

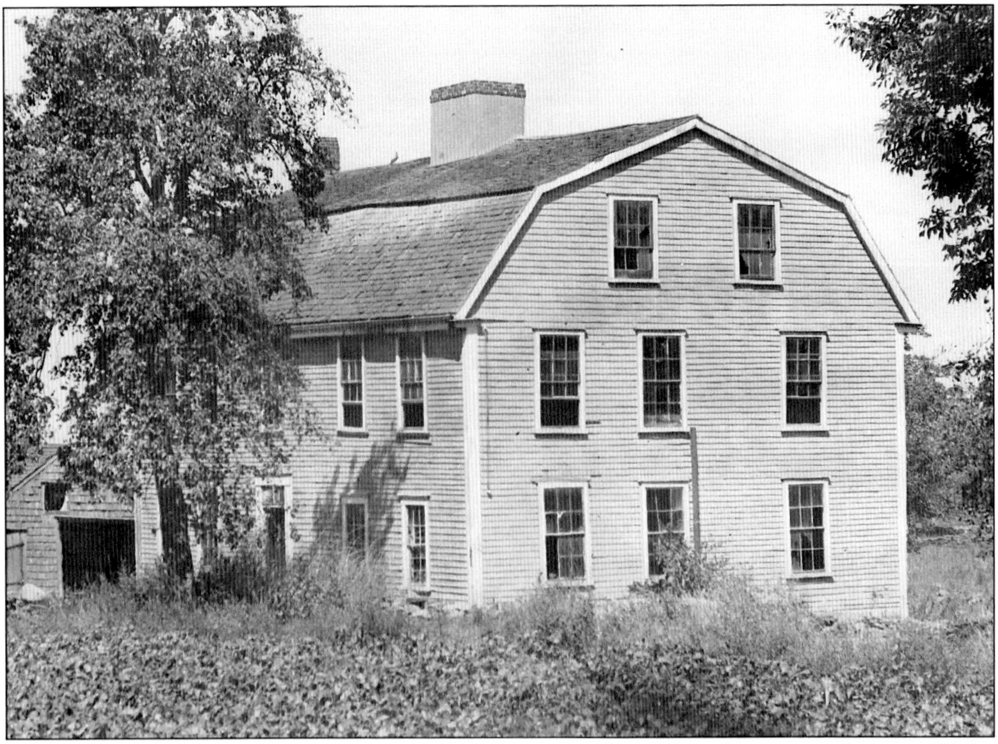

The house at the top of Turkey Hill. British forces were met here when they came ashore in 1776.

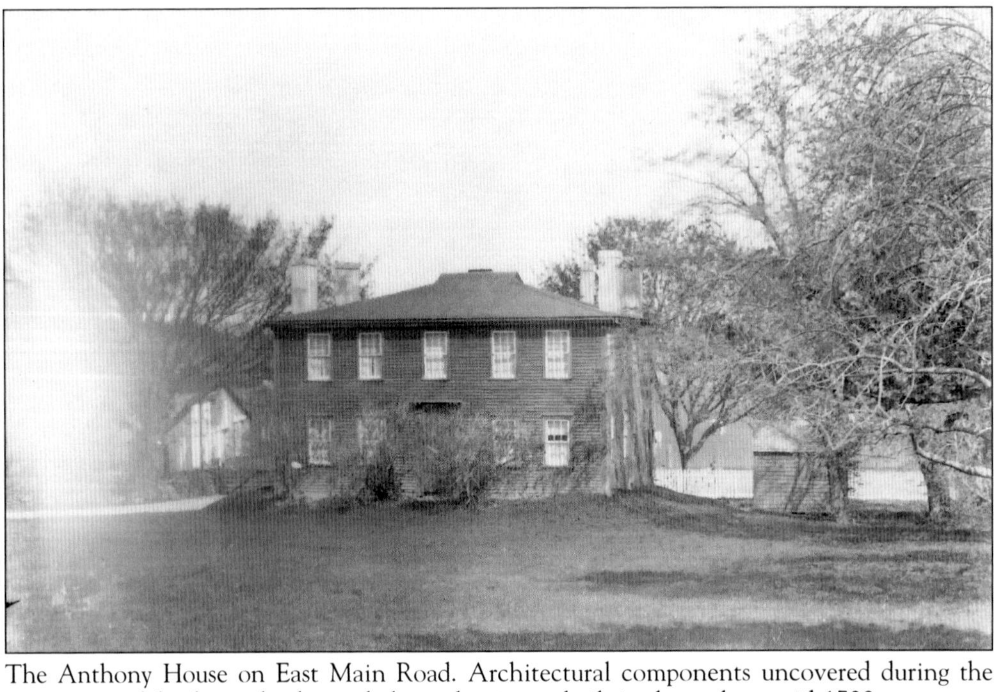

The Anthony House on East Main Road. Architectural components uncovered during the restoration of this house lead us to believe that it was built in the early to mid-1700s.

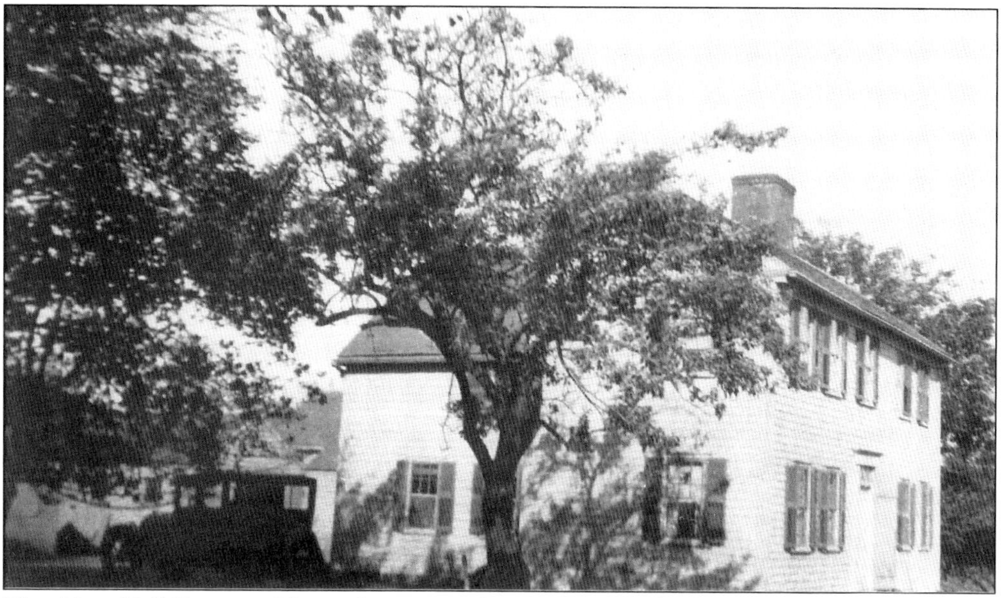

The Almy-Hall House on Union Street near Saint Marys Pond. The rear of the house was built in 1720; the later addition was built in 1780. The house was a stop on the Boston to Newport mailcoach run. (Photograph courtesy of Dot Piermont)

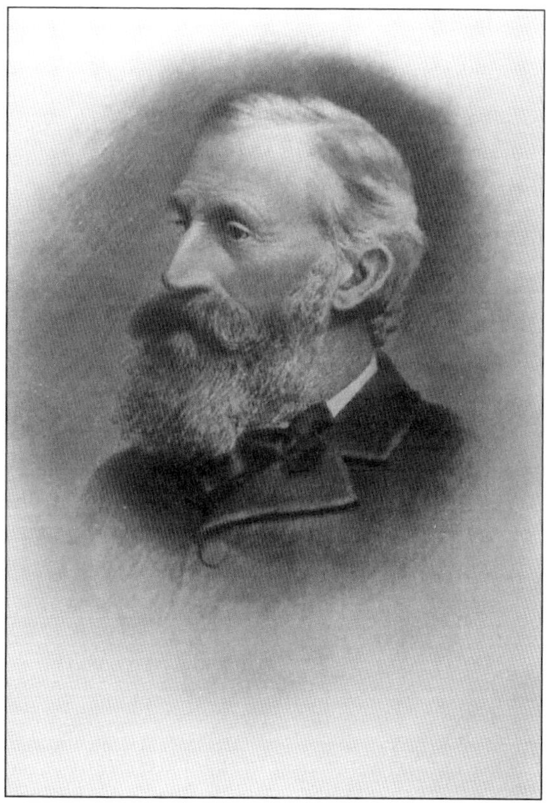

John F. Chase, a very influential citizen in Portsmouth during the latter half of the 1800s. Born in 1829, Chase tilled the soil for a living but was also very active in politics. During his life he held various township offices and was in the Senate from 1877 until 1879 and the House of Representatives from 1884 until 1888 (see p. 81).

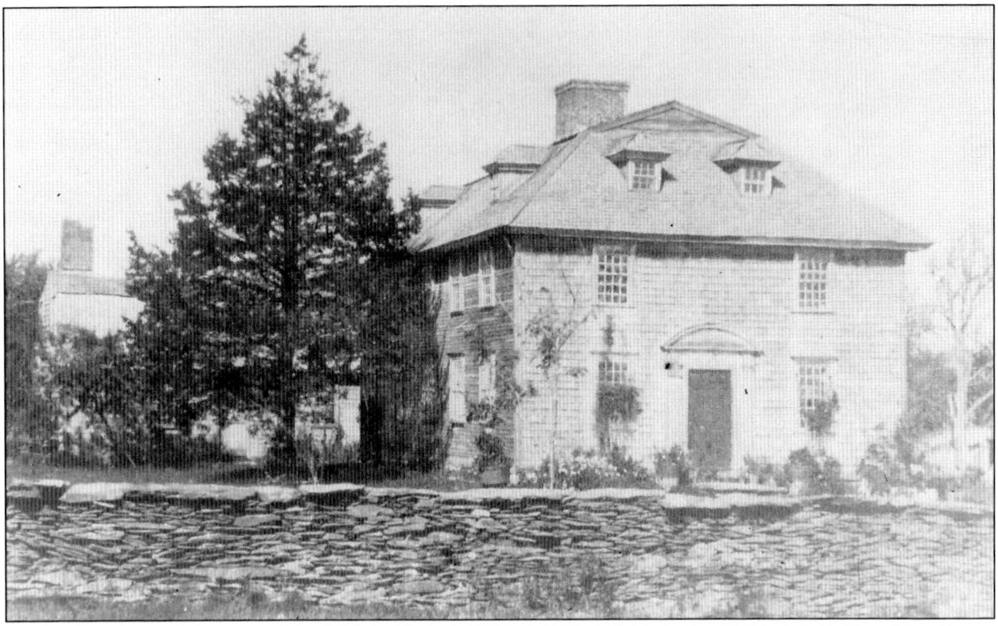

The Metcalf Bowler House. Bowler's country estate was located off Wapping Road and was built in the early 1700s. Bowler was a wealthy East India merchant. He was very involved with civic duties, at one time representing Portsmouth in the General Assembly and serving as a judge on the Supreme Court of the Colony in 1776. Bowler was also a signer of the Rhode Island Declaration of Independence.

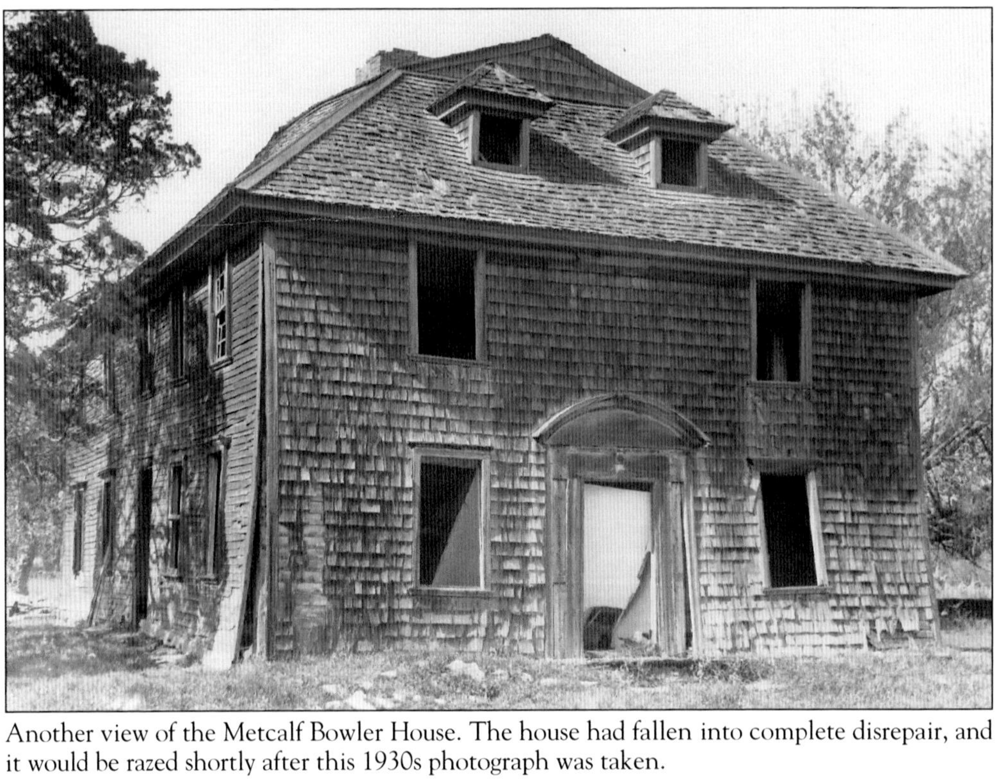

Another view of the Metcalf Bowler House. The house had fallen into complete disrepair, and it would be razed shortly after this 1930s photograph was taken.

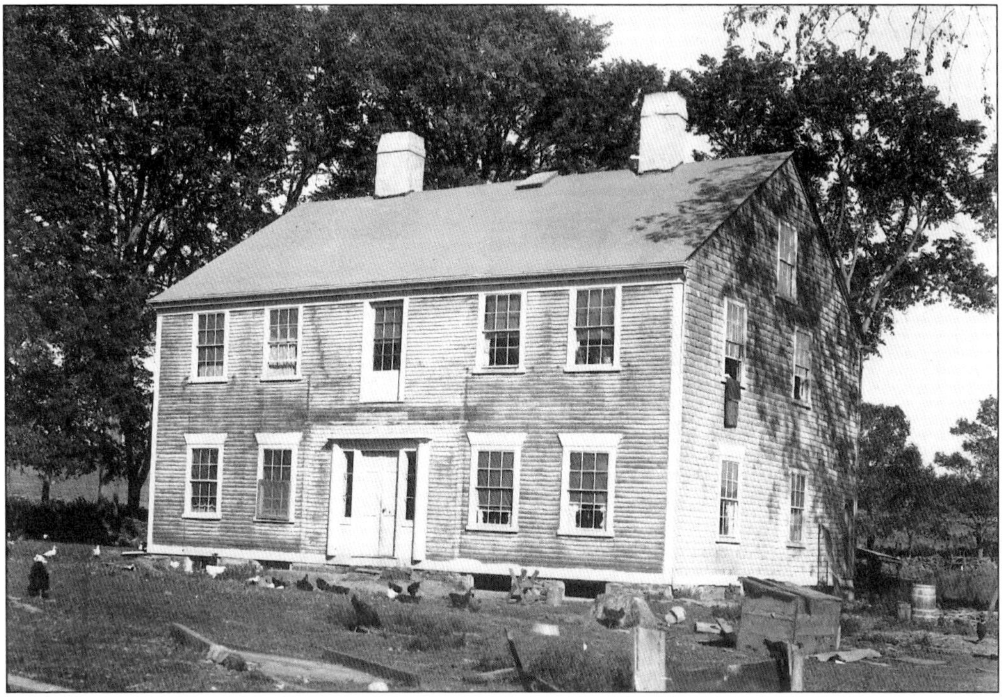

The Stoddard House near Weavers Cove. On December 8, 1776, the British Army landed at Weavers Cove and the following morning took possession of Newport. Today Weavers Cove is maintained as a water access facility equipped with a handicapped accessible boat dock.

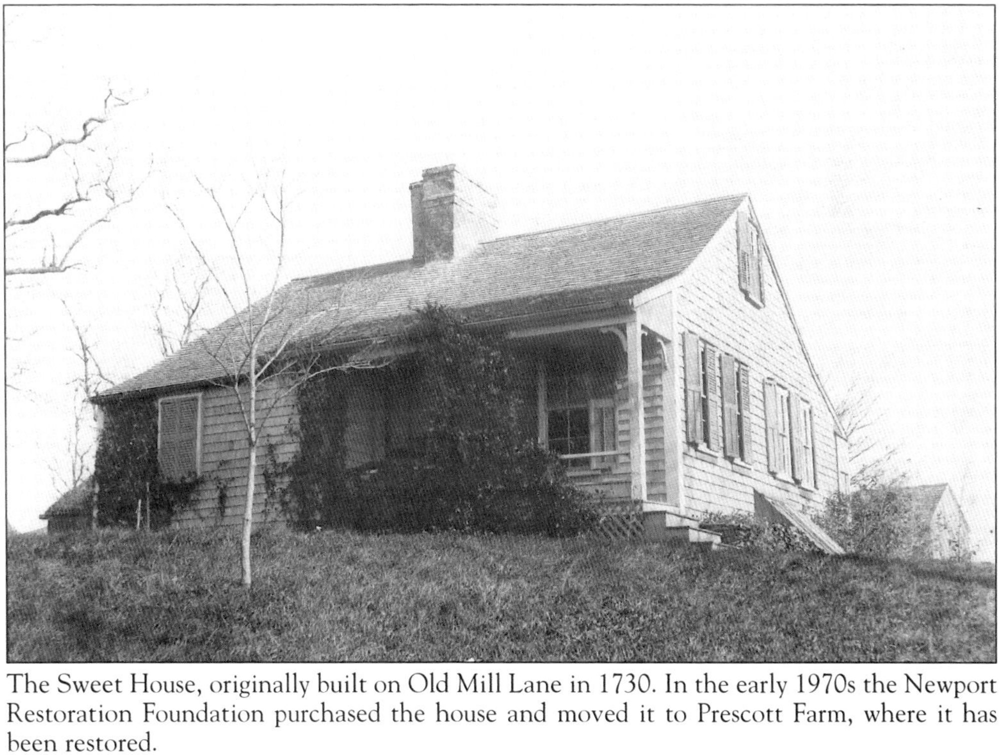

The Sweet House, originally built on Old Mill Lane in 1730. In the early 1970s the Newport Restoration Foundation purchased the house and moved it to Prescott Farm, where it has been restored.

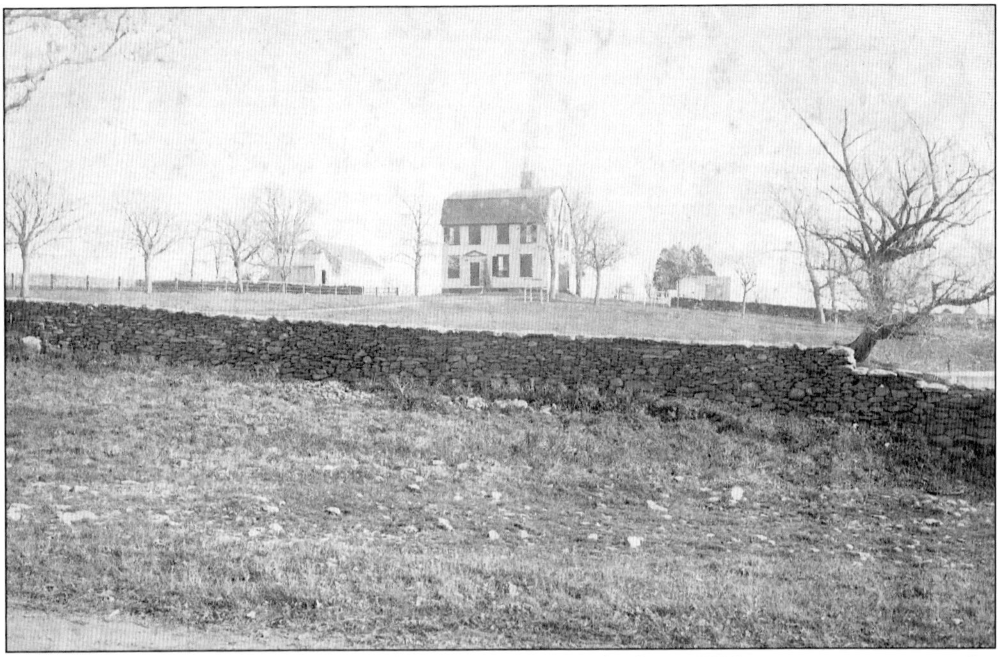

The Overing House, also known as the Prescott House, built in 1730 as a country estate. On July 9, 1777, Colonel Barton and a group of men rowed across the bay from Warwick Neck, carefully avoiding British warships stationed along the coast.

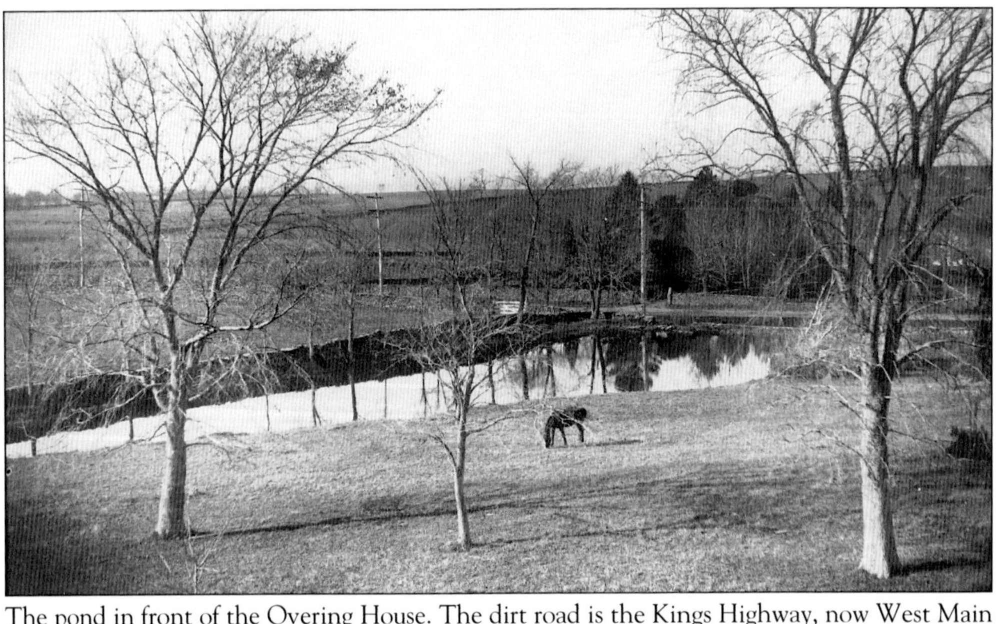

The pond in front of the Overing House. The dirt road is the Kings Highway, now West Main Road, and the land across the street is the Coggeshall Farm. After rowing ashore in Portsmouth the Barton's men made their way to the Overing Farm and proceeded to capture General Prescott in the middle of the night. He was supposedly taken out of the house in his nightshirt and brought back to Warwick. The object of the enterprise was the eventual exchange of General Prescott for General Lee.

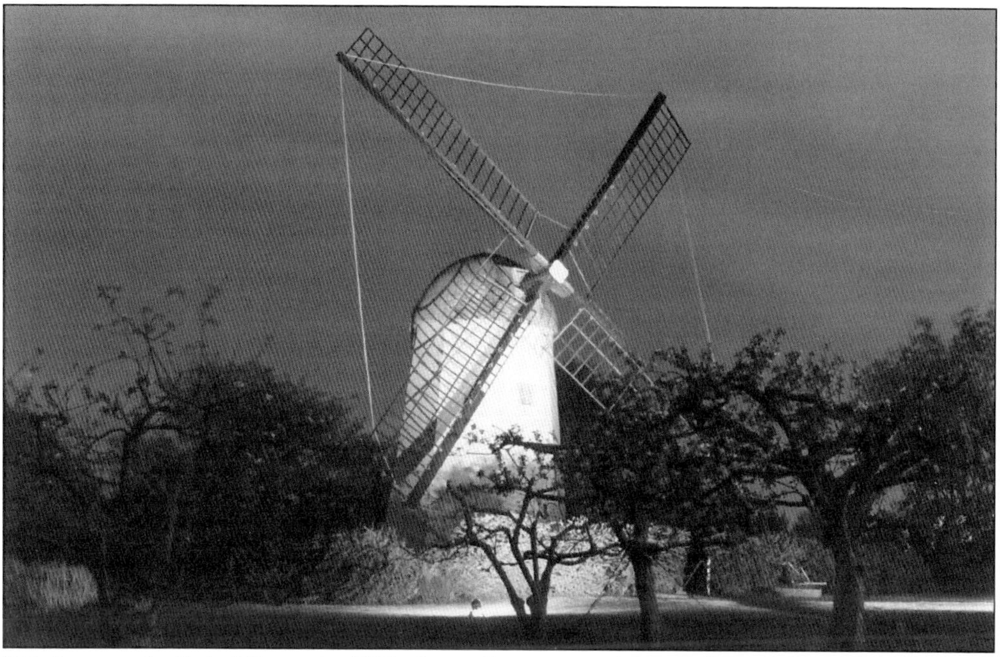

Wind power. Built in Warren in 1811, this mill was moved across the ice into Fall River where it rested in the Highlands area for a while. Robert Sherman eventually purchased it and had it moved to Quaker Hill, and then to Lehigh Hill. The mill changed hands many times, but was finally purchased by the Newport Restoration Foundation in the early 1970s and restored to an operational status. It is now, along with a guard shack and a country store, seasonally open for tours. (Photograph by Rob Lewis)

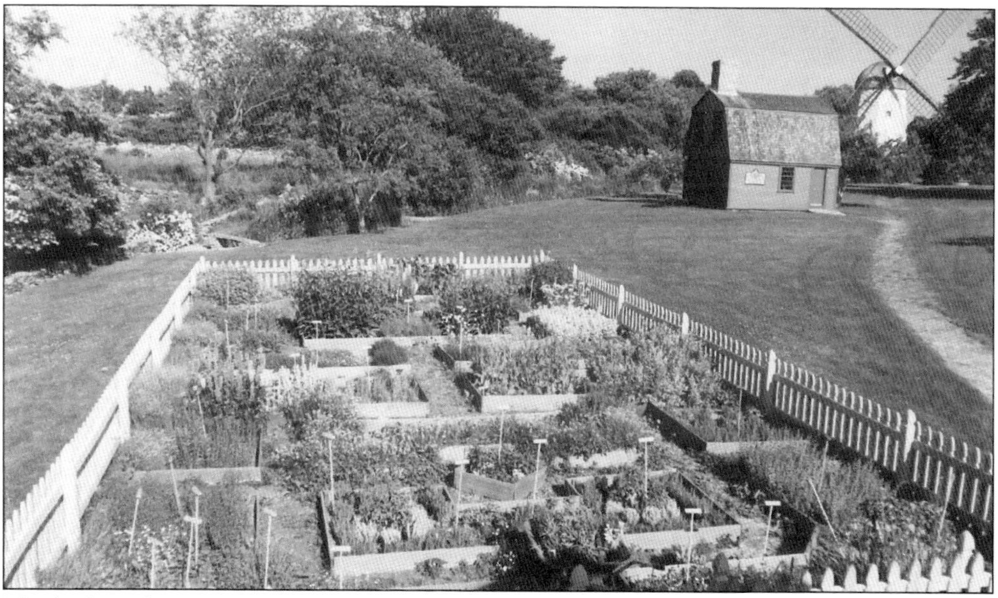

The herb garden at Prescott Farm. The small red building was originally attached to the back of the Overing House and served as a guard shack when the General stayed at the house. During the farm restoration the guard shack was moved downhill; today it houses colonial artifacts and is part of the tour of the farm. (Photograph by Rob Lewis)

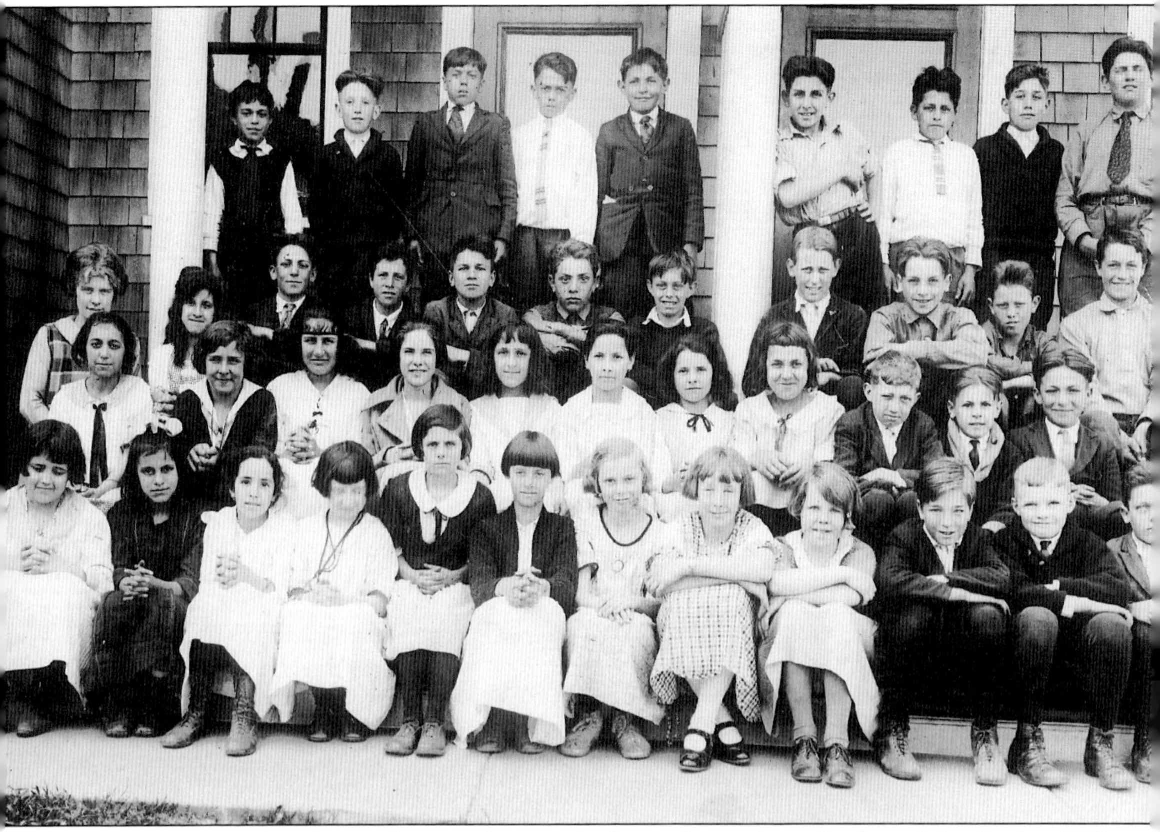

Where's Waldo? This graduation photograph shows the sixth grade class of the Quaker Hill School in 1924. Alton Sherman is in the third row, fourth from the right. The teacher ,Miss Caswell, is also in the third row, all the way to the left. The Quaker Hill School was built in 1915 across from the town hall. Today the building is home to the Portsmouth School Administration. (Photograph courtesy of the Peter H. Sherman family)

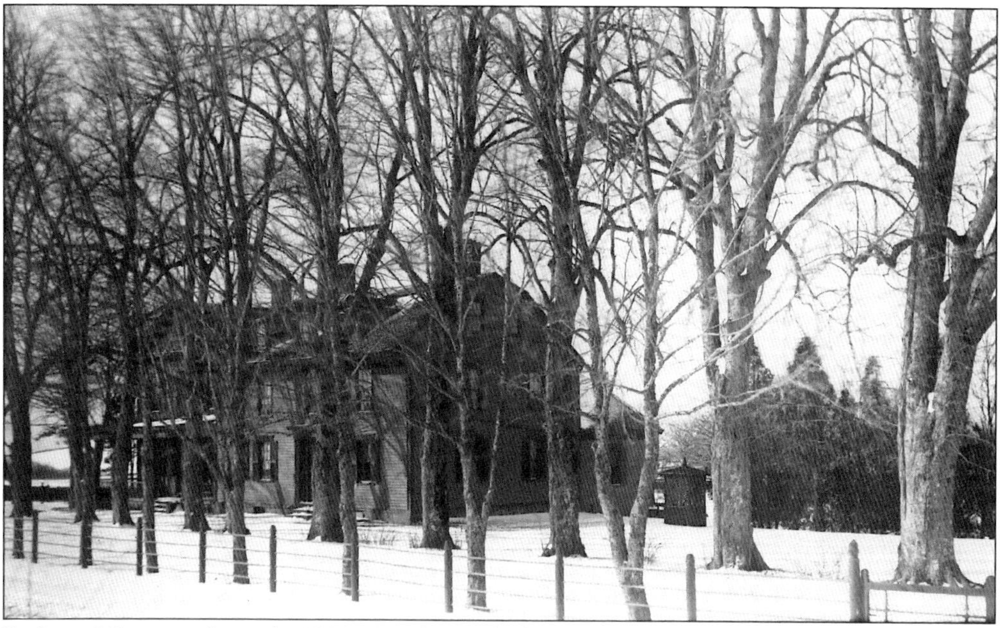

Redwood Farm in the early 1890s. In 1743, Abraham Redwood Jr. purchased a country estate from his father-in-law, Daniel Coggeshall, located on the west side of West Main Road near the intersection of Union Street. The gardens surrounding the house were 1.5 acres and were said to have been magnificent. Many of the plants came from his sugar plantation on Antigua, West Indies, and included such exotic fruits as viz oranges, lemons, limes, pineapples, and tamarinds.

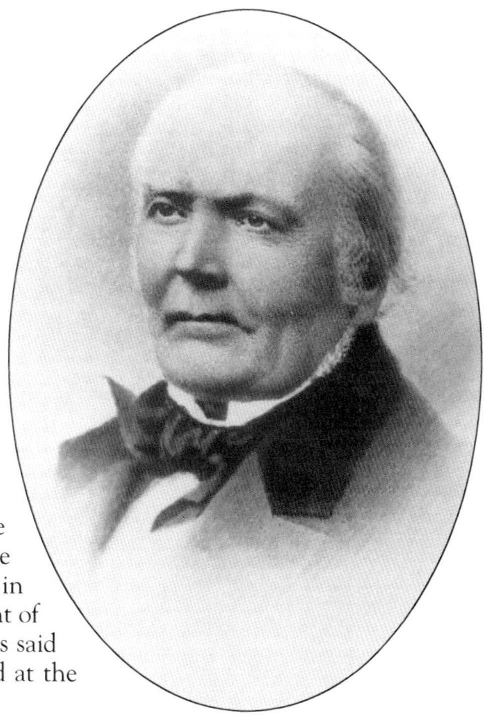

Joshua Coggeshall, born in December 1788 on the family farm in Portsmouth. He spent his life in the healthful pursuit of farming, served several terms in the General Assembly, and was also the president of the Portsmouth Town Council for years. He was said to be a kind and intelligent man and worshiped at the Friends Meeting House.

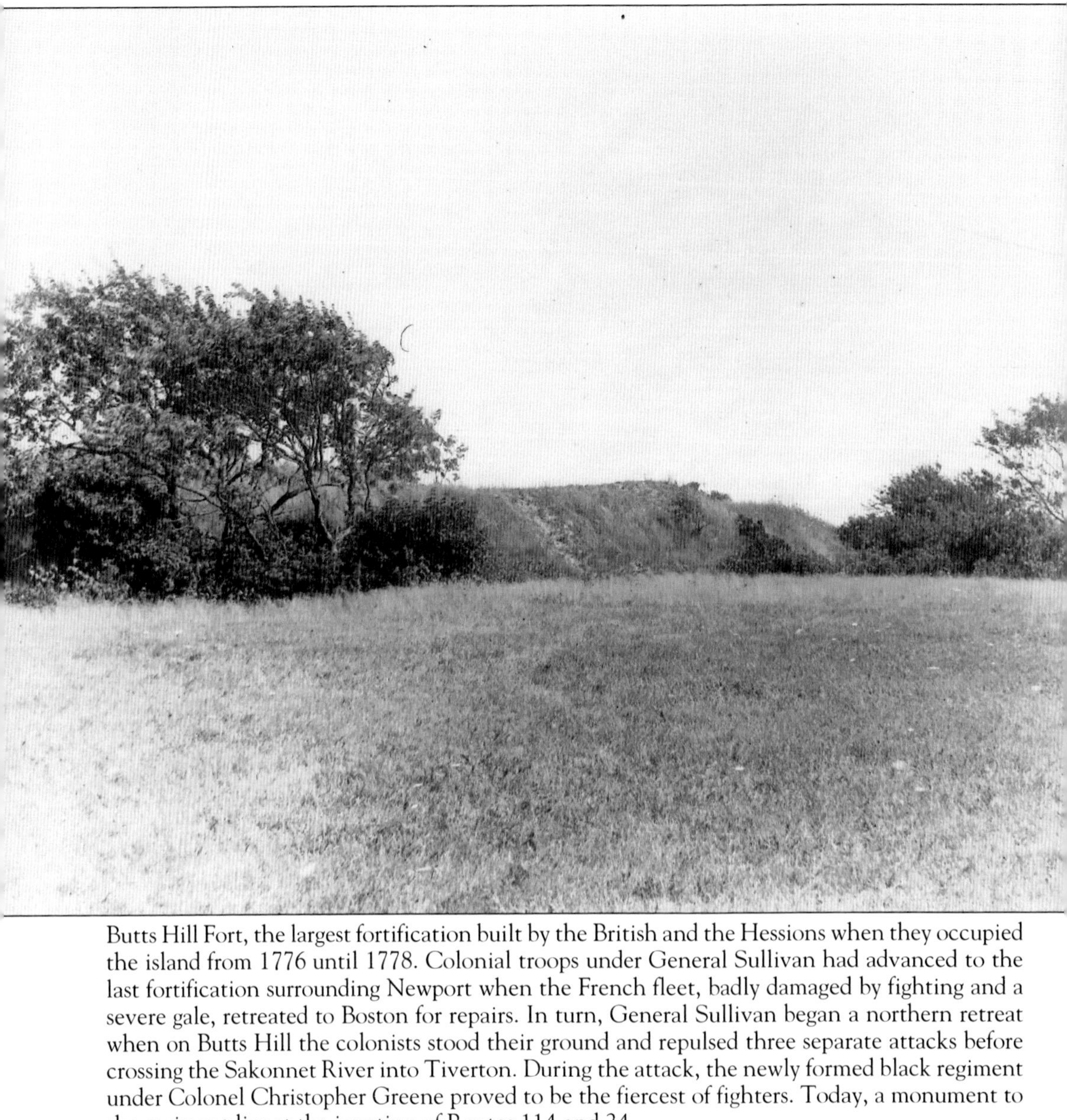

Butts Hill Fort, the largest fortification built by the British and the Hessions when they occupied the island from 1776 until 1778. Colonial troops under General Sullivan had advanced to the last fortification surrounding Newport when the French fleet, badly damaged by fighting and a severe gale, retreated to Boston for repairs. In turn, General Sullivan began a northern retreat when on Butts Hill the colonists stood their ground and repulsed three separate attacks before crossing the Sakonnet River into Tiverton. During the attack, the newly formed black regiment under Colonel Christopher Greene proved to be the fiercest of fighters. Today, a monument to the regiment lies at the junction of Routes 114 and 24.

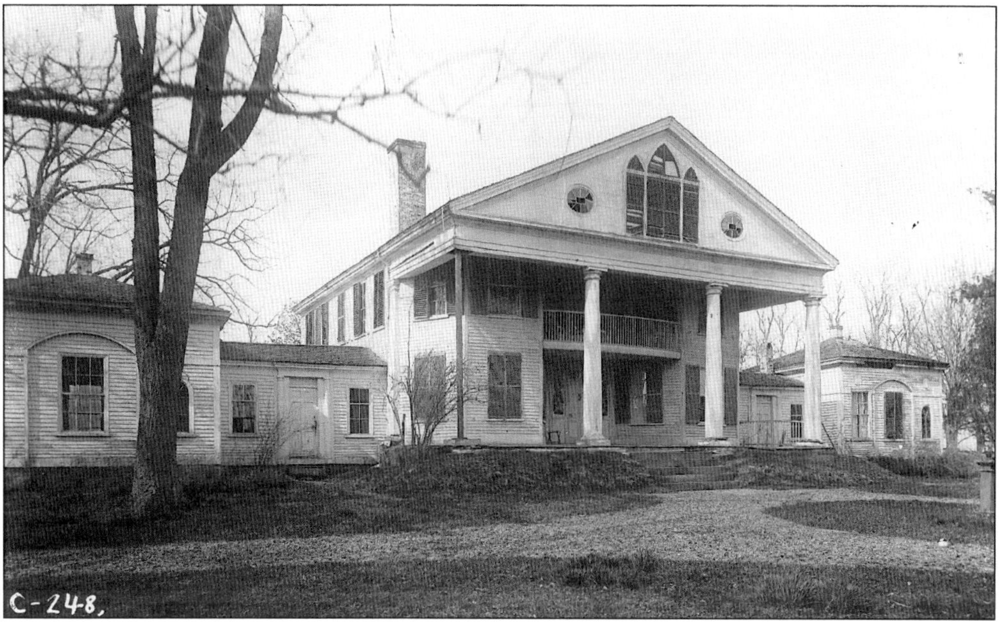

The height of country living. Vaucluse Farm was built by Gervais Elam in the early 1700s. Sometime after 1777 his nephew, Samuel Elam, inherited the estate and remodeled the house in the Greek Temple style with a Doric portico and side wings. It was later the home of Thomas Robinson Hazard.

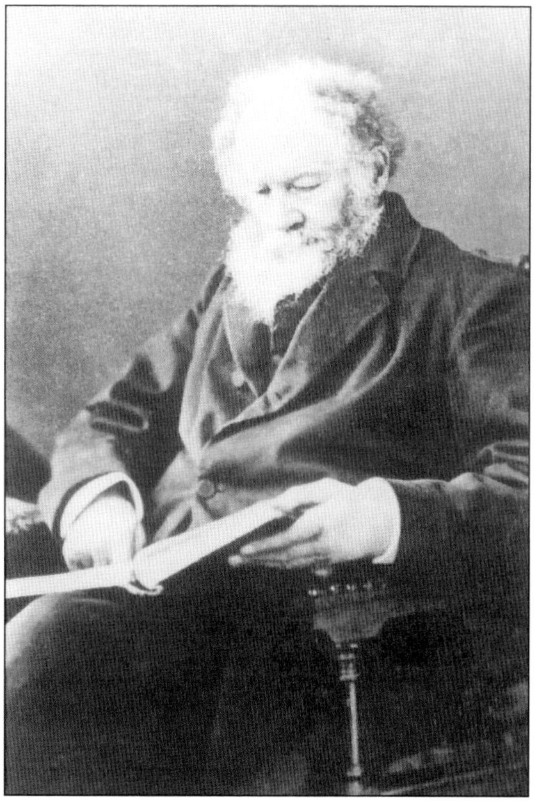
Thomas Robinson Hazard, born in January 1797. Hazard earned his living in the fledgling business of woolen manufacturing. In the late 1830s he purchased the country estate Vaucluse and resided there from 1842 on. He visited every public poorhouse in the state, gave a full report to the General Assembly, and was instrumental in bringing reform to the system. He also played a part in the founding of Butler Hospital.

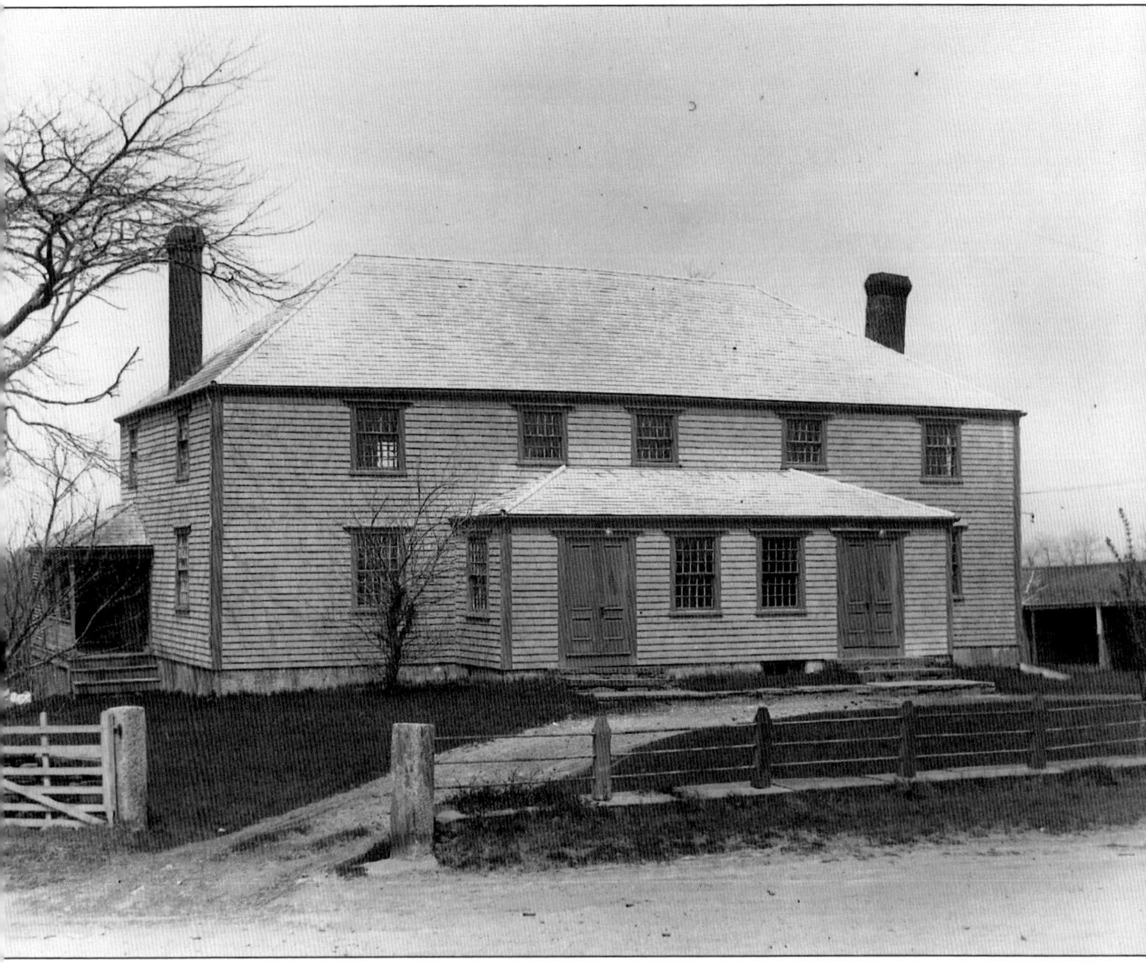

The Friends Meeting House at East Main Road and Hedley Street at the top of Quaker Hill. The Quakers were the first ecclesiastical presence in Portsmouth, having meetings as early as 1672. By 1692 they had purchased a lot with a house on it in which to meet. In August 1699 a new lot at the top of Quaker Hill was purchased and soon after the meetinghouse, which still stands today, was erected.

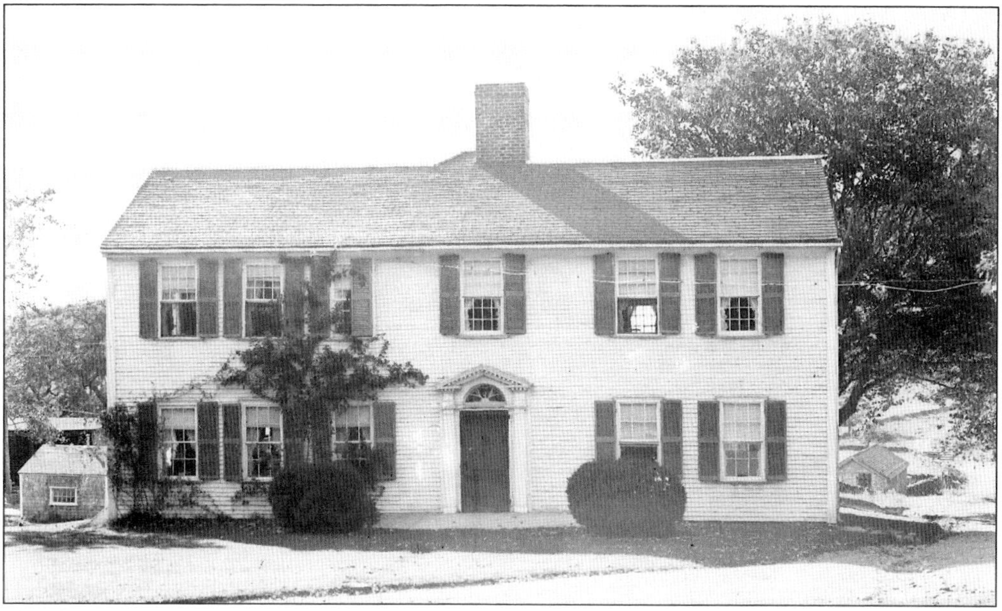

The house located on the estate of Bradford Norman. From 1932 until 1942, Mr. Norman served as the president of the Newport Savings Bank. In later years he was president of the Peoples Library and a trustee of Long Wharf.

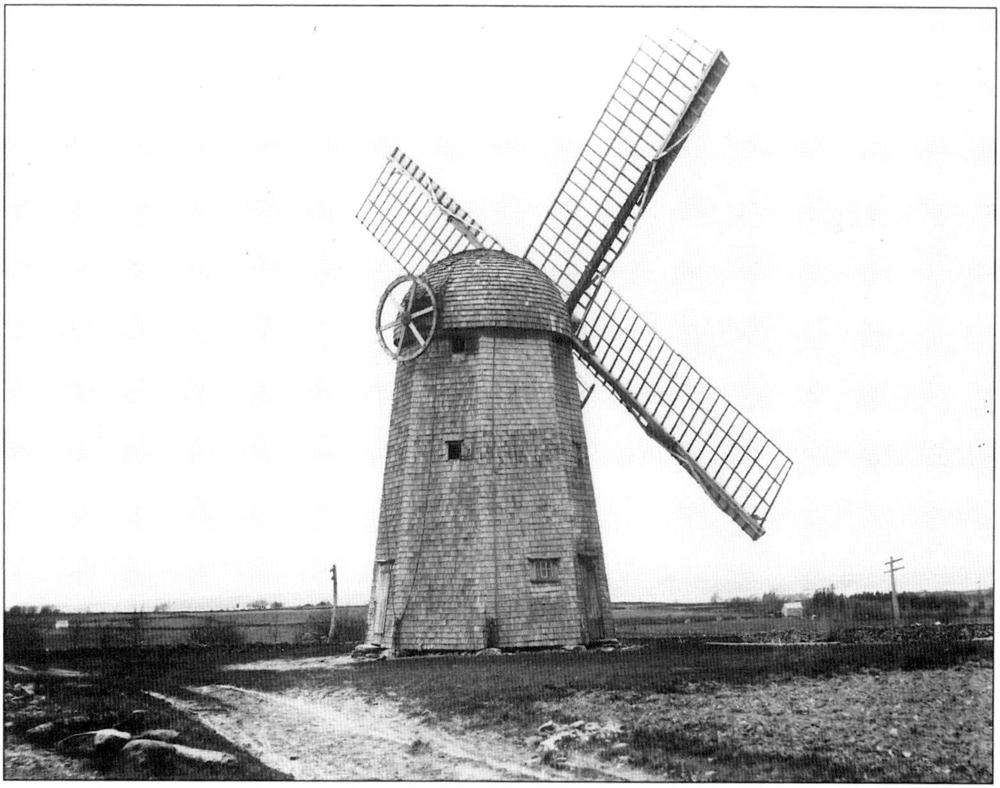

The Hathaway windmill on Quaker Hill in a photograph taken in 1900. Not much is known about the origin of this mill, but by 1910 it had been damaged and was non-functioning.

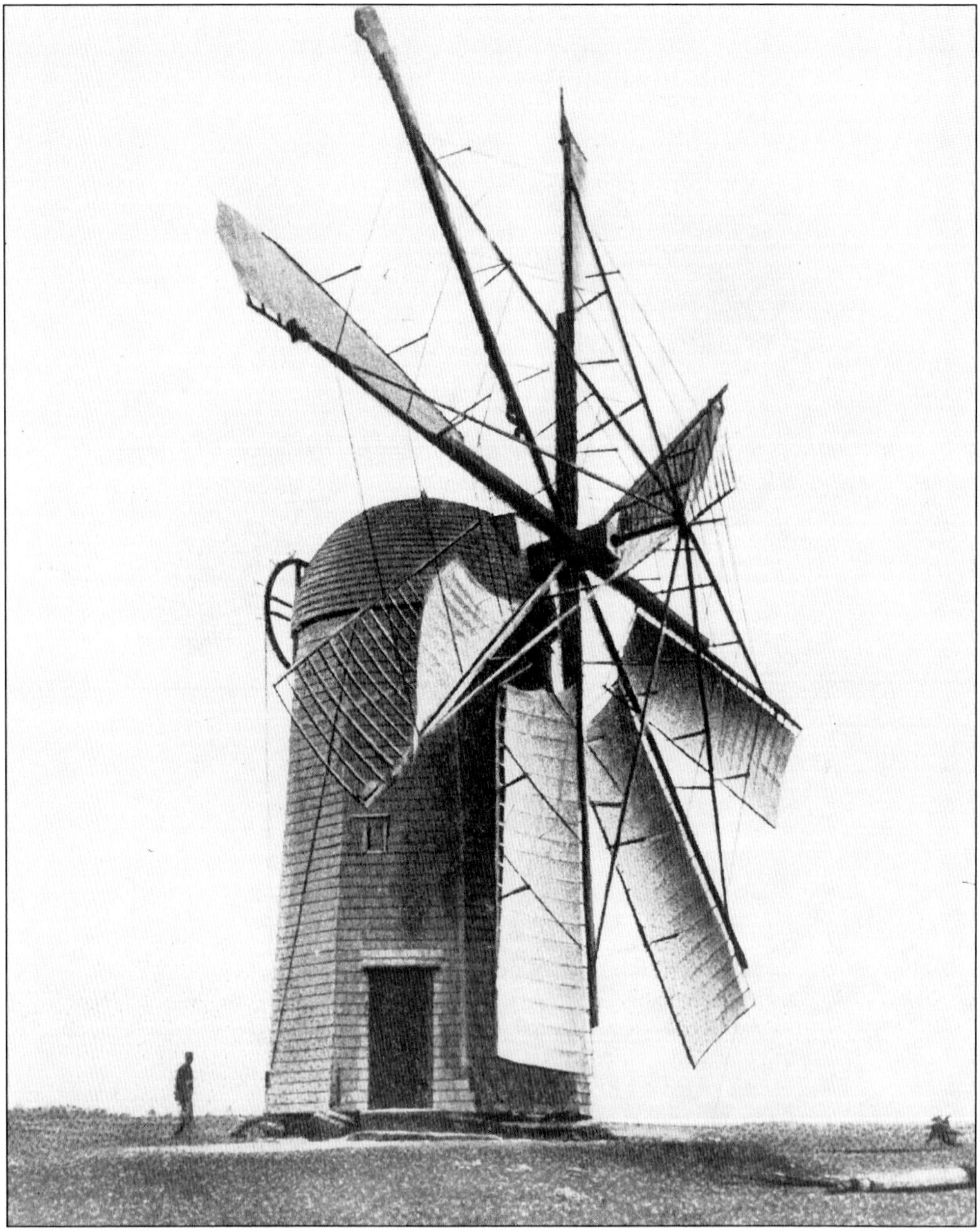

Boyds Windmill, built for John Peterson in 1810 on West Main Road at Windmill Lane, now Mill Lane. In the mid-1800s William Boyd rented, and then purchased, the windmill, which the Boyd family operated for the next three generations. In 1901 Benjamin Boyd remodeled the windmill to have eight arms with sails instead of the original four. This photograph was taken after 1901 and before 1916, when the mill was converted to gasoline power.

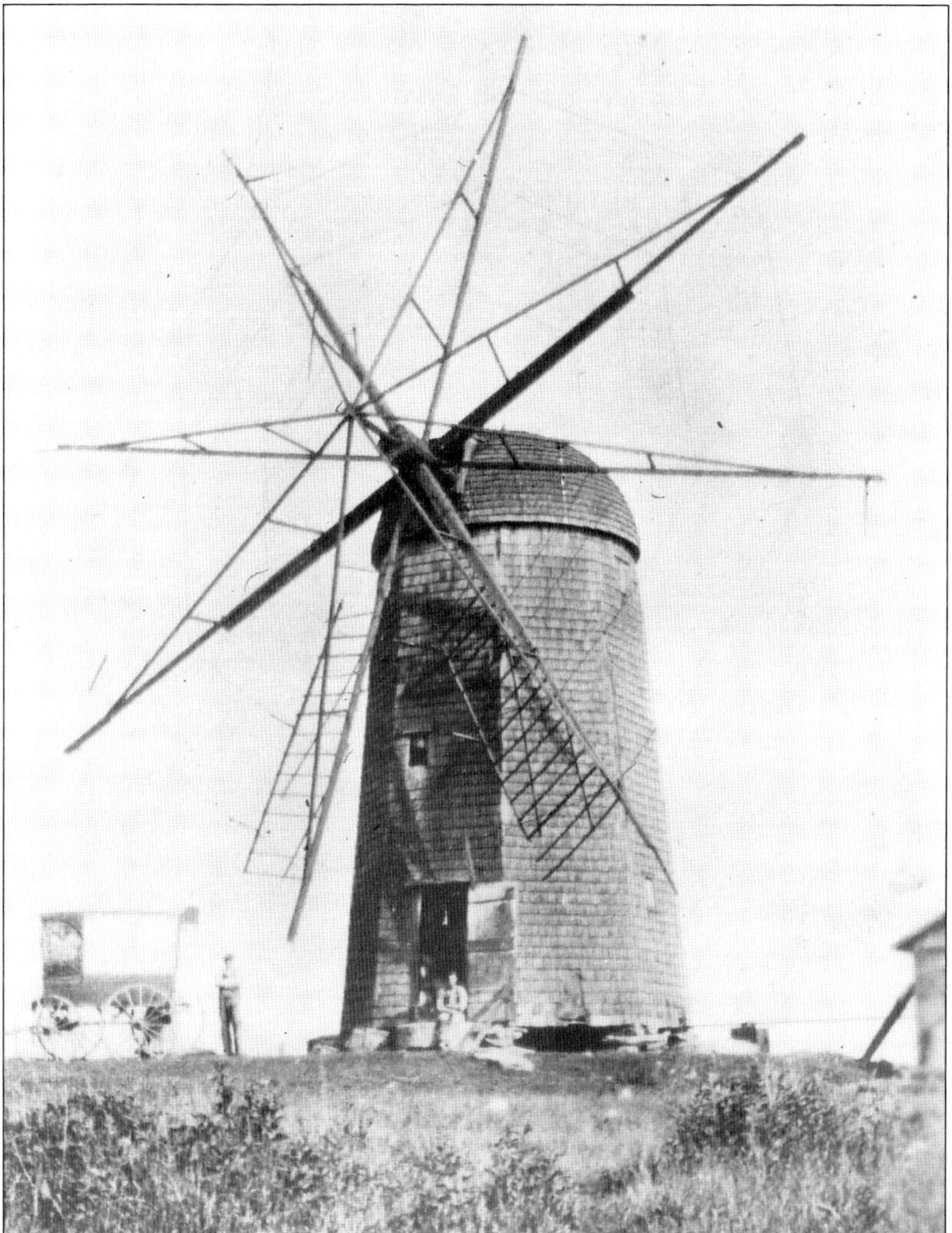

The Boyds' wind-powered gristmill, shown here still operational but abandoned for a more modern convenience—gasoline power. The Boyd family donated the windmill to the Middletown Historical Society, who moved the structure to Paradise Valley Park. It is in the process of being restored to an operational capacity for use in the education of milling history.

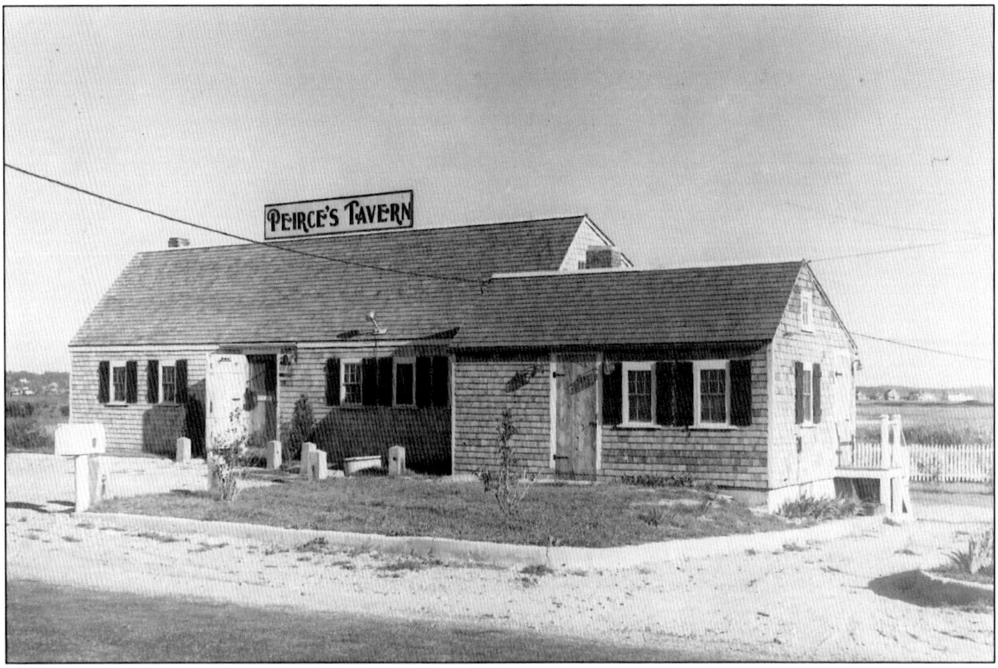

Peirces Tavern on Anthony Road, located on the east side of what is now Route 24, approximately across from the Bay Point Inn.

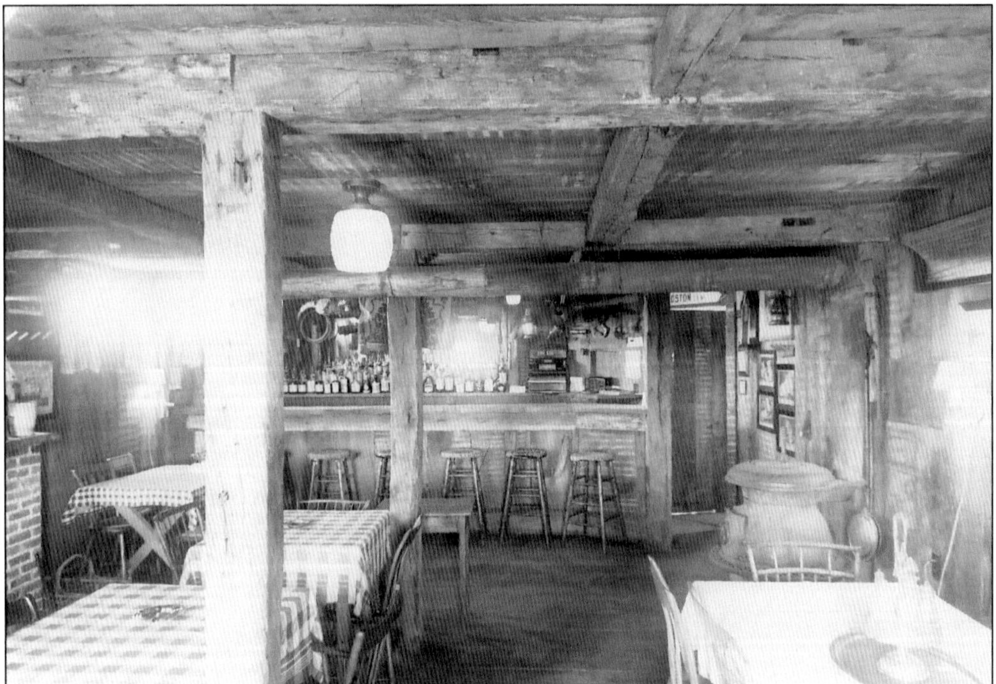

An interior view of the tavern. In September of 1954, during Hurricane Hazel, the tavern burned to the ground.

Five

Conanicut

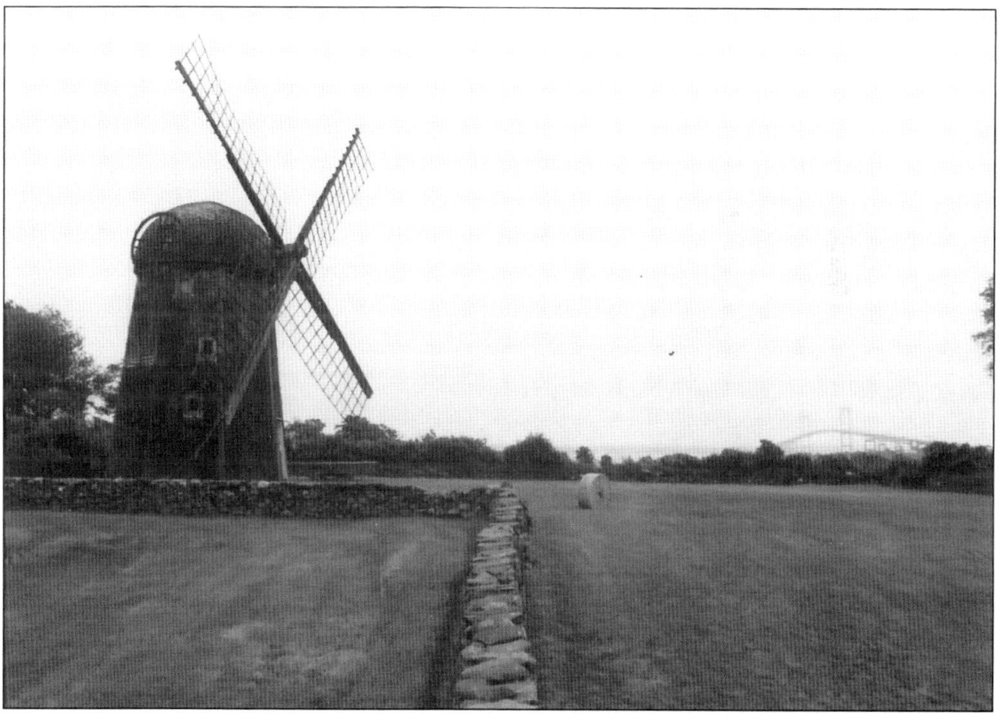

The Jamestown windmill, built in 1787 and operated until the 1890s. Over the years it fell into disrepair, but in 1904 a move was started to save the structure, and in 1912 the Jamestown Historical Society was formed. The new society, together with the Windmill Association, restored the windmill. (Photograph by Rob Lewis)

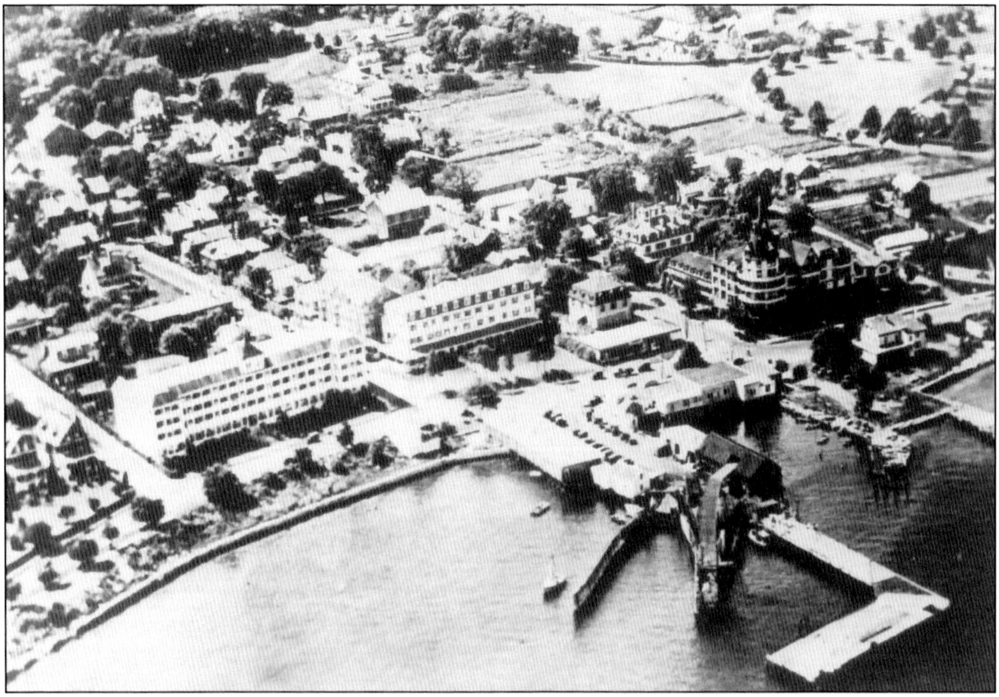

East Ferry from the air. The boat slip for the Jamestown to Newport ferry can be seen in the bottom of the photograph. Also evident is the buildup of resort hotels around the ferry landing.

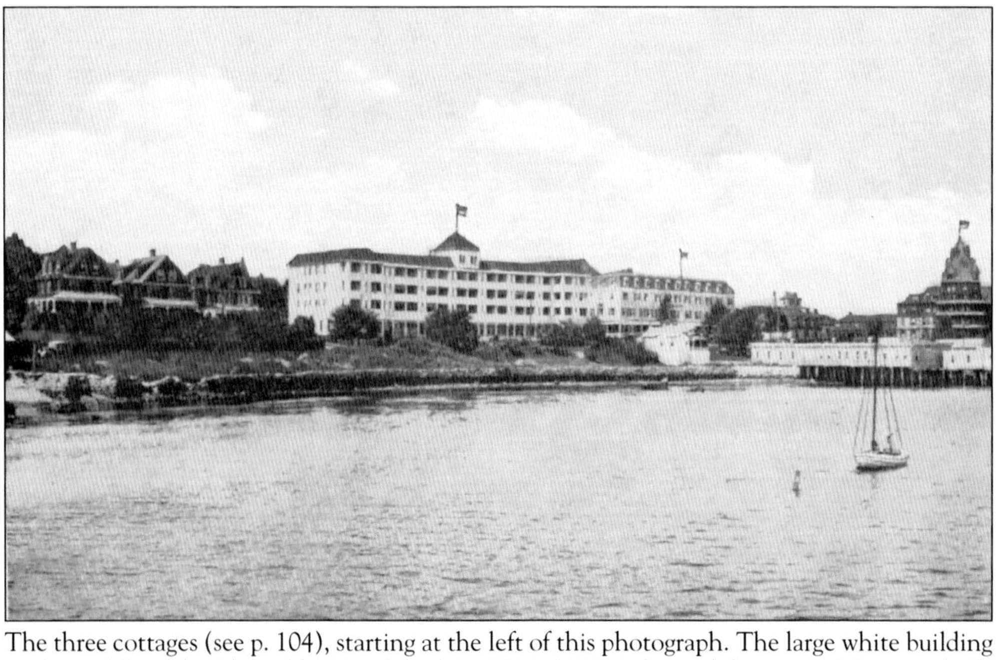

The three cottages (see p. 104), starting at the left of this photograph. The large white building in the middle is the Thorndike Hotel, built in 1899–1900. It burned down in 1912, was rebuilt the following year, and finally demolished in 1937. At one time the first floor housed the Jamestown Pharmacy.

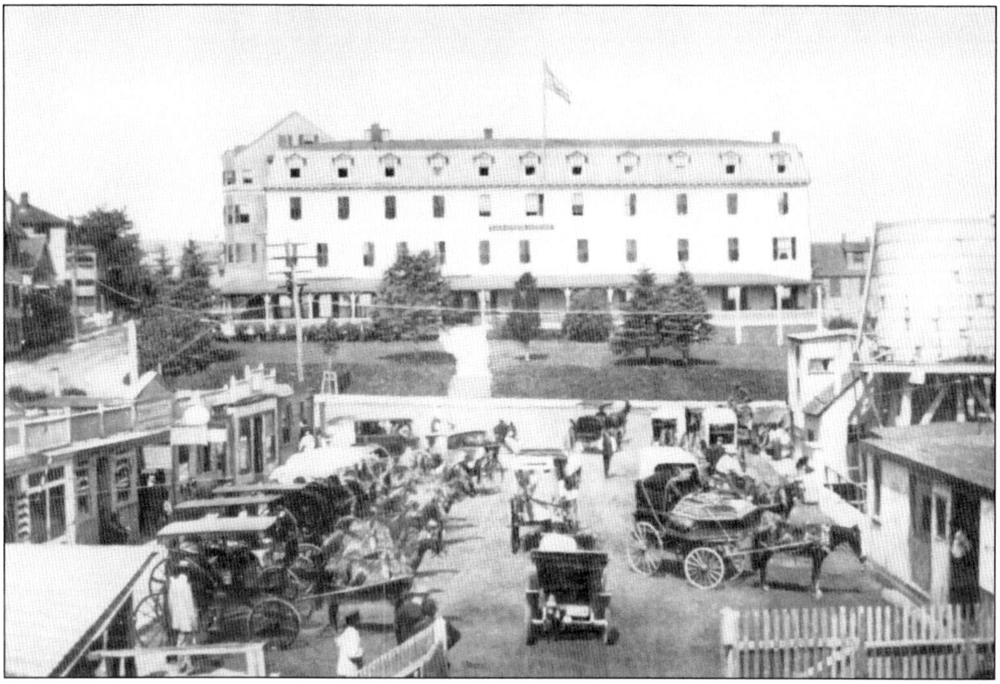

East Ferry landing around 1900. Passengers disembarking from the Newport ferry were greeted with the sight of the Gardner Hotel. Built in 1883, it was razed in 1941.

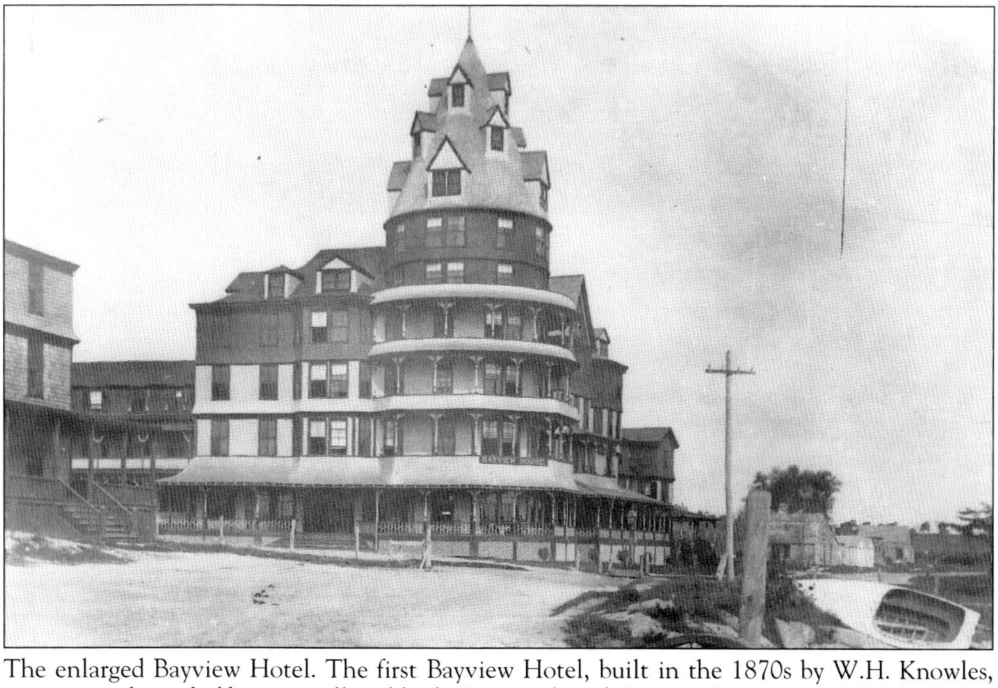

The enlarged Bayview Hotel. The first Bayview Hotel, built in the 1870s by W.H. Knowles, was two-and-one-half-stories tall and had a Mansard roof. In 1899 his son Adolphus built this enlarged Bayview, which could accommodate two hundred guests. It served as a hotel until the 1960s. In 1985 it was demolished, but in 1988 the Bayview Condominiums were built to resemble the original building.

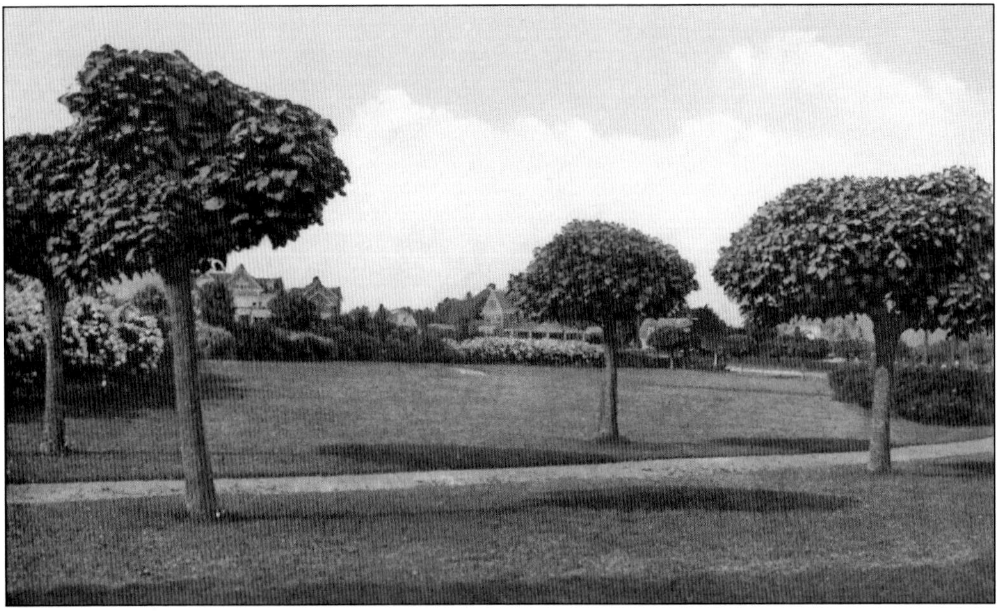

Shoreby Park in the late 1890s. Shoreby Hill was formerly known as Greene or Quaker Farm, and was subdivided and developed between 1896 and 1900. By 1899 ten houses had been built on the hill.

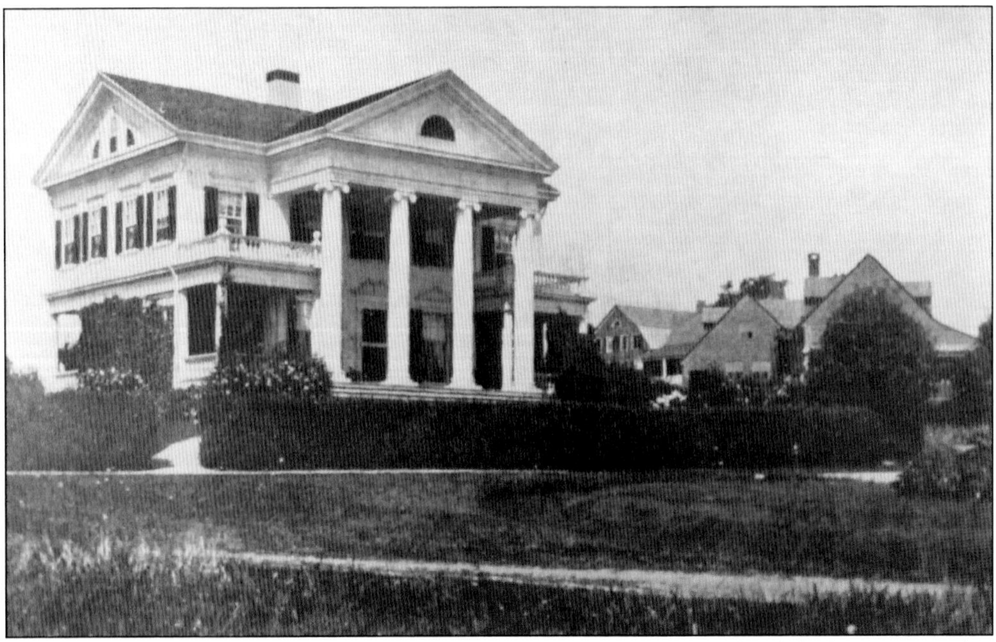

The Charles H. Bailey House, built on Shoreby Hill in 1898. The style of the house was a big departure from the less formal, shingled residences that were more common to the development. During the 1970s the Clifford Largess family occupied the house.

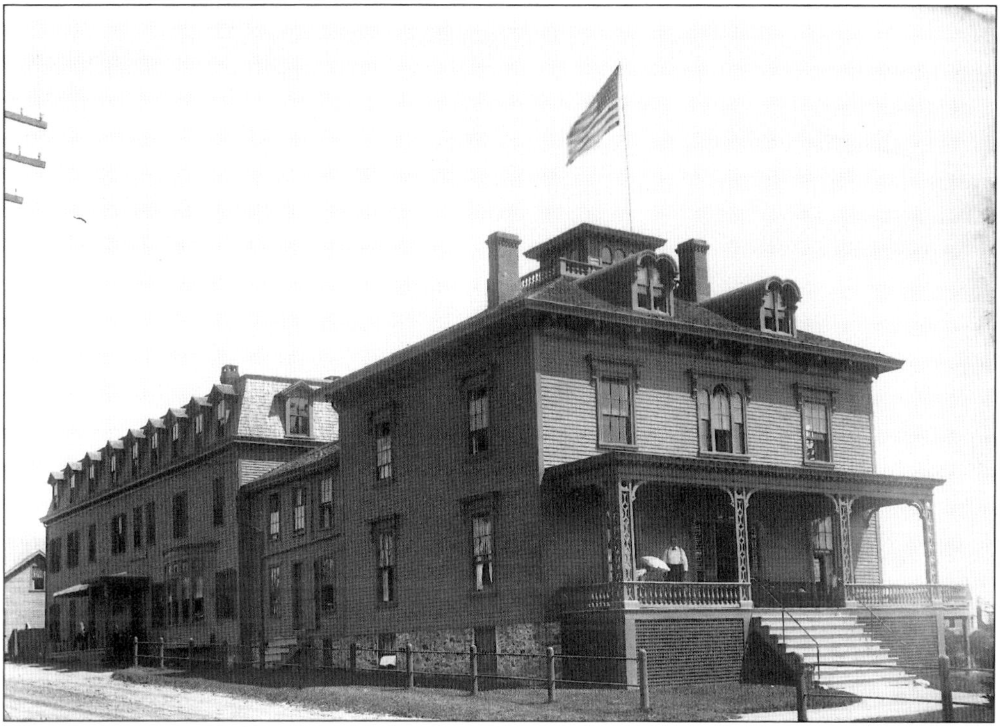

The Bay Voyage Hotel. The main part of the hotel was built in Middletown in the 1860s. In 1889 the house was cut into two pieces and floated across the bay on barges. In 1890 it was enlarged to offer thirty more rooms. It is still open as a hotel and restaurant.

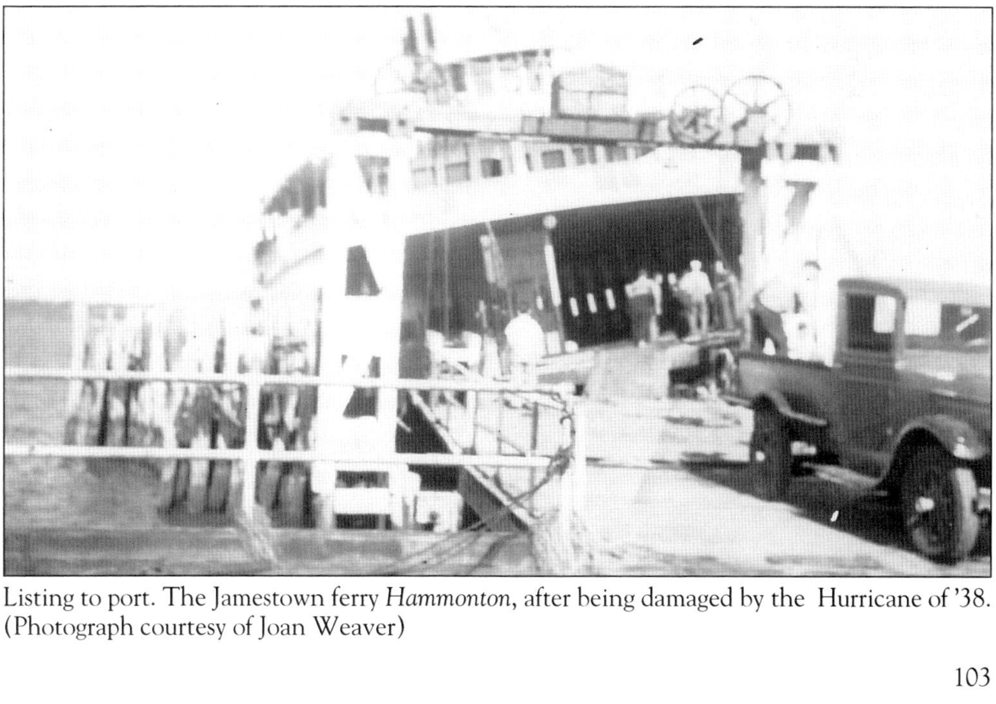

Listing to port. The Jamestown ferry *Hammonton*, after being damaged by the Hurricane of '38. (Photograph courtesy of Joan Weaver)

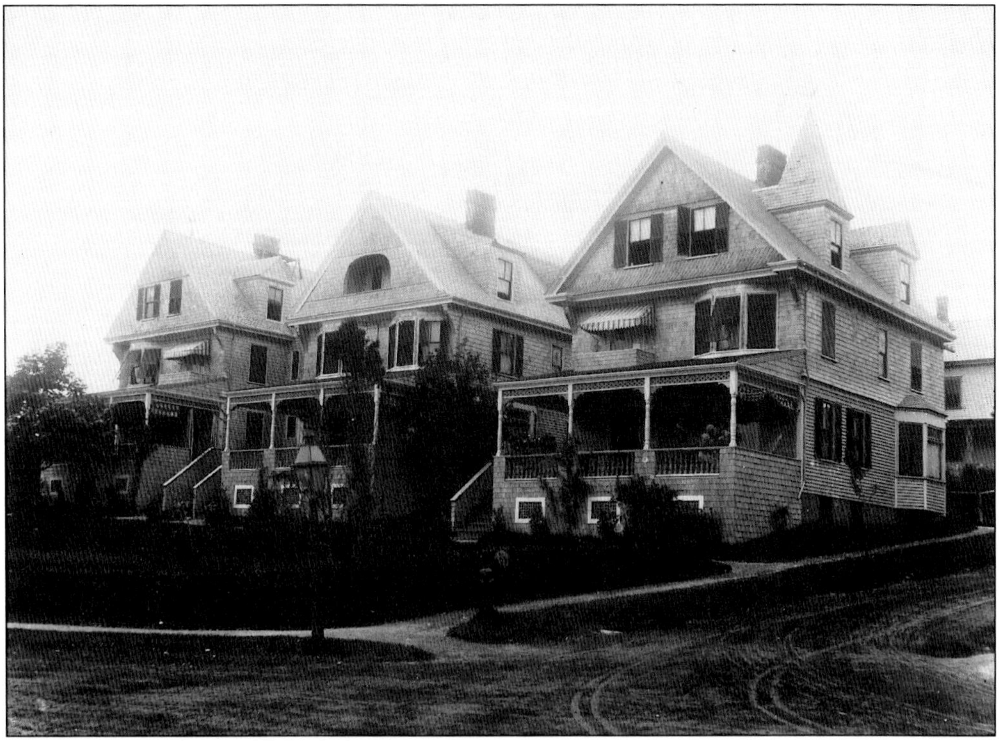

The Horgan Cottages, also known as the three sisters, built in 1897–98 by Patrick Horgan. When they were first built they were rented out by the Thorndike Hotel as part of the hotel's accommodations. They were named after Horgan's three daughters—Myra, Betty, and Nina—who, after their father's death, each inherited a cottage.

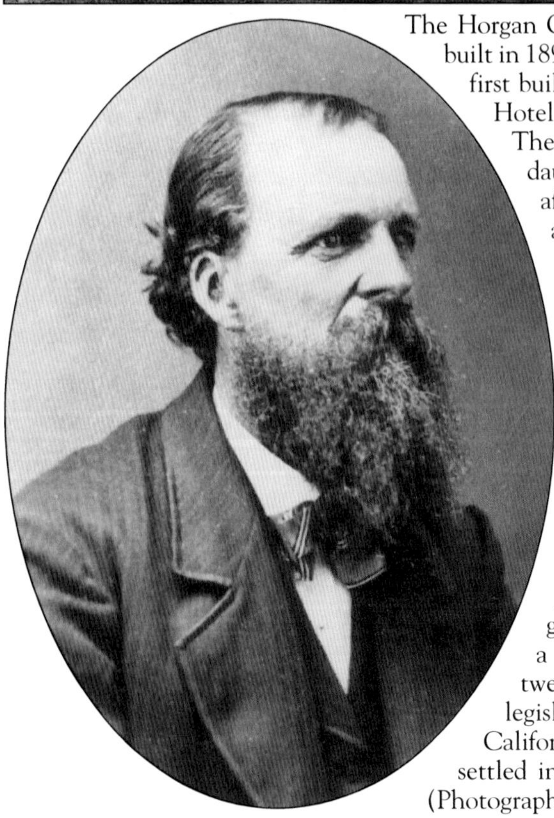

Samuel Elhorn Weeden, born in June 1832 on the farm that bore three generations of Weeden's before him, in a house built in 1687. When Elhorn was twenty-two he began two terms in the state legislature. In 1858 he crossed the country to California, returning home in 1865. He finally settled in Illinois on a farm in Onarga township. (Photograph courtesy of Donna Weeden)

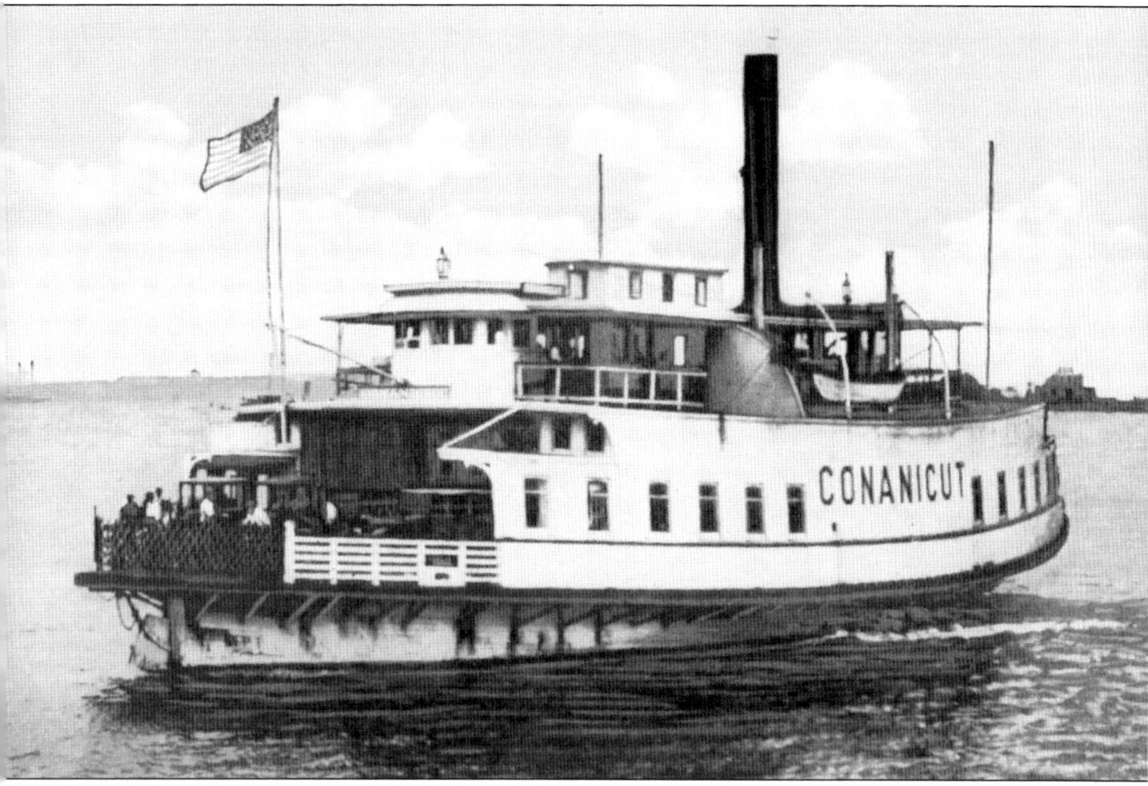

The *Conanicut*, built in 1886 to replace the *Jamestown*. The *Conanicut* was damaged by fire in 1914, rebuilt, and put back into service until 1927, when it was replaced by the *Governor Carr*. Jamestown probably had the first ferry system in the country. Of the more than seventy-five ferries that plied the waters of Narragansett Bay from 1640 to 1969, over one third had a landing in Jamestown. For over forty-six years, from 1797 to 1844, the fare stayed at 10¢ one way.

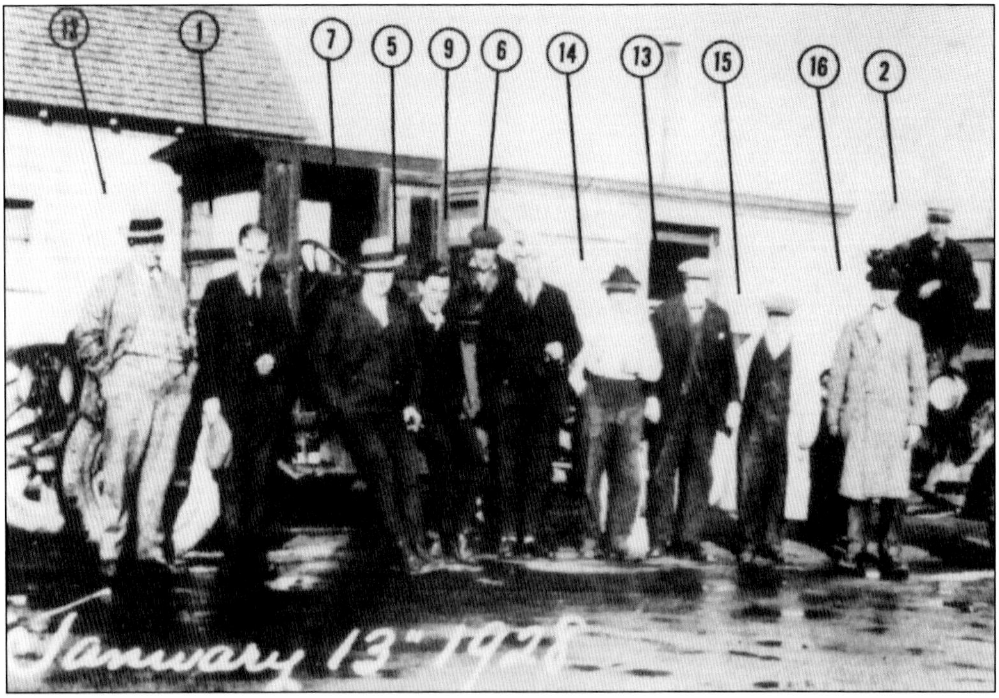

A photograph from a 1960 calendar, printed by the E.R Vieira Coal and Oil Company to salute the local businessmen of Jamestown. They are, from left to right, Archibald Clarke, Charles Haywood, Leroy Meredith, Harry Pitchers, Norman Caswell, Isaac Clarke, Herbert Hammond, Perry Brown, Herbert Barlow, Vernon Head, and Ernest Vieira Sr. (Photograph courtesy of Joan Weaver)

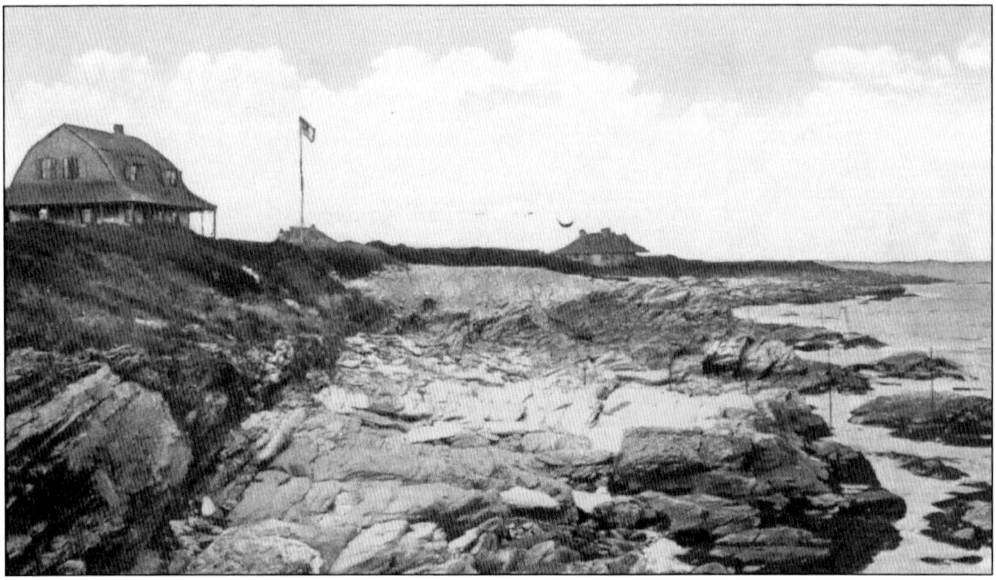

The Robert Goelet fishing camp, a private club limited to the original seven members. In the background is the Grey Ledge Tea House, built as a studio in 1895. From 1912 until the mid-1920s, it was used as a tea house for private parties. It was privately owned from 1926 until the government appropriated the land in 1941. It burned to the ground in 1942.

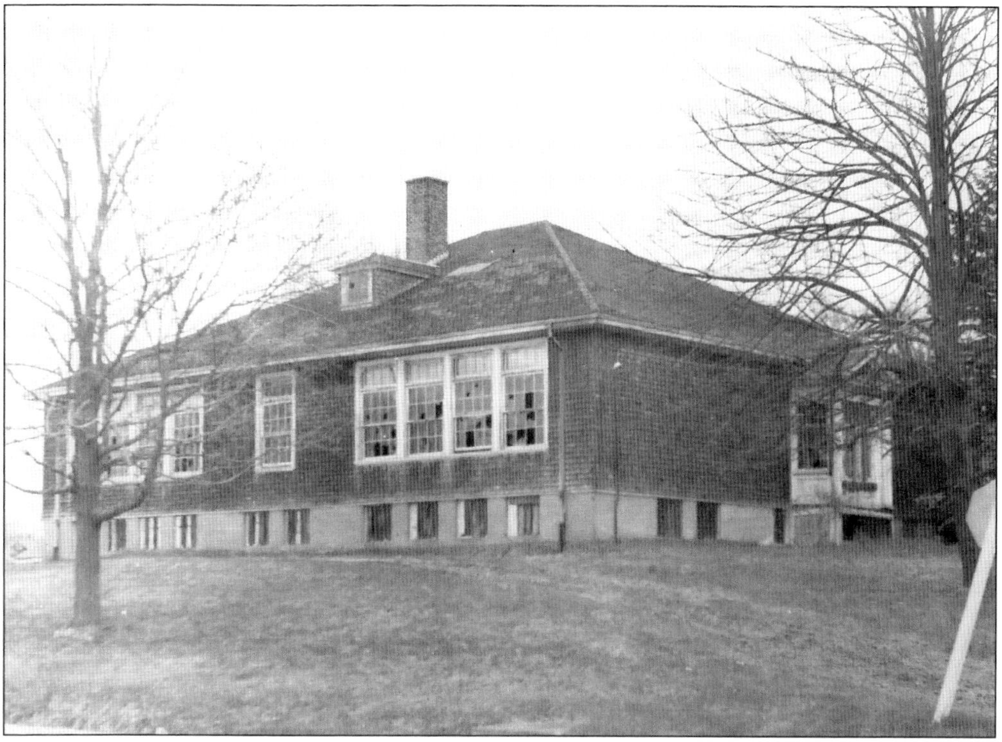

The Thomas H. Clarke School, opened in September 1923. Clarke was a superintendent of schools in Jamestown for over a decade. Today this is the site of the library.

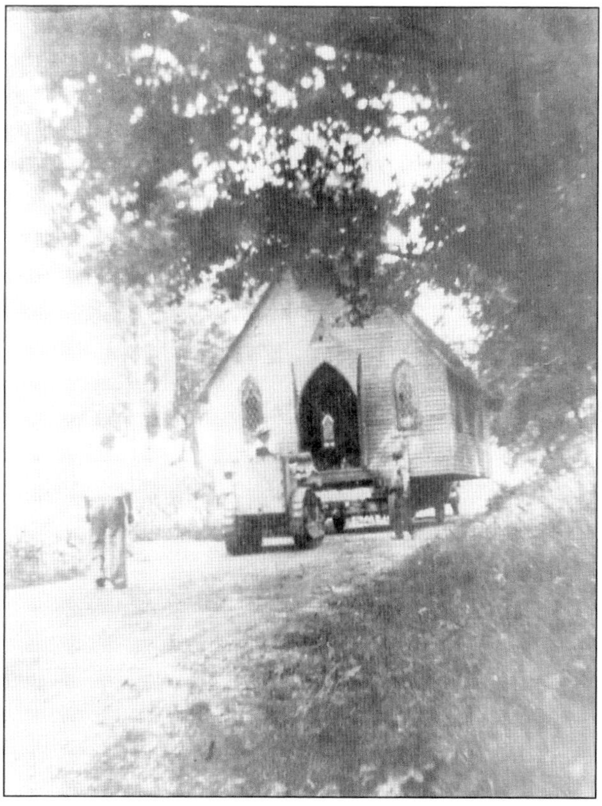

The movable chapel, 1898. Reverend Charles Preston had the idea to have this chapel built. In the summer it was moved to the north end of the island to accommodate the many summer residents. In the winter it was moved south, closer to the body of year-round residents. In 1915 it was made a permanent foundation. In 1933 it was moved once more, this time to be restored and used as a private residence.

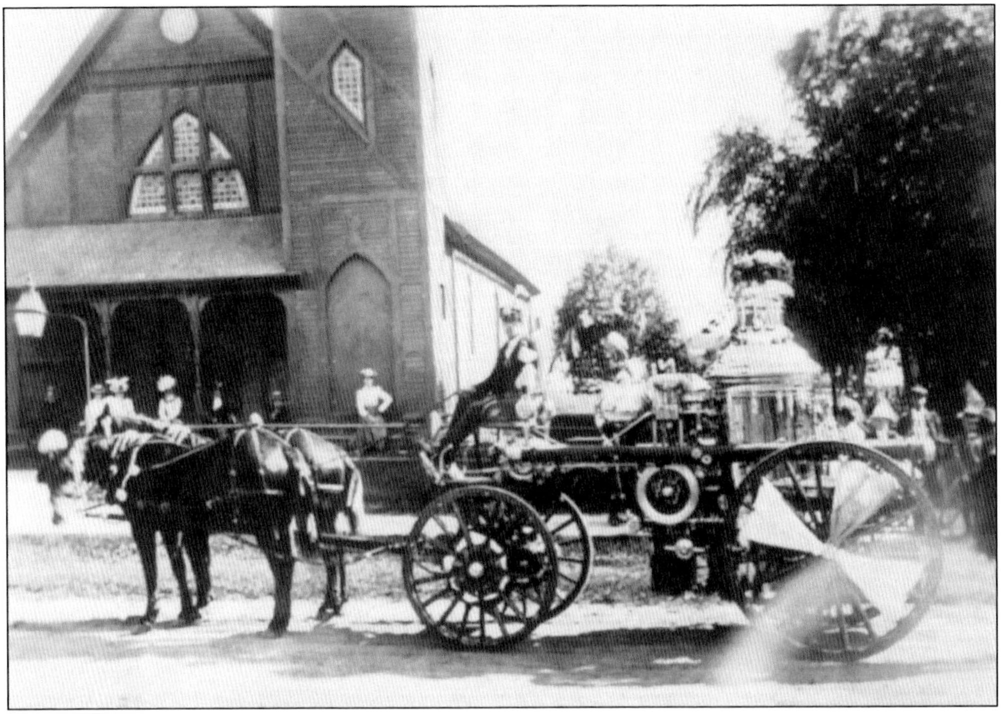

Jamestown Day in the 1890s. Every year between 1897 and the early 1900s Jamestown held a huge event, which included a parade of carriages (eventually replaced by automobiles), exhibitions, and grand prizes that were given away. (Photograph courtesy of Joan Weaver)

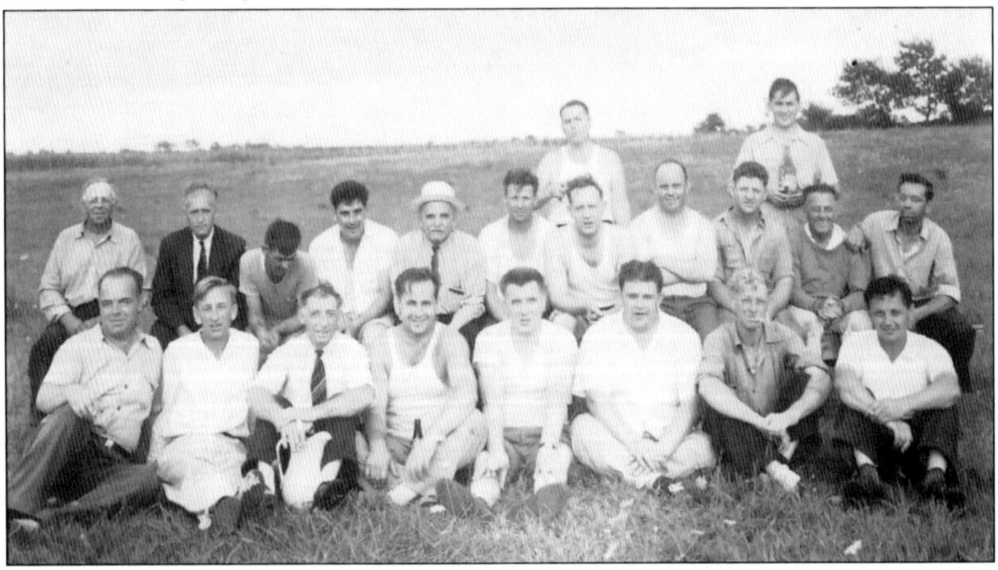

The Jamestown Volunteer Fire Department at their first annual picnic in 1942. The following, from left to right, have been identified: (front row) George Barker, Mert Hull, Charlie Dowling, Harry Boroch, Clinton Duffy, Sam Smith, Glass Littlefield, and Albert Lathan; (middle row) Herbert Wright, Eugene Kirbey, Lloyd Wright, Ernest Vieira, Jessie Teft, Manuel Guimary, Alfred Richardson, Charlie Manders, Bill Turillo, Walt Marley, and John Silvia; (back row) Harry Lark and Joseph Chesbro. (Photograph courtesy of Joan Weaver)

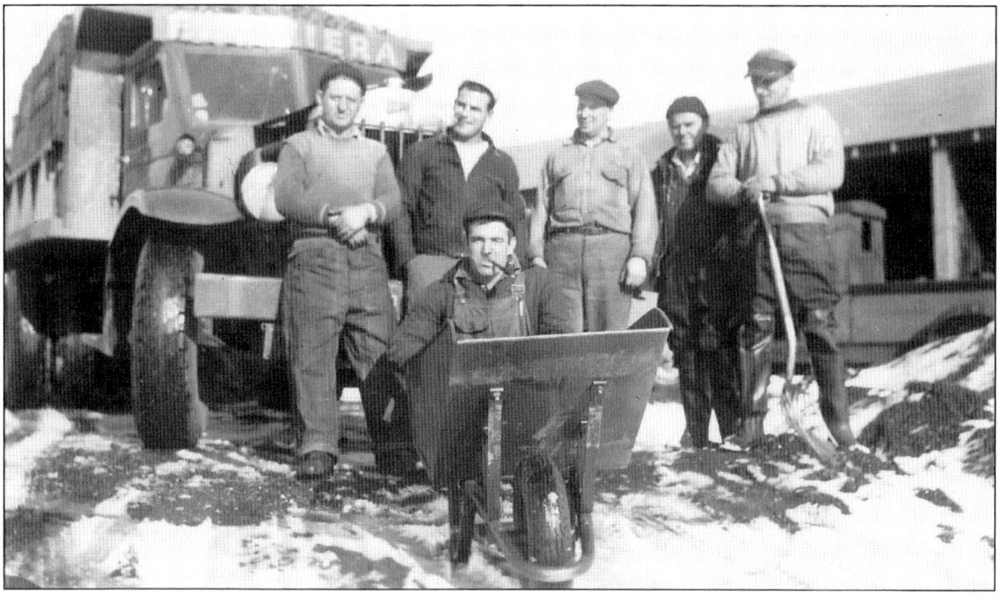

Employees of the E.R. Vieira Coal and Wood Company. Kneeling in front is Joseph Botelho. Standing, from left to right, are Bill Theroux, Alfred Vieira, Manuel Guimary, Emeziah Gorton, and Joe Godena. The company was a family-owned business for almost six decades, from 1922 until it was sold in 1981, and was one of the oldest and most respected family businesses on the island.

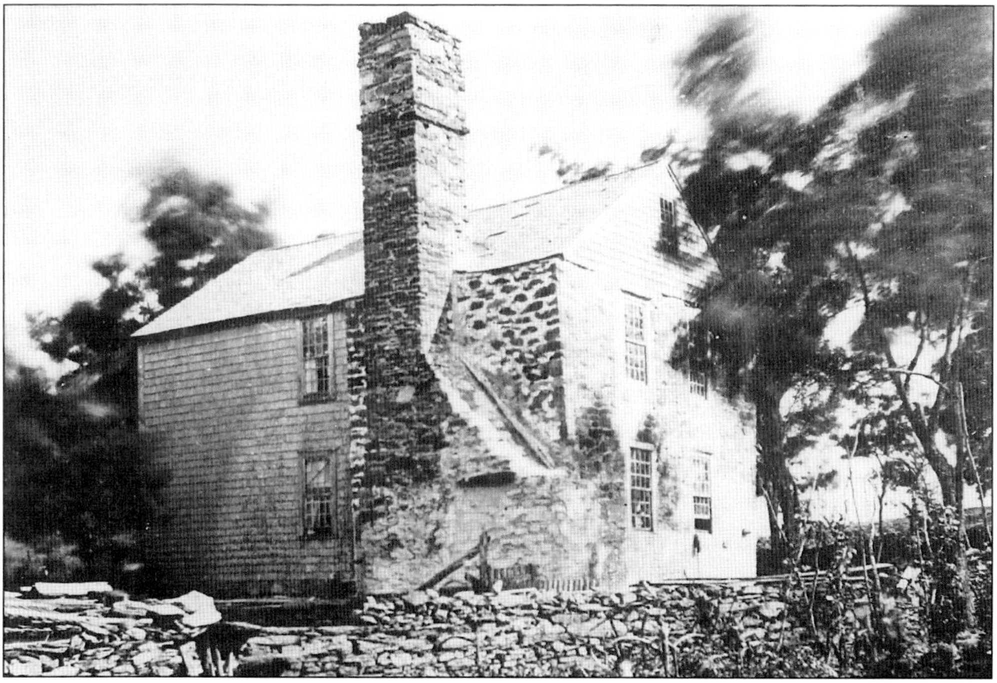

The half-stone house, built by Governor Caleb Carr about 1686. This house featured a great stone chimney, which fell in 1885 after a severe gale. The house, however, remains standing today.

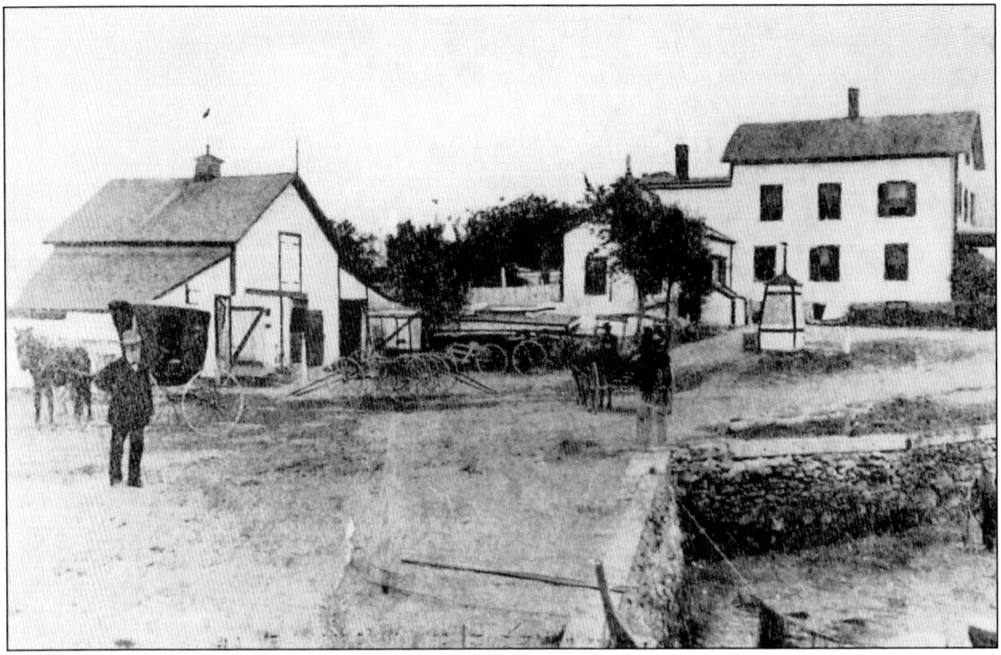

West ferry in the 1880s, located at the west end of Narragansett Avenue (which in earlier times was called Ferry Road). Ferry service was almost continual from the early 1640s until 1940, when the Jamestown Bridge was opened. (Photograph courtesy of Joan Weaver)

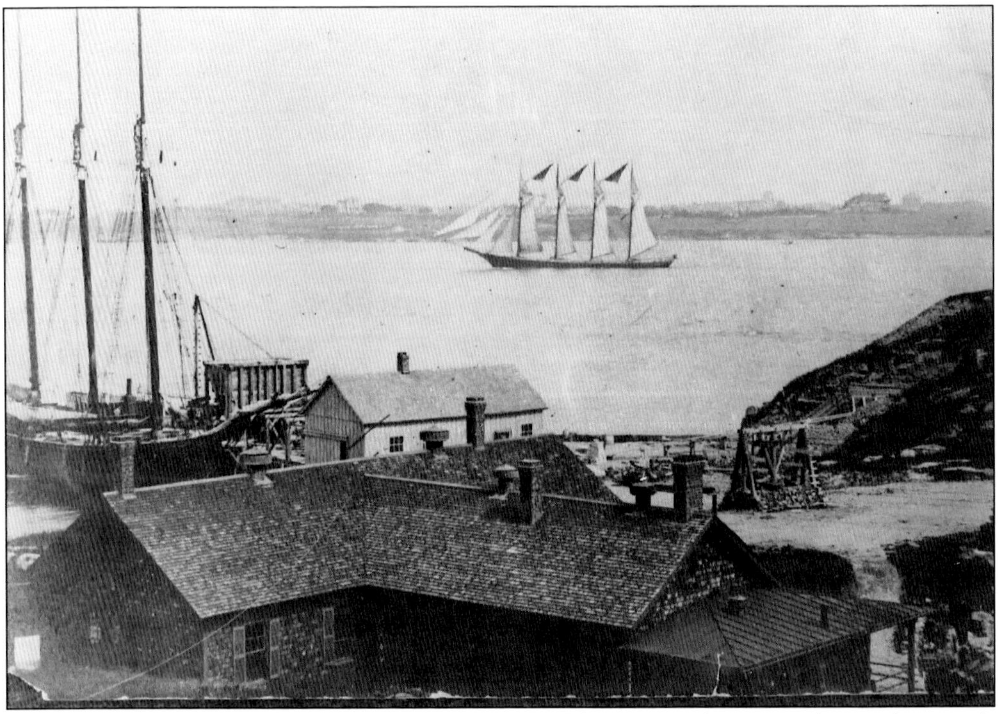

Wharton's Shipyard, *c.* 1905. This shipyard was used by J.S.L. Wharton to house the vessels that carried him and his guests to his home, Clingstone (see p. 116). In 1931 the property changed into the hands of his son Charles, who ran a commercial shipyard here until 1973.

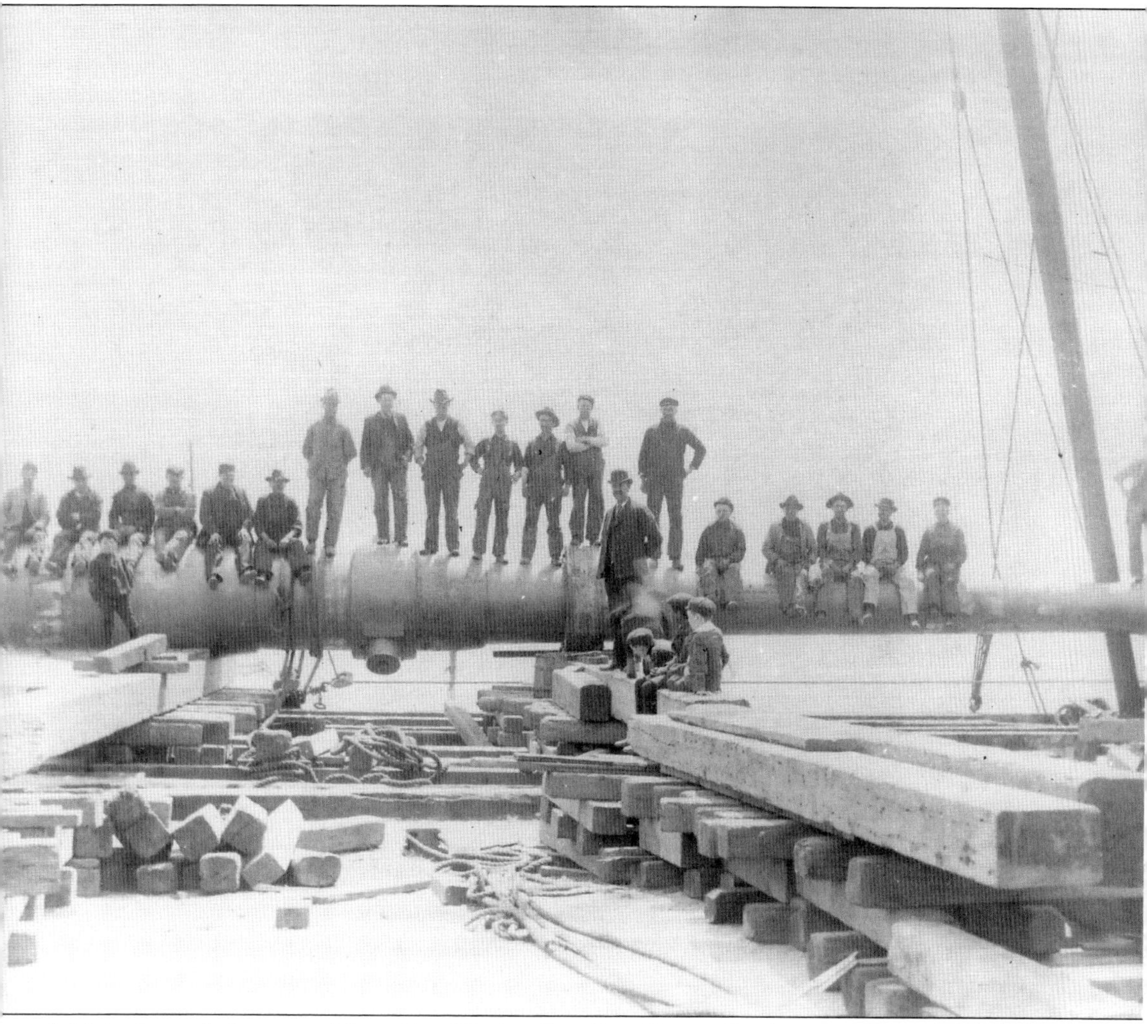

A 16-inch gun being moved from Fort Wetherell to Fort Getty. The first use of Fort Wetherell as a fortification goes back to the Revolutionary War, when colonists positioned cannons behind hastily erected earth works. The government purchased the area in 1799. Shortly after the Spanish-American War, it was dedicated in honor of Captain Alex Wetherell, who lost his life in Santiago, Cuba. Fort Getty was acquired in 1900 and construction of fortifications began a year later. It was dedicated in May 1903 and named after Colonel George Getty, a participant in the Civil War.

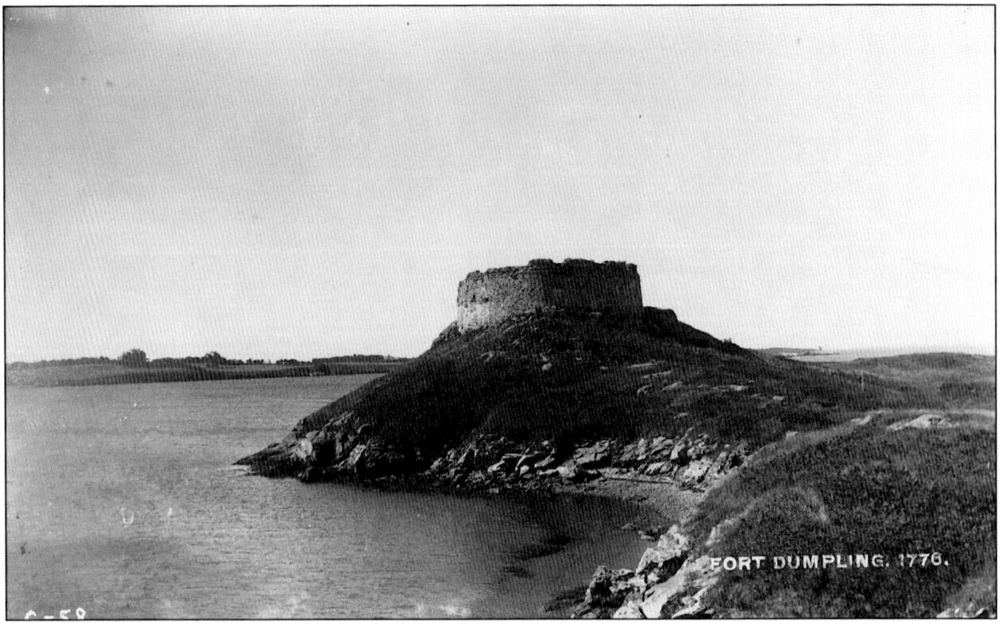

Fort Dumpling. Built in the late 1790s, Fort Dumpling was damaged by target fire from Fort Adams in the 1850s. It was finally demolished in 1898–99.

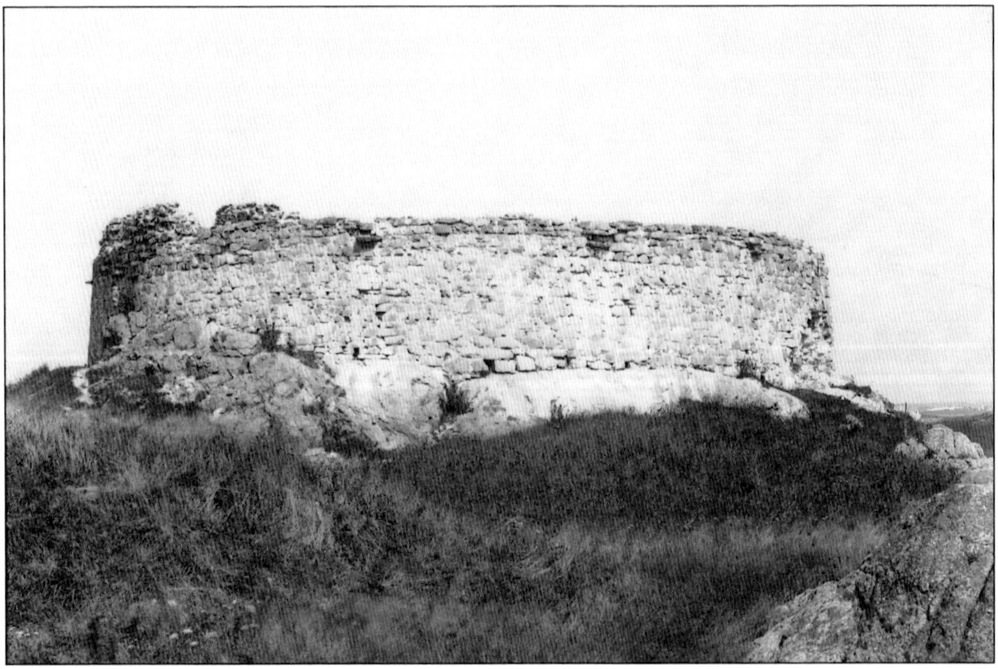

A close up of the fort. Its usefulness as a fort was short lived when Fort Adams was built in the 1800s, although it was written about many times as a must see when visiting the area. A most romantic spot in its day.

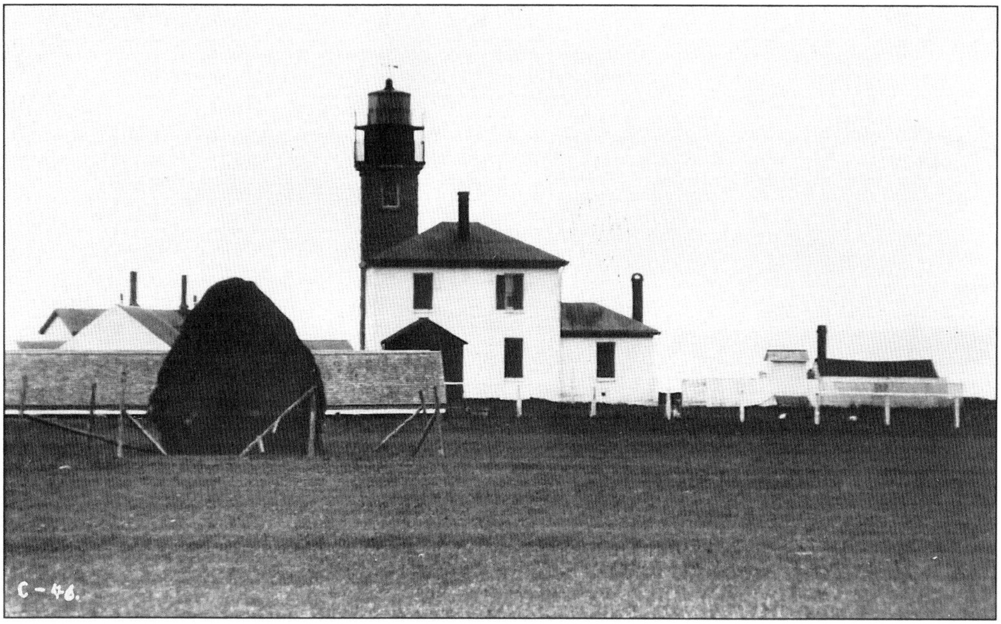

The Beavertail light, always at the forefront of technology. A watch house first appeared at Beavertail Point in 1705. By 1712 a beacon had been erected, and in 1750, a 60-foot tower was built of wood. It burned three years later and in 1755 a stone tower replaced it. The British destroyed it during their evacuation and it stayed in darkness until the mid-1780s when it was repaired. It remained in service until 1856, when Beavertail light was built. In 1818 it was fitted with a gas-burning light but returned to burning oil a year later. In 1931 it was converted to electricity.

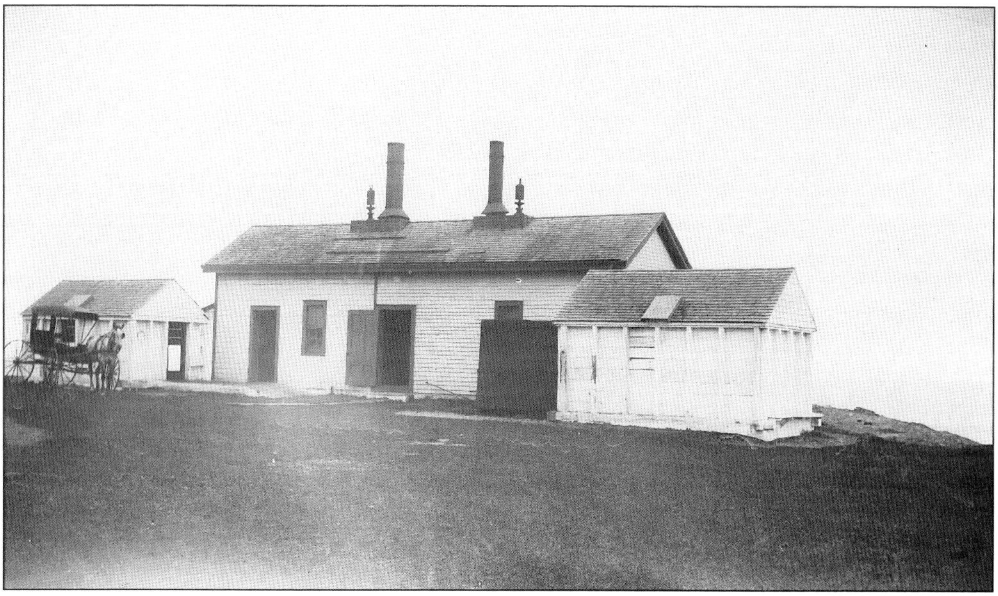

The steam whistle-fog horn shed. In 1851 a fog trumpet was installed. In 1866 a reed trumpet was put into service, which was in turn replaced by a steam whistle in 1881. During the Hurricane of '38 the whistle house was washed away, revealing the foundation of the original 1750 structure.

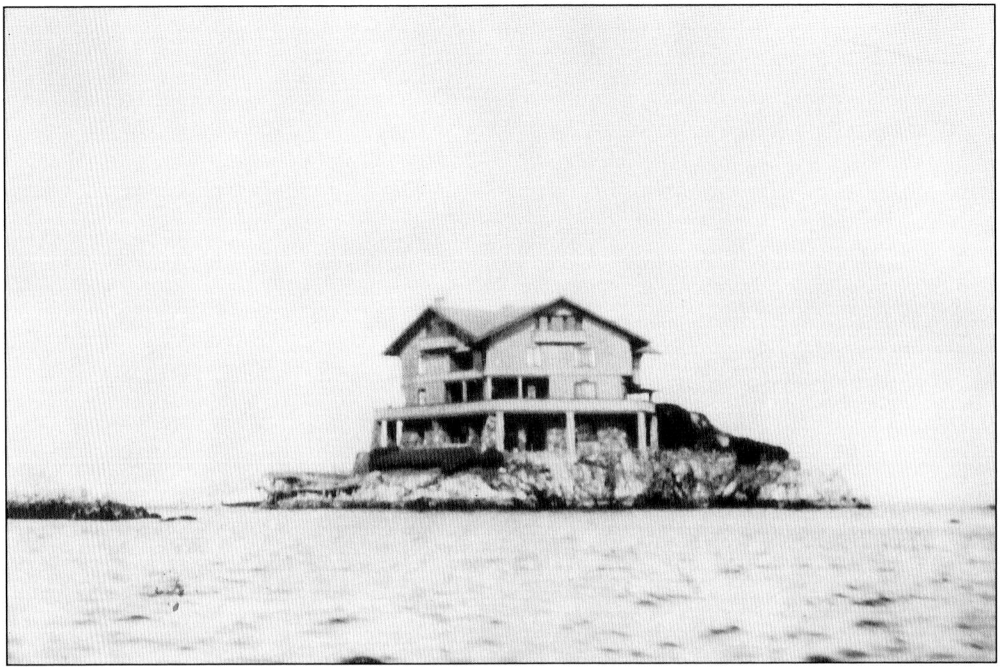

Clingstone, located on a rock just off the coast of Jamestown, in the area known as the Dumplings. Built in 1904–1905 by J.S.L. Wharton (see p. 110), this house sat empty for decades, until 1962, when Boston architect Henry Wood purchased it and made extensive repairs. The cost to build the twenty-three-room house in 1904 was under $40,000.

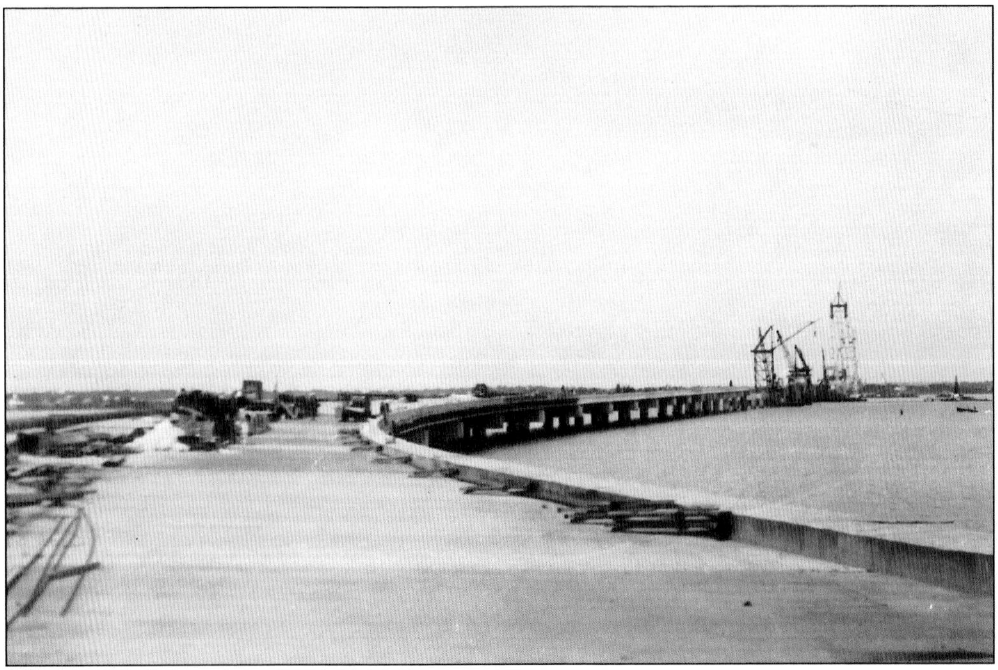

The Narragansett Bay Bridge, completed in under two years at a cost of 3 million dollars. Some compare this to the Jamestown-Verrazano bridge which replaced it in 1992, and took over seven years to complete at a cost of over 168 million dollars.

Six

Prudence Island

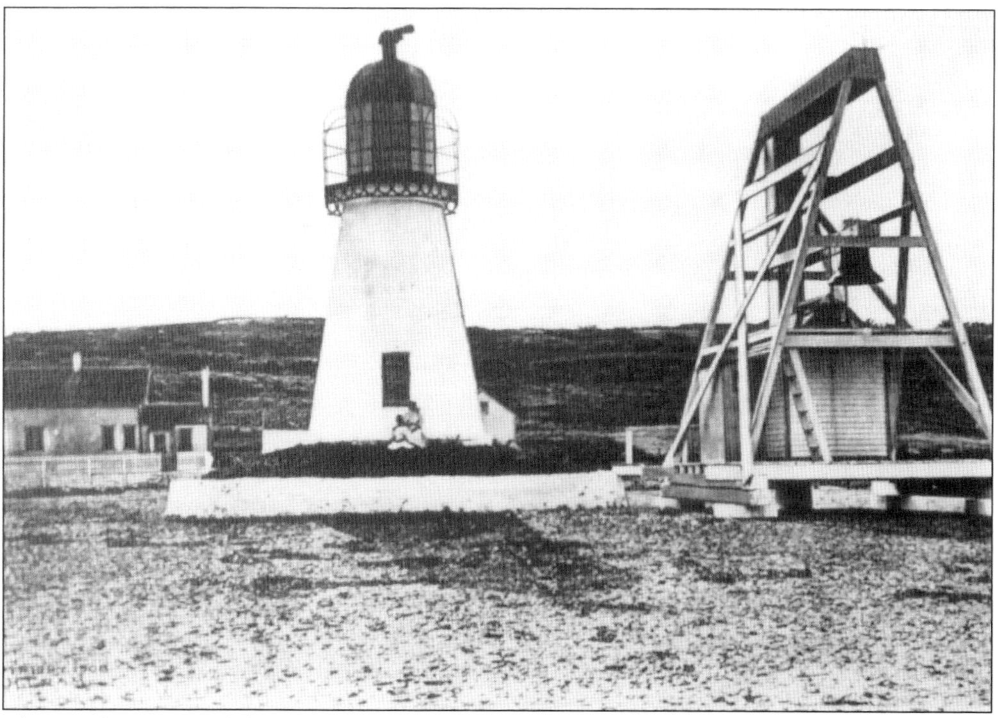

The Sandy Point Lighthouse in the 1890s. This island, first known by the Native Americans as Chibacuwese, was purchased by Roger Williams in 1637 and named Prudence Island. The Sandy Point Lighthouse, originally built at the north end of Goat Island in 1824, was floated up the bay by barge in the early 1850s and has served the island since. (Photograph courtesy of Donna and Joe Bains)

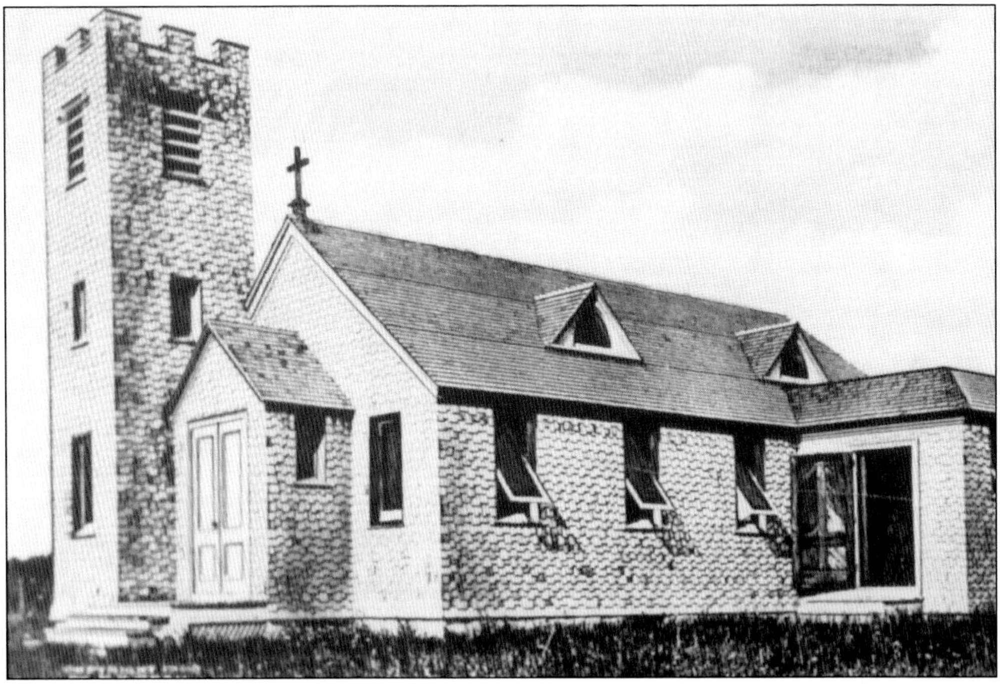

The Episcopal chapel. In September 1897 two lots were purchased at Prudence Park by a trustee for the church of the Holy Ghost. In August 1902 the cornerstone was laid and the church was completed soon after. In Charles Matum's book, he surmises that this was the first church built on the island. (Photograph courtesy of Donna and Joe Bains)

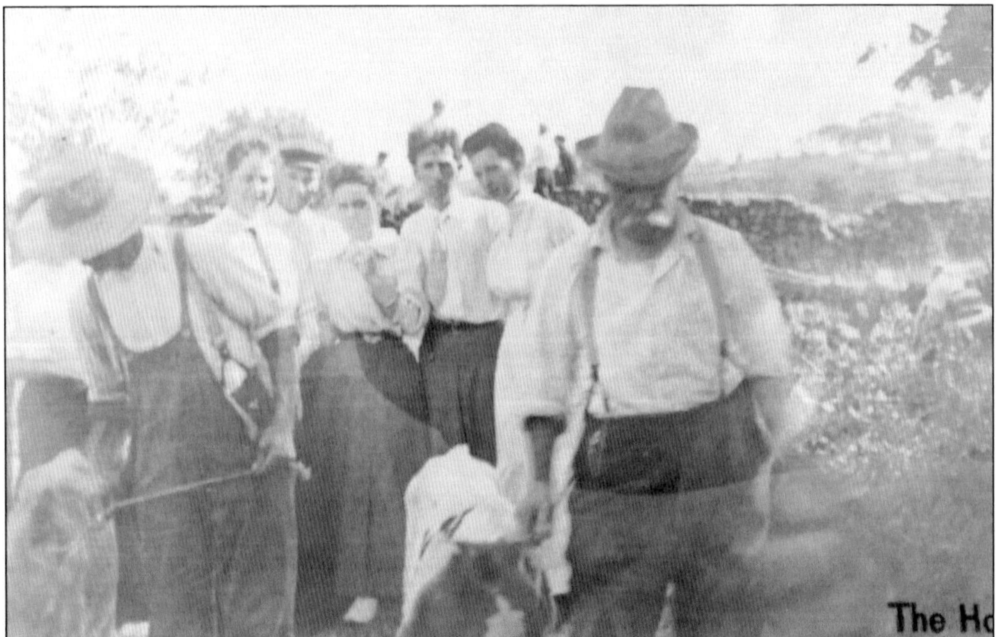

Madison Cram (to the right) and other family members at the Homestead, one of the first guest houses that opened on Prudence Island at the turn of the century. (Photograph courtesy of Donna and Joe Bains)

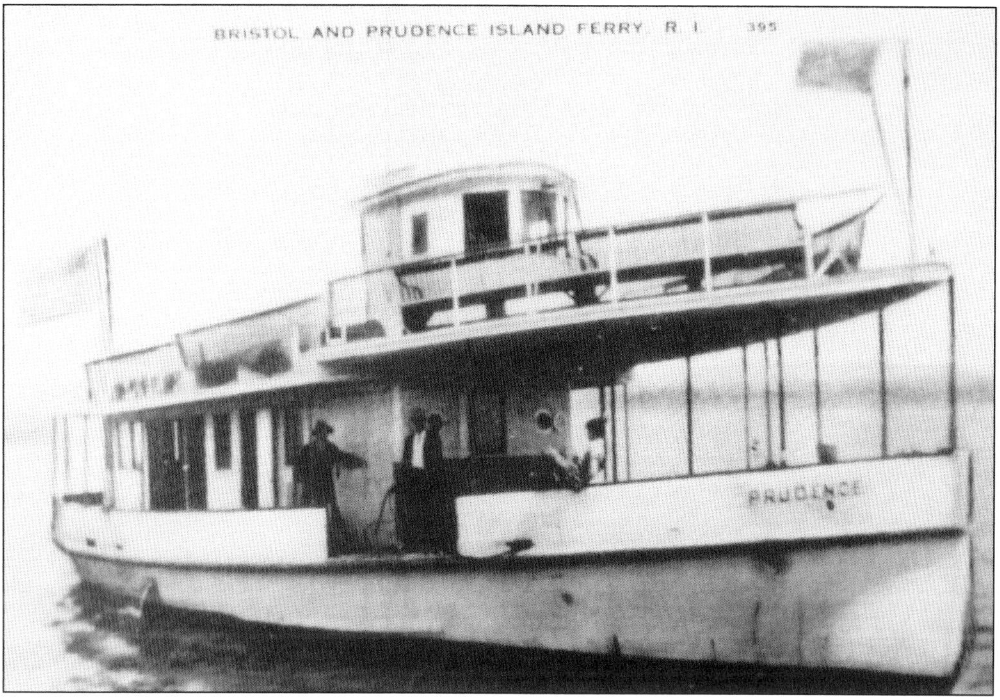

Dear *Prudence*, the Bristol to Prudence Island ferry. The *Prudence* traveled the waters of Narragansett Bay for over four decades. (Photograph courtesy of Donna and Joe Bains)

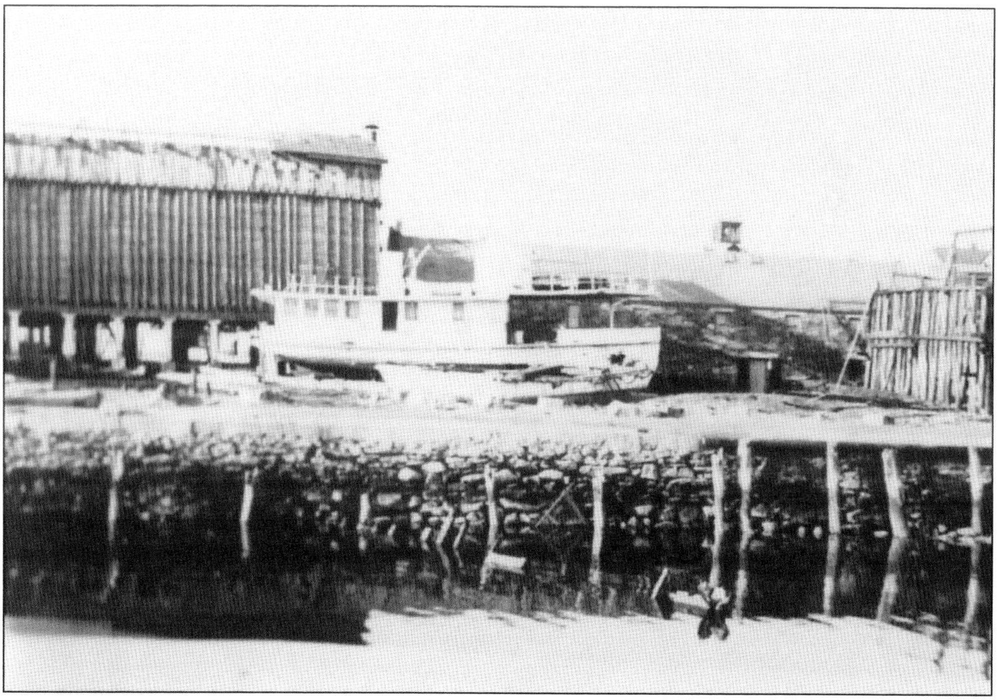

The Prudence Island ferry after it washed up onto a dock in Bristol harbor during the Hurricane of '38. (Photograph courtesy of Donna and Joe Bains)

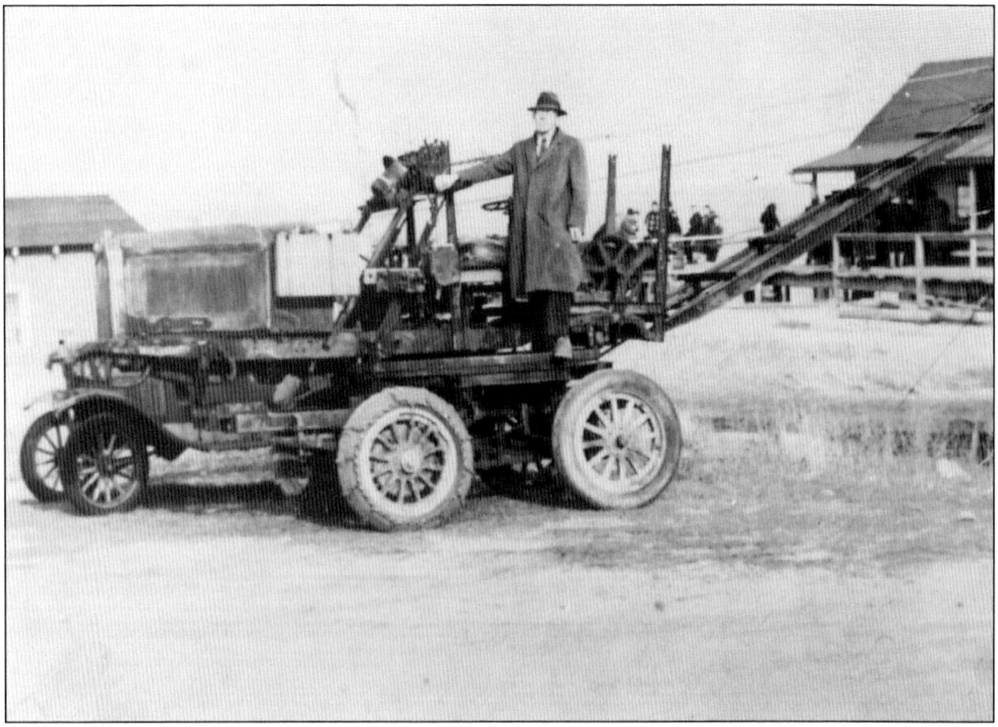

Milton H. Chase around 1937, standing on the octopus, an invention of his. Made from two old tractors and various spare parts, Chase used it to dig holes and erect utility poles. He also took care of the Sandy Point Lighthouse, on and off, from September 1938 until the early 1950s. (Photograph courtesy of Donna and Joe Bains)

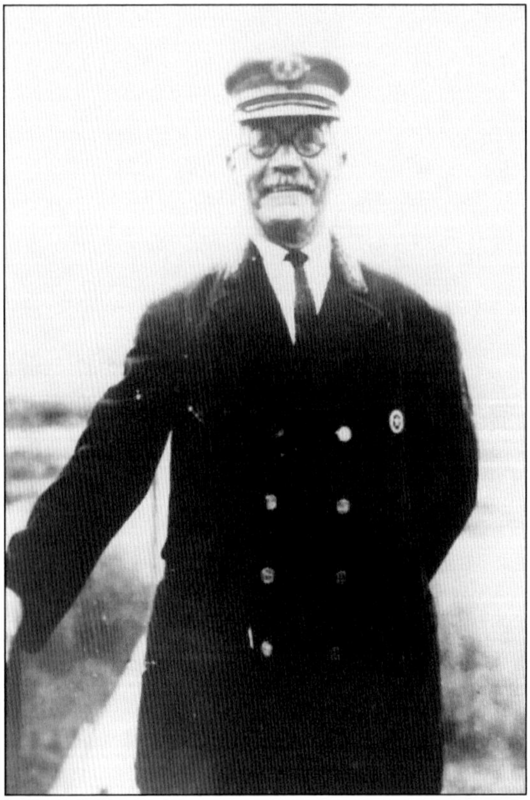

Martin Thompson, the Sandy Point Lighthouse keeper from 1905 until his retirement in 1933. Thompson perished in the 1938 hurricane when he tried to seek refuge in the lighthouse from the storm. (Photograph courtesy of Donna and Joe Bains)

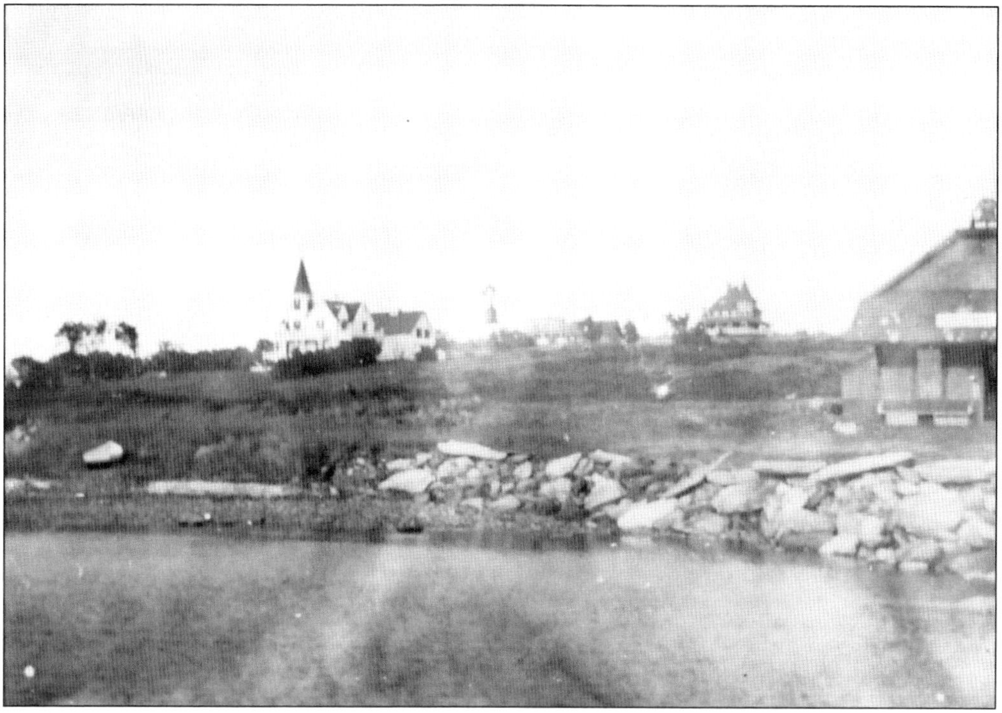

Prudence Park, located on the center of the west shore. Originally the Sweet Farm, 380 acres of land were purchased in 1874, and two years later the first homes were built. (Photograph courtesy of Donna and Joe Bains)

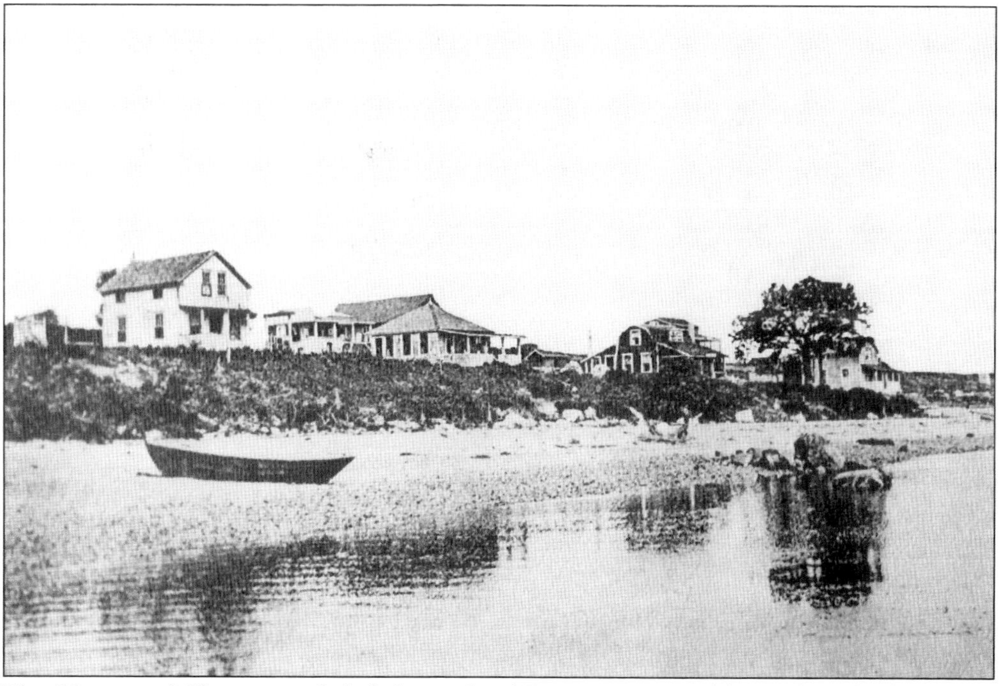

The Homestead Plat, situated slightly south of Potters Cove and located on land formerly belonging to Madison Cram. (Photograph courtesy of Donna and Joe Bains)

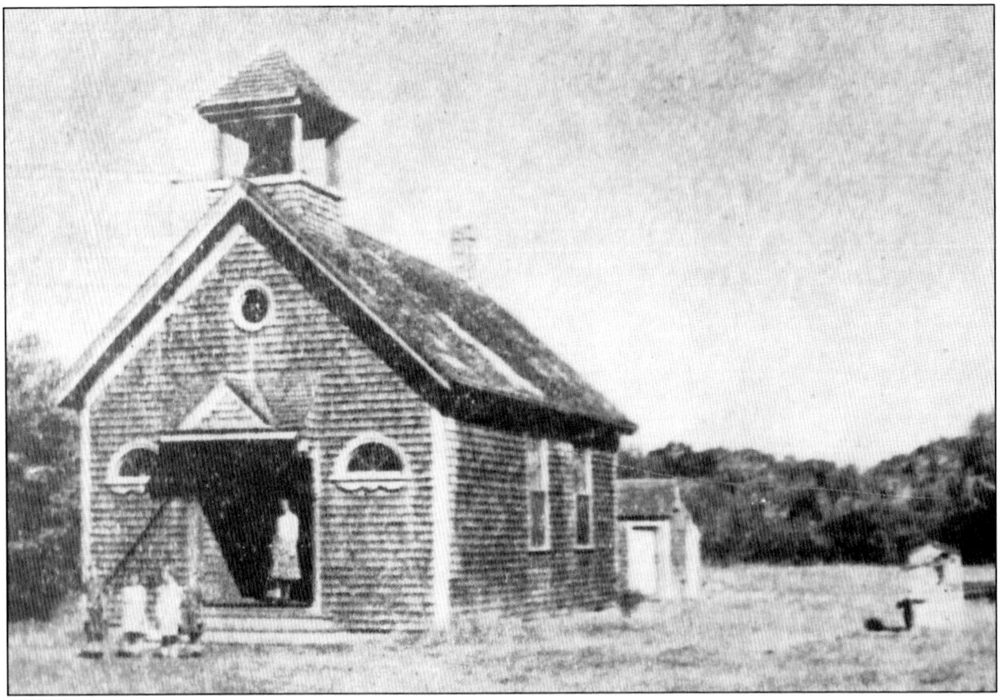

The 1896 schoolhouse, one of four that have been built on this site. The first school building was erected here in the 1760s. It was burned by the British forces during a battle on the island in 1776 or 1777. Two more schools were built on this site, one in 1782 and the one shown here in 1828. The present building was erected in 1896. It was open until 1982, when it closed for seven years, but it re-opened in 1989. (Photograph courtesy of Donna and Joe Bains)

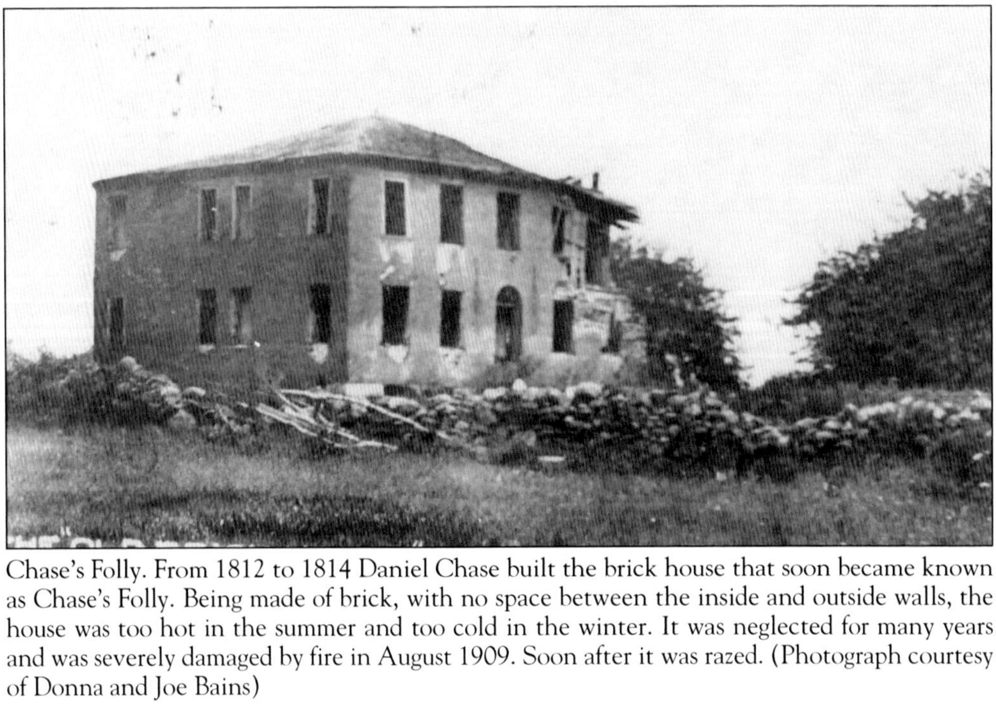

Chase's Folly. From 1812 to 1814 Daniel Chase built the brick house that soon became known as Chase's Folly. Being made of brick, with no space between the inside and outside walls, the house was too hot in the summer and too cold in the winter. It was neglected for many years and was severely damaged by fire in August 1909. Soon after it was razed. (Photograph courtesy of Donna and Joe Bains)

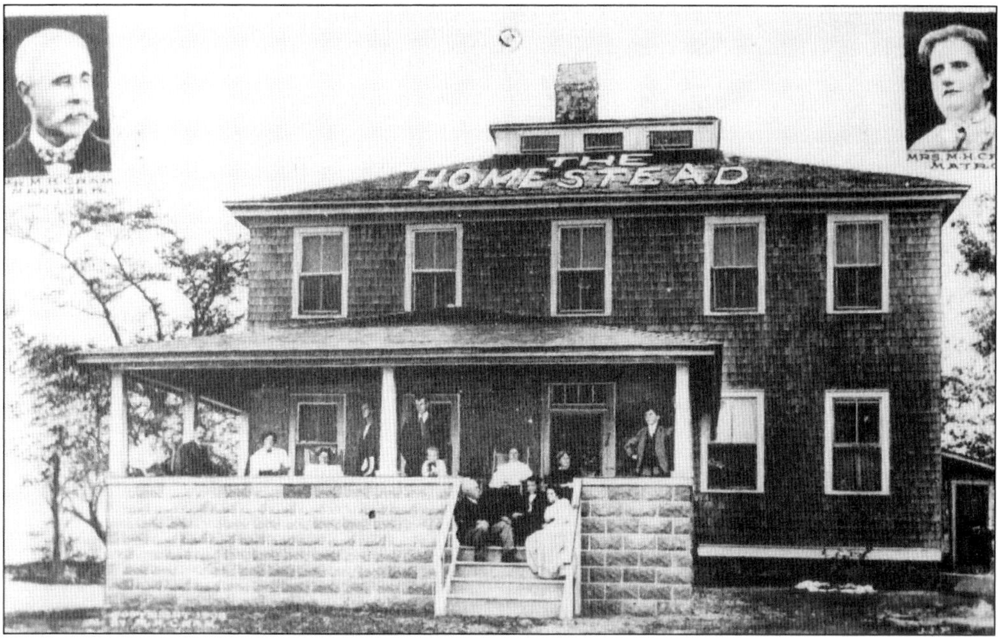

The house originally known as the Darius Chase House. In the early 1890s it was operated by the Crams as a boarding house, the second one to be opened on the island. (Photograph courtesy of Donna and Joe Bains)

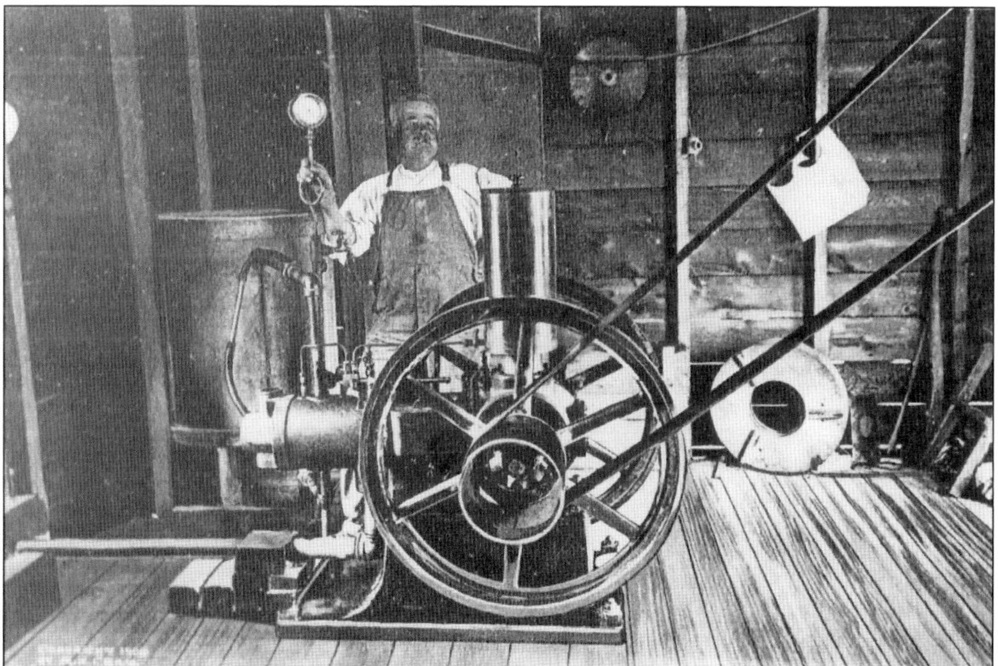

Madison Cram in the pump house of the Homestead Inn. One had to be resourceful living off the mainland, and Mr. Cram was said to be a master at it. (Photograph courtesy of Donna and Joe Bains)

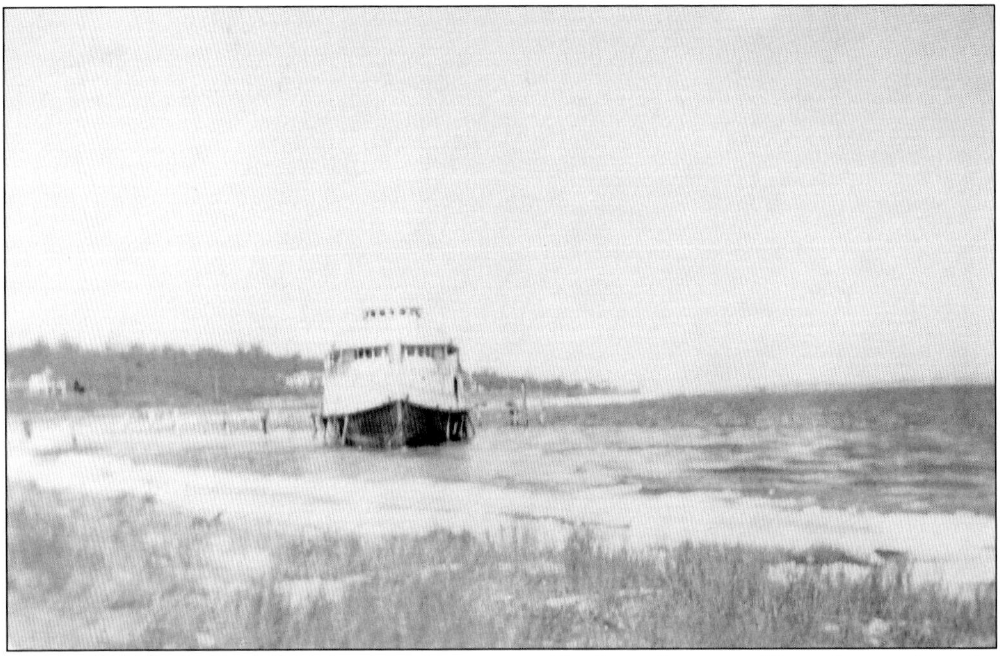

Shipwrecked. The Monhegan ferry was being towed back to the port of Providence when she began to take on water and became stranded in this spot for years. In the late 1930s for two or three seasons she was used as a dance hall. (Photograph courtesy of Donna and Joe Bains)

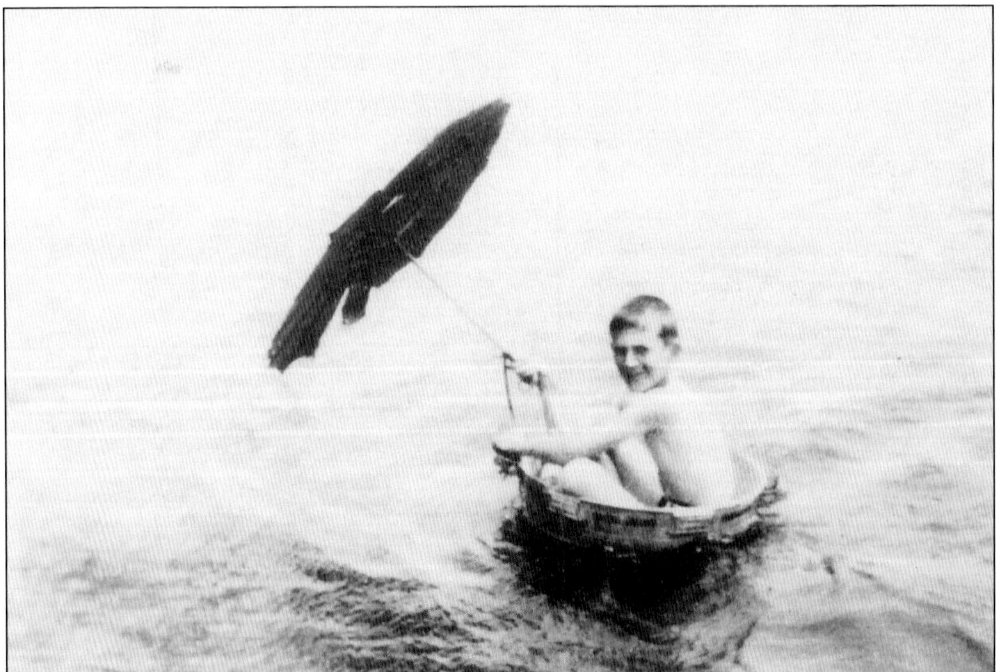

An early Prudence Island postcard featuring one of the Richardson boys. (Photograph courtesy of Donna and Joe Bains)

Seven

Remaining Bay Islands

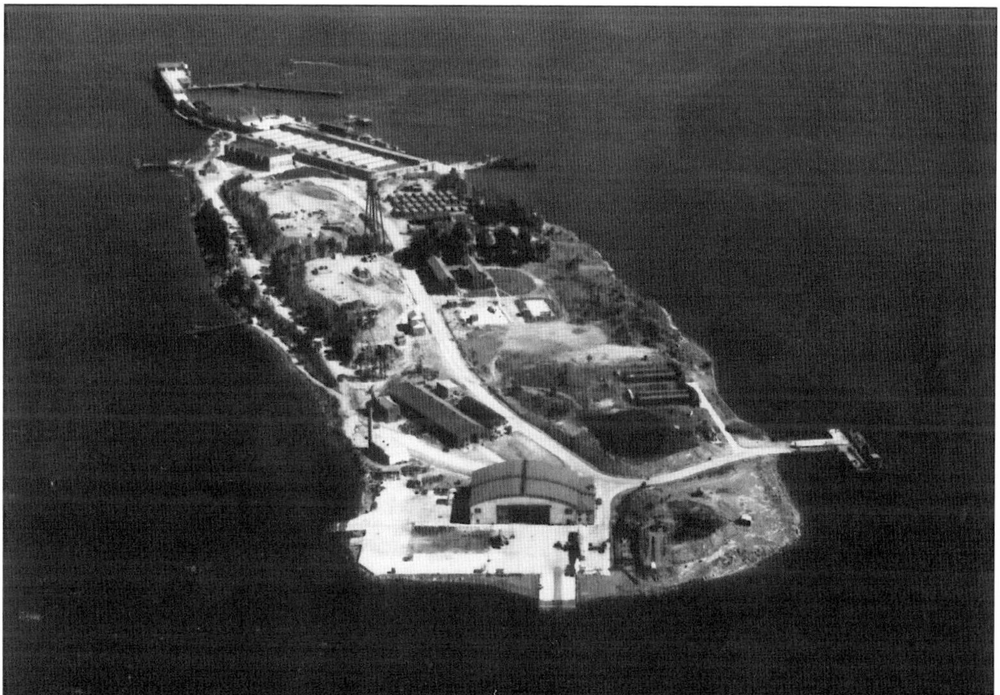

Gould Island. The Native American name was Aquopimokuk, and it was purchased from them by Thomas Gould in 1657 to be used as pastureland. In 1918 the Navy acquired the land and developed it into a facility for testing and repairing torpedoes and storing explosives. In 1921 two seaplanes were assigned to the island to experiment with air-dropped torpedoes; the hanger and one of the planes can be seen at the southern end of the island. In 1941 a degaussing station was installed for the purpose of demagnetizing ships. Today the Navy owns part of the island; the rest is part of the Bay Island Park System.

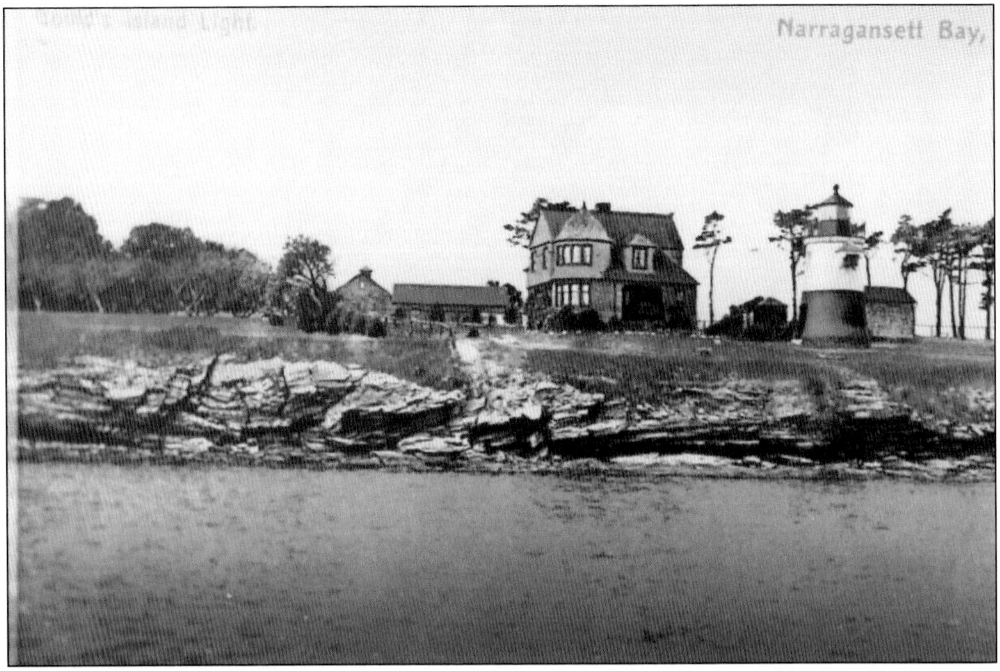

The Gould Island Lighthouse, built at the southern end of the island in 1889. The light was 47 feet above water and had a visibility of 12 miles. The lighthouse was operational until 1947 and was demolished in 1960.

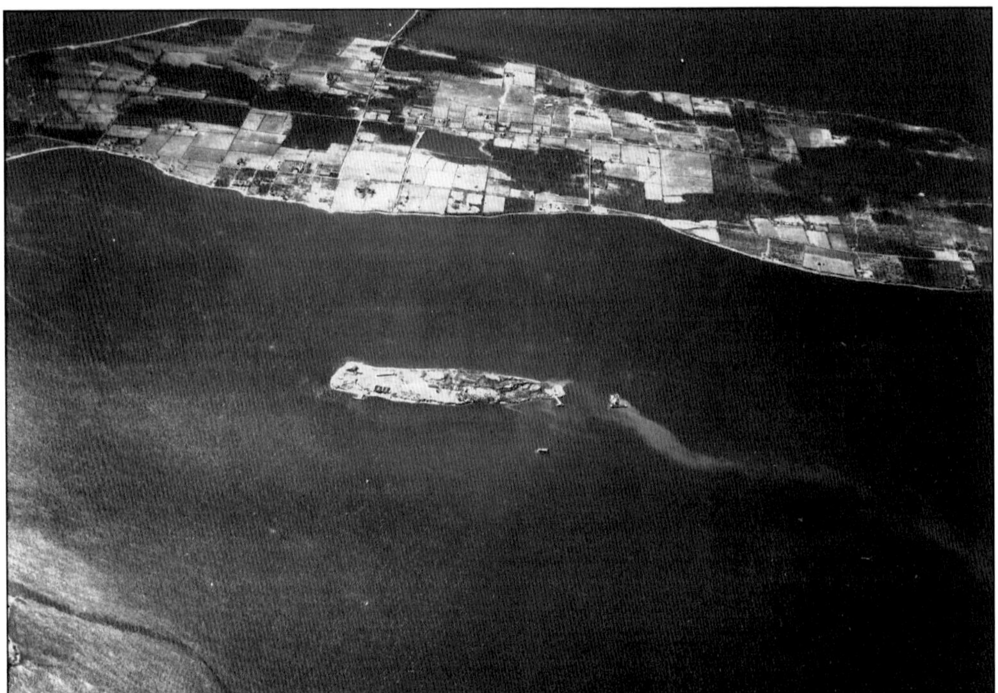

Gould Island from an altitude of 10,000 feet on November 3, 1942. Conanicut Island is in the distance with the Jamestown Bridge at the top of the photograph.

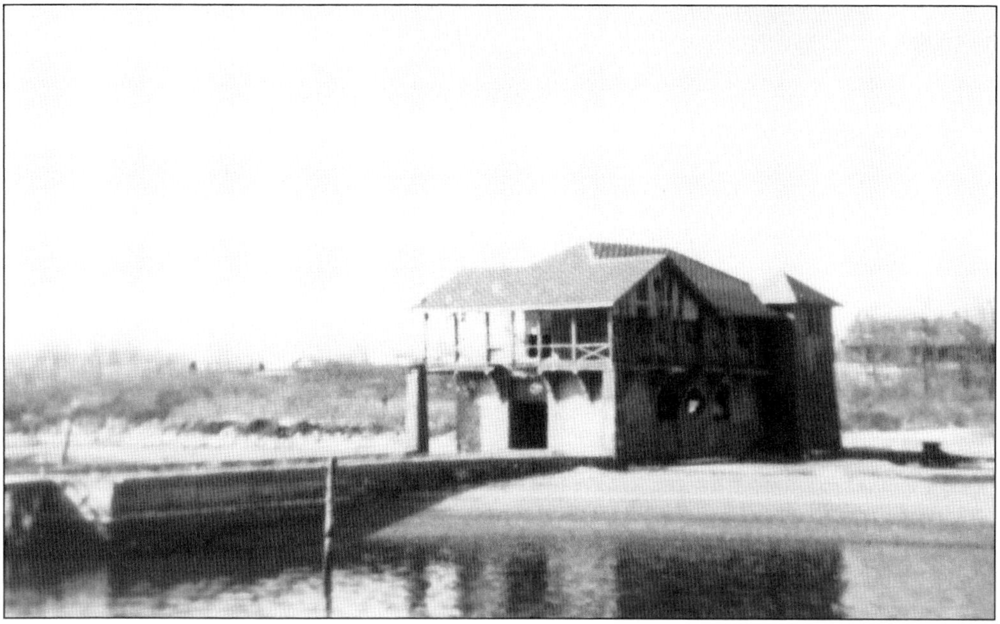

The boathouse for the Knight estate on Hog Island. The Knights owned the island in the 1890s. It was first purchased from the Wampanoags in 1646, whose name for the island was Chiseweanock. The early settlers kept swine on the island—hence its name. Many of the smaller islands were used for the containment of livestock because of the ample grazing, and because there was no need to erect walls or pens for the animals.

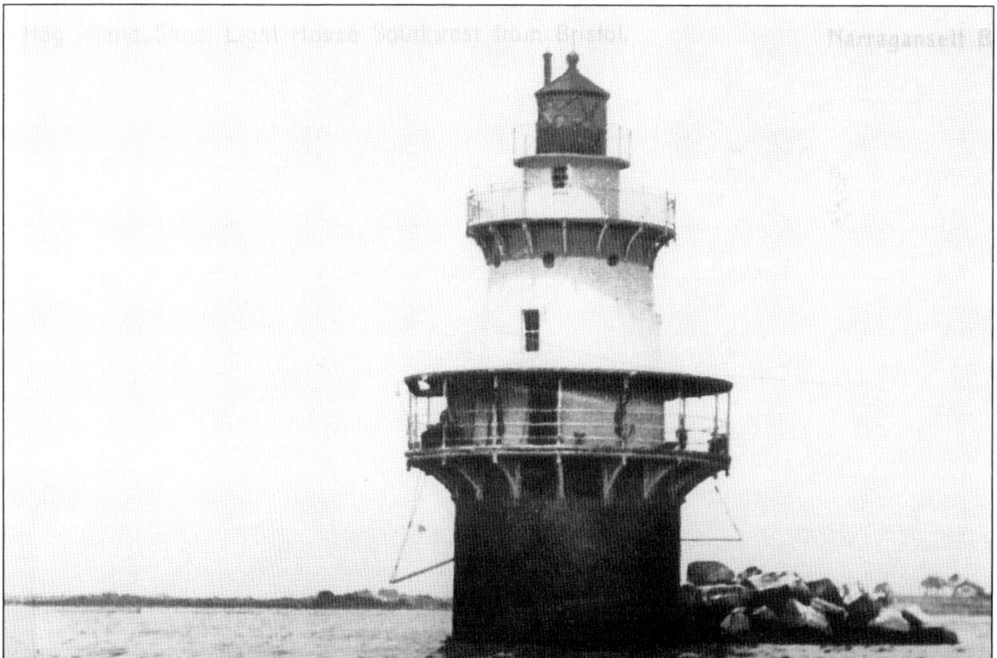

The Hog Island Shoal Lighthouse, built in 1901. The view is from Portsmouth with Hog Island in the background.

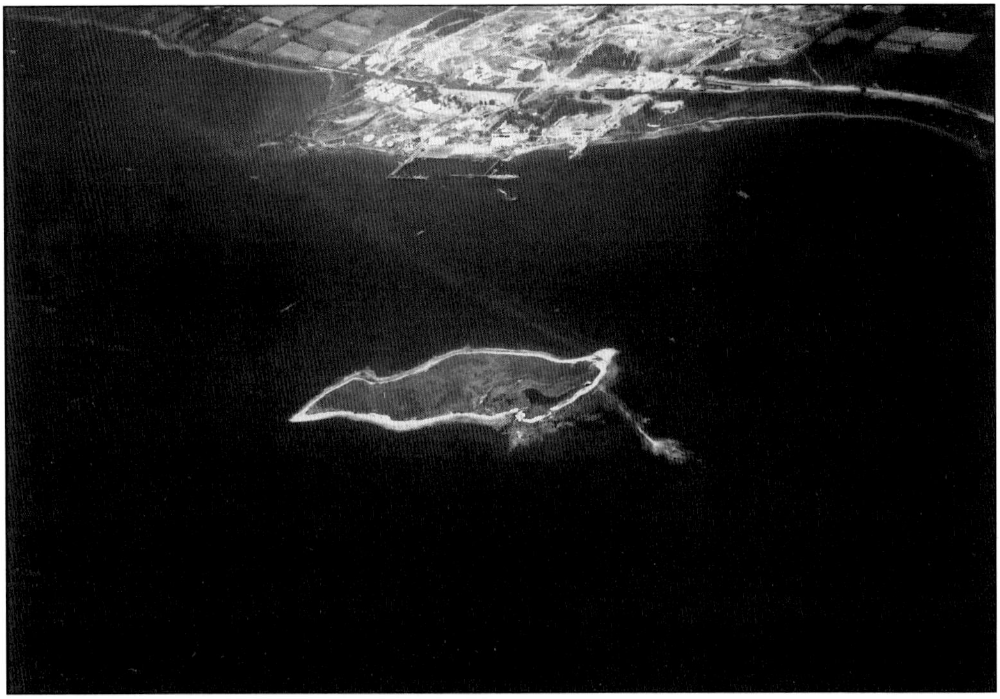

Dyer Island with Coddington Point in the upper half of the photograph. this island was purchased from the Native Americans by William Dyer to be used as pastureland. (Photograph courtesy of the Naval War College Archives)

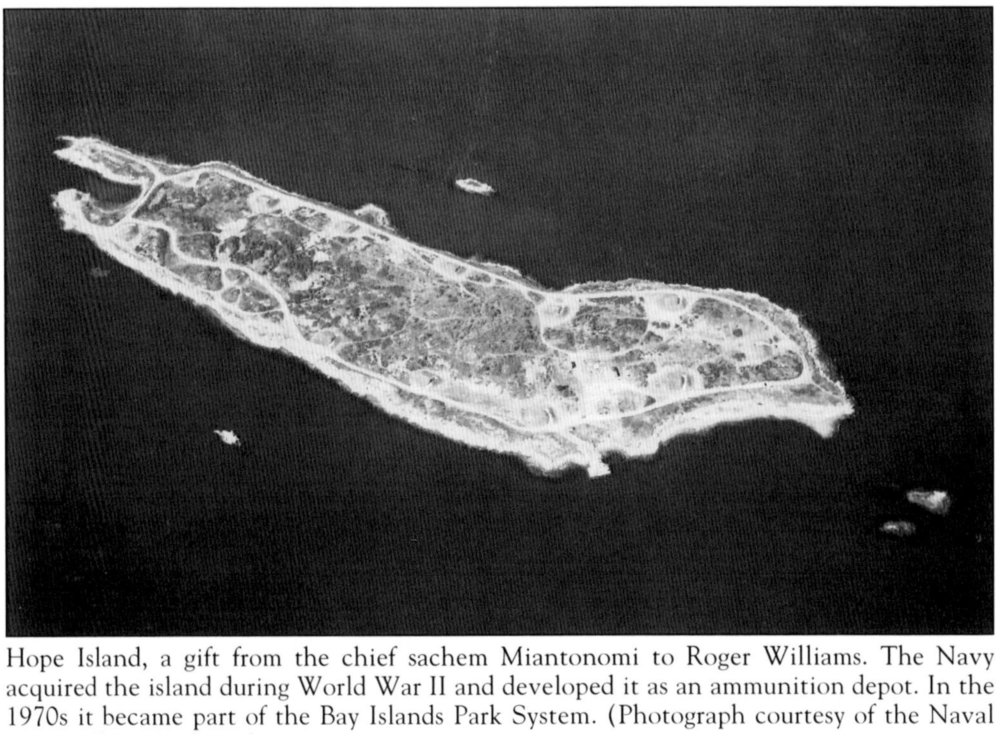

Hope Island, a gift from the chief sachem Miantonomi to Roger Williams. The Navy acquired the island during World War II and developed it as an ammunition depot. In the 1970s it became part of the Bay Islands Park System. (Photograph courtesy of the Naval War College Archives)

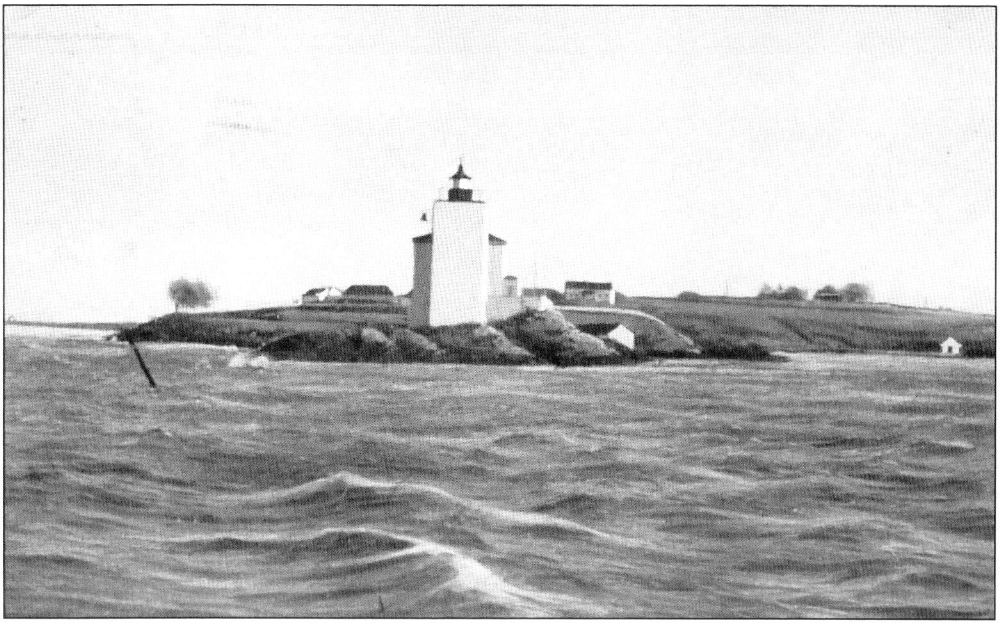

Dutch Island. In early times Dutch traders would meet here with local Native Americans for the purpose of trading. The 80-acre island was acquired by the government in 1863. Soon after this a small fortification was built, which remained little used until the Spanish-American War in 1898. The fort was named after Lieutenant John Greble, the first officer killed in the Civil War. Deactivated in 1906, it was used again in World War I and World War II, but was permanently dissolved in 1947.

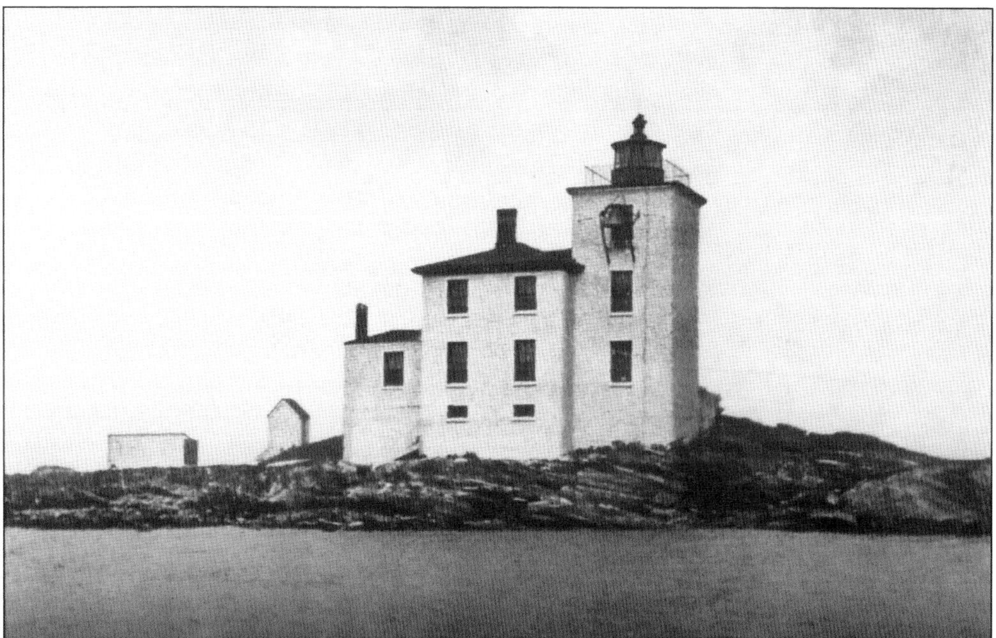

The Dutch Island Lighthouse, built in 1857. It replaced an earlier light built around 1825. In 1931 the beacon was automated.

Acknowledgments

As with my first book on Newport, again I am indebted to Benjamin Cobb Reed Jr., the Executive Director of the Newport Restoration Foundation, for the opportunity to use the vast photographic archives that the foundation has amassed. The photographs not only provide a valuable tool for the restoration of old homes but are glimpses of our past, frozen moments of time. There were many people, some who I approached and some who approached me, who allowed me to borrow precious photographs of ancestors to be included in this volume. I will attempt to name them here, but forgive me if I forget anyone: Mike Allen of the Middletown Police Department, Evelyn Cherpak, Curator of the Naval Historical Collection at the Naval War College, Charlotte Johnson, the Executive Director of the Rose Island Lighthouse Foundation, June and Don Occaso, Donna Weeden, Helen Jones, Lorraine Davol, Dot Piermont, Dot Hogan, Ralph Arnold Jr., and Doug Baker.

Some families went above and beyond to dig up family treasures. Among them were the Peter H. Sherman family of Middletown and the Viera family of Jamestown, especially Joan Viera Weaver.

The most elusive photographs were of Prudence Island, and it seemed that my photo deadline would come and go when Joe and Donna Bains of the Prudence Island Historical and Preservation Society came to the rescue. Joe gave me access to his personal collection of family photographs and postcards, a generous offering that led to Prudence Island having its own chapter.

Again, as with the first book, I was consumed and I have Bob Lennon to thank for holding up the fort during the months of chaos. Dawn Lyon Cullinan drew the map for reference to the introduction. Mary Jackson pointed me in the right direction when I would call her with questions, and Pat Dennett was always helpful at the NRF office. Last, but not least, thanks to the staff at Arcadia Publishing, especially Jamie Carter, who are true professionals at what they do, and a special thank you to Jim Jackson (for his computer expertise) and to Mary Ellen O'Neil, MEO, who again came through at the end.